Guillermo Cabrera Infante
and the Cinema

Juan de la Cuesta
Hispanic Monographs

Series: *Estudios de literatura latinoamericana* «Irving A. Leonard» Nº 3

Guillermo Cabrera
Infante and the Cinema

by

Kenneth E. Hall

The University of North Dakota

Juan de la Cuesta
Newark, Delaware

Parts of Chapters 1, 3, 4, and 6 were published in the article cited below, for which permission to use is acknowledged here:

"Cabrera Infante and the Work of Alfred Hitchcock,"
World Literature Today,
Copyright © 1987 by the University of Oklahoma Press

To my grandmother, Mrs. J. L. Estes

Contents

Acknowledgments

I AM GRATEFUL TO Wake Forest University for its generous support of my work on this book. The Research and Publication Fund at Wake Forest provided me with a substantial publication subvention. I thank the Director of the Fund, Dean of the Graduate School Gerald W. Esch, for his assistance in obtaining the subvention. The Provost of Wake Forest, Dr. Edwin Wilson, was very helpful in this regard as well as in others; I value his help as well as our friendly conversations during my time at Wake Forest. Ms. Kim Waller of the Grants and Contracts Office at Wake Forest was also of assistance to me in connection with funding possibilities.

I wish to acknowledge the generous assistance of Dr. Lanin A. Gyurko, my dissertation director, whose patience and helpful and prompt responses to my drafts were indispensable to the project. His advice and encouragement concerning publishing the book are also appreciated. I would also like to thank the other members of my committee, Dr. Eliana Rivero, who was very generous with her time and suggestions—including conversations and notes on my drafts from which I quote in the book—and Dr. José Promis, for his expeditious reading of the later drafts.

Further acknowledgments concerning the dissertation from which this book was derived are in order. The personnel at the University of Arizona Film Library, particularly Mr. Vic Ferguson and Ms. Betty Jeanne Ginn, were quite helpful. Mr. Ferguson was especially generous in assisting me to locate films.

Several members of the Department of Spanish and Portuguese at the University of Arizona, including Professors H. Reynolds Stone, Karen Smith, Karl Gregg, and Frances Aparicio, and Ms. Martha Yeager Velásquez, were quite helpful to me. My colleagues Randy Webb, Silvio Sirias, and Rafael Saavedra, patiently encouraged me. The opportunities to view films through the UCLA Archives and at

The Library of Congress were also of great help to the study. I also thank my typist, Ms. Linda Harper.

In the process of converting my dissertation into the present book, numerous people and institutions were of assistance to me. I am grateful to several members of the Department of Romance Languages at Wake Forest University. Dr. Milorad Margitic for his helpful suggestions regarding publishing. Drs. Mary Lusky Friedman, Jane Albrecht, and Byron Wells were also helpful in this regard. Dr. Shasta M. Bryant provided me with assistance and encouragement. Dr. Byron Wells also helped me with French problems, especially with the clarification of a quotation from Barthélemy Amengual as well as with computer questions. Drs. Susan Linker and Whang-Bai Bahk, of the Department of Romance Languages, and Dr. Win-Chiat Lee, of the Department of German and Philosophy, offered support and encouragement. Mr. Dirk Faude, director of Media Services at Wake Forest, was helpful in locating the film *Mr. Arkadin* for me and with setting up film viewings for me. Finally, I owe many thanks to the late Mrs. Mickey King, secretary of the Department of Romance Languages at Wake Forest, for her advice on computer problems, help with proofreading, and general encouragement and assistance.

I also thank my proofreaders, Ms. Susan Hall, Ms. Susan Knight, Ms. Stephanie Sams, and Ms. Angela Burleson, all Wake Forest students, Mr. Robert Dickson, and Ms. Ursula Hovet, of the English Department at the University of North Dakota. I wish also to acknowledge the assistance of several members of the Modern and Classical Languages Department at the University of North Dakota, including Drs. Ralph Koprince and Gene Dubois in obtaining computer resources for me, Mrs. Graciela Wilborn in helping me to find a proofreader, Drs. Paul and Lucy Schwartz for their kind accommodation regarding computer equipment, and finally Dr. Ralph Koprince again for aid with computer questions and friendly encouragement. Dr. Manuel Cachán helped me to see an error in the book regarding *La Habana para un Infante Difunto* and assisted me with a passage of *Tres tristes tigres* concerning the film *El Vampiro*. Dr. Michael Anderegg of the English Department, as well as D. Gene DuBois, were of help to me in checking the Preface. Dr. María Salgado, of the Department of Romance Languages at the University of North Carolina at Chapel Hill, read the dissertation prior to my revision of it for publication and offered useful suggestions regarding publishing.

I wish to thank the audio-visual staff at the University of North Carolina at Greensboro Library who helped me to see films. The Duke University Library was also helpful in this regard. The assistance of several staff members at the Wake Forest University Library is appreciated. Ms. Carrie Thomas, from Interlibrary Loan, was patient and helpful. I also wish to thank Ms. Helen Rifas and Mr. Charles Getchell, from the Reference Department.

The book was prepared using Nota Bene software, versions 1-3. The staff at Dragonfly Software, the makers of the program, have been of great help to me. I wish to extend general thanks the Technical Support Staff. Of especial assistance was Mr. Charles Garrett, who helped me with some problems encountered in preparing my index. His preparation of index files in improved format from my originals was indispensable to the project.

Special thanks go to Mr. Guillermo Cabrera Infante for granting me an interview as well as more extended conversation and very entertaining company with him and his wife. His generous responses to my questions were of much help to the project. His generosity in writing a preface for me is greatly appreciated. I also wish to thank Dr. Ardis Nelson for her suggestions and help, particularly with locating Mr. Cabrera Infante, who was a visiting professor at Wellesley College in 1985, and with notifying me about the 1987 Puterbaugh Conference on Cabrera Infante at the University of Oklahoma and asking me to appear on a panel there, an experience which gave me ideas for the book as well as the publication of an article. Professor Ivar Ivask and Mr. David Clark were of kind assistance regarding my appearance on the panel and the publication of the aforementioned article.

I wish to thank several friends for their encouragement and assistance. Luther Wood, Suzi Montgomery, Bill Keppel, Bob Kirk, W. A. Armfield, and especially Tom Montgomery were all helpful with encouragement and suggestions. Many thanks are due to my parents for their help and encouragement.

Dr. Thomas Lathrop, my editor, has been of great help with his suggestions and his kind patience in making corrections and changes in the text and proofs.

Finally, I thank Mr. George W. Bauer, the Director of *World Literature Today*, for his timely response to my request for permission to reprint my *"Cabrera Infante and the Work of Alfred Hitchcock,"* from the tumn, 1987 number.

K. H.

BY MYSELF

G. Cabrera Infante

At the beginning of *The Band Wagon* there is an auction. It is in fact a Dutch auction. The auctioneer is Douglas Fowley, an actor who can play the sedulous ape better than Cheetah did with Tarzan. Fowley was the irascible film director who instructed silent stars on sound techniques, in *Singin' in the Rain*, with the immortal coaching, coaxing lines, "Talk to the mike in the bush! In the *bush!*" He is now desperately trying to sell "the famous stick and silk hat" worn by the unforgettable star of so many musicals. What's his name? The Auctioneer begins with "A dollar?" There is no response from the audience. He then proposes fifty cents, then a quarter, then a dime. Silence is his echo. Now he begs in despair: *"Anything?"*

Later a man is seen traveling on the 20th Century incognito—or is it merely unknown? He is hiding behind a newspaper, probably an old issue of *Variety*, while two other passengers talk of great stars, like Ava Gardner, and washed-ups (a word deep into the heart of Hollywood: it is used *five* times in *Bullets or Ballots* and even the undercover agent in the underworld, Edward G. Robinson, dies as he pronounces it for the last time, "Washed-up") like Fred Astaire, who now comes out from behind his newspaper, gets up and offers each of his critics an exploding cigar!

In New York there are journalists on the platform and Astaire comes up for air. He thanks the photographers for their attention—but it is Ava Gardner they are actually expecting. Fred (can I call him Fred?) leaves the train, alone and lonely and begins to sing "By Myself" in a melancholy mood.

Is this why my introductory note is called "By Myself"? Perhaps. Which means yes but not exactly. Read on, reader. Read on.

Later in a fun fair (a pun pair) Astaire dances and sings "A Shine on Your Shoes" together with Leroy Daniels. Astaire is impeccably dres-

sed (but not in top hat, white tie and tails) in a pearl gray suit, in felt hat
and felt song and looking slight and small, while Leroy is an enormous
black bootblack in a loose Hawaiian shirt and flamingo pink socks.
Together they produce one of the happier moments in that cornucopy
of music and dance and shapely legs that is the *The Band Wagon*, a
masterpiece of the genre. A musical is happiness at twenty-four frames
per second. Was happiness a place called Broadway? Yes, it was. At
least it was in the movies. In this movie happiness is on Broadway,
though it is not a play or a movie but a penny arcade where you can
have all the fun in the world, including a giant music box and a shoe
shine to boot. In "A Shine on Your Shoes," as opposed to "By Myself,"
see above, I'm less myself because I'd rather identify with Leroy
Daniels, a bootblack who was a born dancer, than with Fred Astaire, a
trained dancer who has his toe-shoe shined: I would never be in his
slippers. Rather than a song-and-dance man I would want to be a
stand-up comedian who writes his own material. I like to shine my own
shoes.

But I began with Fred Astaire because he is a curious phenomenon.
A song-and-dance man (a Hollywood scout on Broadway had originally
reported him to the studio: "Can't act, can't sing, can dance a little"),
sometimes a mere hoofer or a tap dancer and later little more than the
ideal partner of lovable, sexy Ginger Rogers in movies labelled then as
cheap entertainment, with the passing of time he became a popular
legend. When Astaire's career began Vaslav Nijinsky's days as a dancer
were over. But he became a high-culture legend: the greatest ballet
dancer ever. In 1983 Jerome Robbins, no hoofer he, staged a ballet
tribute not to Nijinsky but to Astaire. Of Astaire the song man Oscar
Levant, who went from classical to pop sitting on the same stool, said
this: "Fred Astaire is the best singer of songs the movie world has ever
known." Before the tribute Robbins had said in the Soviet Union, when
a dance columnist asked him which dancers had influenced him the
most, "Oh well, Fred Astaire." The journalist was not surprised: "Mr.
Balanchine had just said the same thing." Balanchine, the archpriest of
highbrow dancing, probably the best choreographer the century has
seen, Stravinsky's favorite dance partner, said even more: "He is like
Bach. He has the same concentration of genius." He was not talking of
Stravinsky, he was talking of Fred Astaire—and so was Margot Fon-
teyn, who should have praised her famous partner first: "One of the
great dancers of all time. A genius."

But what about the boys in the corps de ballet? Rudolf Nureyev calls Fred Astaire "the greatest American dancer in American history." And Mikhail Baryshnikov jumps on the band wagon: "He is a genius ... A classical dancer like I never saw in my life!"

Meanwhile only yesterday Nijinsky reincarnated in a horse. Two legs good, four legs better.

There are some other questions relating to low entertainment and high art that my books (not even those garrulous TTTs) never answered because, among other things, they were never asked. But now I might do. I mean I might ask some of the questions myself. When (and why) *The Odyssey*, a poem for the ear of the many, became a classic for the eyes only of the elite? Why (and when) *Oidipous Turannos*, a popular play in Athens ("Standing room only"), became *Oedipus Rex* and hence a highbrow tragedy that was obviously just a bedroom sittrag? Its protagonists were a wondering King, a widow Queen and a wandering foreigner who was a social climber with eye problems in later life. He was known as Bigfoot. He had a dutiful daughter. It should have been Feydeau's favorite farce and not Freud's Greek primer. When and why Shakespeare, so popular with the Elizabethan riffraff (women were not safe in the stalls then: they were not even safe on stage!), became a playwright for the featured few he scorned in his plays? *Hamlet* was written in fact by a stage manager concerned with his actors getting the best accommodation when they toured. The main character envies the players' popularity and he says so. He worries that the actors, just as in Hollywood, play only "the brief chronicles of the time" and he rejects social conscience. Neorealism is not for him but perhaps he would praise Capra. The playing prince is not only an expert in amateur theatricals ("Speak the speech," he orders the leading actors, "as I pronounce it to you," just like the voice coach in *Singin' in the Rain*) but he has the gall to write "new material" into an old play like any film producer "getting in on the act," the Jimmy Durante axiom Igor Stravinsky loved to quote: once more funny music hall feeding serious music. That, ladies and gentlemen, is what is called an interpolation. A word Julius Marx loved more than he loved other words by Marx. The former not the latter was called Groucho when he laughed. Or made us laugh. It was a long trip from German philosophy to vaudeville and then to Hollywood. But he made it. Who had the last laugh now? Or the first laugh for that matter? What is the matter? Between who asked Hamlet in turn. Perhaps I should reveal now that *Hamlet* the movie was seen by more people in a year than the entire audience the play had—since it was first staged by the man who was a production manager with a piece of the action.

I'm endorsing Kenneth Estes Hall though he doesn't need any endorsements. But perhaps his book does. I'm not endorsing his book like the trailer that promises an orgasm to the audience ("Coming Soon!") nor as a cigar brand (not even like a cigar band) but because Professor Hall has done a very thorough job, a job of Job's: he at least has read all my books! There is even a timid, tenuous interview which I answered in the Twain manner. I was at the time teaching at a women's college and like Nabokov before me I hated the place, the time and the woman. Otherwise known as the dean, who looked more like a deaconess with a mustache. There were some colleagues, women professors all, who persisted in giving feminism a male name. But not the students, all learning nymphets as in Nabokov's book. By the way he was a professor there for *seven* years and nobody in the campus could tell where he lived! Obviously they were all afraid of saying, "Nabokov slept here."

I have a calm qualm about the book though. I refer to some quotes from writers other than Dr. Hall, either about my books or about Cuba, though I don't write about Cuba but about Havana mostly. Though I endorse the Hall book wholly I must take exception to those commentaries that are merely opinions but not even qualified ones. Ken Hall is not old enough or has not consulted the opinions of bona fide Cubans (I cannot of course include Alejo Carpentier among them: he is dead now) to counterbalance stories that are mostly fiction posing as truth. To say (allegedly BC, Before Castro) that Cuba was an American fiefdom is not to know Cuba at all—or to try to disfigure her best profile. Very few writers in Cuba this century were USA-oriented. I believe I am one of the few to exalt Mark Twain together with Faulkner and Hemingway, who was almost a writer *del patio*. Lino Novás Calvo, one of my more prestigious predecessors, began his career in Spain translating Faulkner but also D.H. Lawrence and only later he translated Hemingway's *The Old Man and the Sea* in Cuba. Though born in Galicia he was more of a Cuban than Carpentier, a Frenchman among the natives. Neither Lezama Lima nor Virgilio Piñera knew any English and they both were oriented to France and to Spain. Nicolás Guillén, before joining the Communist Party, was a popular poet, embedded in Cuban music. And here they have bumped against our Church. Popular culture was never Americanized, as implied. Just the opposite is true. Even after the Forties, with the mambo craze, there was an acrid polemic about American influence in Cuban music—and they talked about an influence that was hardly sponsored by the State Department then, for it was Jazz.

A rude reversal is for real. Cuban music once influenced jazz but after 1961 (Remember the Bay of Pigs?) jazz was not allowed in Cuba. In 1961 I had a television show called *"Lunes* en Televisión." I decided to do a program on jazz. But I couldn't feature a jazz band because it had a saxophone and, according to an agent for the Council for Culture, "the saxophone was an instrument of Imperialism." I retorted: "But the saxophone was invented in Belgium!" The sound policeman said with finality, "You can see why, *compañero*, the Belgians are in the Congo now." What we couldn't foresee at the time was that Cuban music in exile, the sound of salsa, would end up by influencing American pop music. Moreover the exiled sound came back to the island with a vengeance—in the shape of the instrument invented by Adolphe Sax! A Cuban exile is one of the best sax players in jazz today:

> He's a Cuban from Manhattan
> and he calls himself D'Rivera

It is surprising that the USA mainland, being so near, had not been as predominant culturally on the island as claimed in the quotations that I disclaim. Even American inventions like television and the radio (adopted in Cuba as elsewhere) became utterly Cuban. More to the point, that "Guantanamera" sung abroad like a Castroite anthem came from commercial radio. It originated during the 40's in a popular program where it served as a singing Greek chorus commenting on crimes of passion, misadventures and murder! It is of course mistaking la mayonnaise for "La Marseillaise."

In fact there is much more Russian penetration in Cuba today than there was an American influence. The Cuban army is as dependent on Russia now as it depended on the United States before. The only difference is that Batista had an army of less than 50,000 men and Castro has an army of more than a million Cubans! There are now more schools of Russian (and of German, Polish and Czech) than there were free schools of English in the 50's. There are more students in Russian universities today than there ever were in the USA. But Russia is some seven thousand miles away and Key West less than ninety.

Fidel Castro once claimed as a Hegelian *après la lettre*: "History will absolve me," and a journalist quipped: "But not geography." Accordingly the Cubans listen to American radio stations and even watch American television late at night for better reception and less interference. As it was thirty years ago, Cubans prefer American movies. No wonder. Or all wonders. It was the rainbow more at hand then, it is to look over the rainbow now. They have learned to follow the yellow bright road. In Cuba yellow is the color of hope.

Of the books of mine represented in this scholium (*Un Oficio del siglo XX, Tres Tristes Tigres, O, Exorcismos de esti(l)o, La Habana para un Infante Difunto*, and *Holy Smoke* and briefly mentioned, *Así en la paz como en la guerra* and *Vista del amanecer en el trópico*) I like, apart from the parallel views, the chapter on *Holy Smoke* best. Hall has understood that it is a book to be seen and heard.

A word or two before I go. It is about censorship. Kenneth Hall speaks of the hideous Franco censorship. This was a protracted but partial affair. Besides that evil is dead. But there is a worse evil because, like the Frankenstein monster, it's alive! It is *total* censorship. This is practiced in my country with such ability that nothing escapes their dragnets: even a leaflet cannot be printed in Havana and elsewhere in Cuba without the permission of the head of the Comité de Defensa (the Cuban equivalent of Nazi Germany's *Blockleiter*), the Minister for Culture and last but not at a loss for word-counting, the Minister of the Interior. Such censorship would have made Franco's mouth water!

Two of my books were censored in Spain (*Tres Tristes Tigres* and *Vista del amanecer en el trópico*) but they were finally published. None of my books published in Spain and elsewhere has ever been published in Cuba. Furthermore they are not even allowed into the country. A copy of *La Habana para un Infante Difunto* that Seix-Barral, then my publishing house, sent to my father in Cuba never arrived. They sent two more registered parcels from Madrid and Mexico and those didn't arrive either. Kenneth Hall's book will prove that there cannot be less political novels than those two books of mine. *Holy Smoke*, published in England and dedicated to my father, became smoke signals in the hands of the agents of the Ministry of Fear, my least favorite readers.

The old master was right when he claimed that "fear has many eyes and can see things underground." His name is Miguel de Cervantes.

I am an animal lover and when I was young I was the perfect circus buff. Until I saw in Brussels, in the Winter of 62, in a Russian circus, an enormous lion that, when threatened by the tamer's whip, defecated on the spot. It wasn't part of the act: the lion defecated out of fear. You see, the fierce beast had feelings too. It was a pitiful sight and I never visited that or any other circus again. Not even when my young daughters begged me to take them to Billy Smart's in London, where lions roam the streets.

I am a keen fan of those wild-life programs on television in which David Attenborough takes me back to Frank Buck days. He was the American explorer with a motto: "Bring 'em back alive!" Not long ago I saw a scene of fable and feud. Two African deer were trading insults, cursing their ancestors and engaged in dubious battle: antlers crashed with a clash and finally entangled in a horny knot. They seemingly couldn't disengage. Not far from nature's pit one could see a sudden lion. He approached the champions cautiously. Take note: those two were formidable bucks not gentle gazelles. One single buck could have taken care of the lion: this was no king of the jungle but your average hungry prairie hunter. But when the lion saw that the antagonists were deep into the fray of the fight he jumped the nearest combatant from behind and broke his neck expertly. He then proceeded to disengage his quarry clean and took it away in his jaws. The other deer, after some sudden fright, walked into the sheltering bush.

This scene of everyday life in the wild reminded me of literary mayhem, in which critics do battle for a given author or his contrary. They are the deer. The opportunist beast is of course the literary lion. But then I remembered that cowardly lion—

The foundation or foundations of a poetry or a poetic system must take the shape or shade of deeply felt motives as ancient as myth or distant dreams. The instant myth of certain movies or certain actors happens because they are all up there bigger than dreams. In movies vision becomes myth or the stuff dreams are made of. Such are the memories of *Scarface*, in which ape-like Paul Muni, Ann Dvorak (she who devours) and the George Raft who tosses his fate in the shape of a coin. They were present since so long that they are like private dreams in public places. *Scarface* is for me a source of myth, of poetic memory. That is not the case of *Scarface Two*, though both deal with the same kind of stuff and the latter even borrows a few gags from the first version. It is not enough. If the women in *Scarface Two* are all more beautiful than Dvorak (she with a nether world symphony in her name) they don't register. I don't even remember their names. The movie is too contemporary to become myth. It is obvious that you cannot say with movies, as with music, make my myth.

It is not the movies in my life but the life in my movies that my books are all about. Movies are a magma. Or rather an ocean where grey becomes technicolor. Does the fish love water? It is of course a totally irrelevant question. Or as silly if you asked, does the fish hate water? Movies are for me the source of life, life itself. It is an eternity of dreams.

There are very few mistakes in Hall's reading. It is not, as with other scholiasts, a comedy of errors, the scholia cantorum. Like the castrato who wrote of the escapism of my characters. He obviously thought of Houdini. To talk of escape in my books is like talking of escapement in a clockwork. *Escape* in Spanish also means the exhaust of a car or a life exhausted — and then the banter played on. Camera lens, *cámara lenta, festina lens.* Oh video!

TTT and *La Habana* are simply my efforts not to recreate legends about a city but to create the city itself. I want to do for Havana what Baudelaire did for Paris. Or rather what Walter Benjamin said Baudelaire did for Paris. Or as Hemingway briefly noted about Havana: "Looking back, I could see Havana looking fine in the sun." He could also see sometime later "the glow of Havana." He was sailing on the Gulf Stream at the time but I could see Havana from here, wherever that is, like a magnificent vision—or version. What Kenneth Hall calls my mock-epic. Mock-epics are peopled not only by mock-heroes but also by mock-worshippers of heroes and by mock-priests of mock-myths. Mock-epics suit mock-characters. Some of those characters possess, like Hamlet, a tragic intelligence. It is my will and testament that my characters enjoy a comic intelligence. Let me make a brief *dramatis personae*, though *dramatis* does not exactly suit those anti-heroes. Boustrophedon, for his fight against purple patches, all he got was a purple heart. He is the ox of puns. For Cue Utopia became Autopia on cue: where cars in a jam sweeten a cruel dystopia. Silvestre prefers to ride in the suicide's seat: he is the one who leaves in a huff to come back in a jiffy. Códac is an underdeveloped negative hero. Eribó believes that when somebody writes about the Erebus they are misspelling his name: he wears the skin of his drums on his fingertips. They are all in a hurry, though their *magister ludi* is an *esperanto* never a *desperanto*: he who waits. I have weighed my characters and found them wanting—except perhaps La Estrella.

Aping Hemingway, which means aping an ape in the literary jungle, after what he said of *The Unquiet Grave* (a title, by the way, by the way of all flesh), I hope this book has as many readers as it deserves. Then it won't have as many as I believe it deserves—or words to that effect. Bear in mind, reader, that Academia is the last refuge of the critic. *I* should know. I was in Academia once and both Plato and Pluto were my mentors.

Durante, who shares his name with Dante and his beliefs with Socrates (the philosopher who died of box-office poisoning), once said (or sang: nobody can tell for sure, though he was a parody of a song-and-dance man) what is the predicament of every entertainer:

Did you ever have the feeling that you wanted to go?

While at the same time professing:

Did you ever have the feeling that you wanted to stay?

That's otherwise called writer's block.

London,
February 1989

Guillermo Cabrera Infante
and the Cinema

INTRODUCTION

FILM HAS WIDELY BEEN acknowledged as historically dependent upon literature as one of the main sources of both its thematic inspiration and, somewhat less generally, its body of technique. Arthur Knight states in *The Liveliest Art* that "In America, at least, the film was firmly linked to a theatrical tradition from the very outset" (19).[1] As critics such as Knight and George Bluestone emphasize, filmmakers, especially but not exclusively in Hollywood, have long relied on literature, both creative and historical, for plot sources; film adaptations of well-known creative works are quite common. In the area of technique, filmmakers have borrowed extensively from literary practice—note the significant example of Sergei Eisenstein, the great Soviet director and theorist, who performed cinematic exegeses of the descriptions by Leonardo da Vinci of *The Last Supper*, of poems by Pushkin, and of passages from Dickens and Maupassant (*The Film Sense* 3-65, 165-66), and established a theory of montage as the basis for the constitution of the image. Eisenstein stated "that the montage principle in films is only a sectional application of the *montage principle in general...*" (*The Film Sense* 35-36; original emphasis).

Until rather recently, film has not been widely studied for its impact on literature; after all, the phenomenon of film is itself a recent development and has yet to attain to full acclaim as an art form.[2] Much of the influence of film on literature has perhaps been marginal, affecting either "popular" writers like Dashiell Hammett[3] or avant-garde authors such as Robbe-Grillet.[4]

With Robbe-Grillet and the "New Novel," cinematic influence becomes pervasive and, for some readers, excessive in its effect on the narratives of novels such as *La Jalousie* and *Le Voyeur*. The use by Robbe-Grillet of cinematic techniques such as cutting, montage, extreme close-ups, and slow motion makes his work seem almost anti-literary.[5]

1

The movements of the New Novel, of Italian neorealism, and of the French New Wave are all part of the cultural ambience within which Guillermo Cabrera Infante, born in Cuba in 1929, cultivated his creative and critical approaches to film.[6] Cabrera Infante was heavily immersed in the cinema as a child and carried his fascination with movies into adulthood (Cabrera Infante, *Siete voces* 410-17, 444-46). Cabrera Infante says that "'...podía leer en el cine antes que en los libros'" and that "'La primera vez que fui al cine tenía 29 días de nacido, que me llevó mi madre, una loca por el cine...'" (*Siete voces* 410). Cabrera Infante seems to have approached films with a positive fascination with the culture depicted in them, becoming, as a film critic, an avid fan of Hollywood movies.

Cabrera Infante uses film in an encyclopedic and exuberant manner. To echo Andrew Sarris in "Rerunning Puig and Cabrera Infante" (47-48), Cabrera Infante approaches cinematic allusion in an "extensive" fashion, with a Rabelaisian expansiveness not unlike that of Henry Miller with respect to books and art.[7]

The tendency towards cinematic allusiveness opens into an important area of thematic relationships between the narrative art of Cabrera Infante and the fund of narrative in the cinema, especially in its chief incarnation, the great decades of the Hollywood studios. Cabrera Infante declares in *Arcadia todas las noches* that "No es extraño que el cine, arte del siglo, haya producido todos los mitos del siglo: en el pasado ese mismo papel lo llenaron la literatura, la poesía, la pintura." He continues with a definition of myth: "¿Qué es un mito? Una realidad mayor que la realidad..." (31). His works deal with cinema as mythmaker for the Cuban "middle and upper classes";[8] he approaches the cinematic mythos[9] in a fashion somewhat analogous in breadth, if perhaps not in depth, to the mining of Western myth and tradition by James Joyce in *Ulysses* and *Finnegans Wake*. The myth of the small-town girl or boy who "makes it good in Hollywood" is central to the narrative of *Tres tristes tigres*. Cabrera Infante tends to be concerned with the epigonous nature of his characters, with their desire to become images of Hollywood idols or to imitate American culture, consequently losing their cultural center of gravity.

The careful integration of cinematic technique into his work is one aspect in which Cabrera Infante demonstrates the pervasive quality of film in Cuban culture. Despite his use of such techniques, an area which has been documented by critics such as Alvarez-Borland and Nelson, his thematic borrowings seem even more important.[10]

The great importance of film to Cabrera Infante can be understood in terms of film genre and mythology as well as by connecting films and his use of them to Western antecedents. Although cinematic technique is important to Cabrera Infante, this examination of his work will emphasize thematic parallels or influences from films and directors. It is through comparative study of the criticism, fiction, and filmscripts of Cabrera Infante that the nature of his work can best be appreciated. That work cannot be properly evaluated, I believe, without first examining the nature and circumstances of the lifelong interest which the cinema has held for Cabrera Infante.

NOTES

[1] See Knight 19-23 for a historical overview of film and its connections to theater.

[2] Worley (1-28) gives a good overview of the question of film and literature, especially the novel.

[3] Magny supports this view on Hammett (40-43) as well as on other authors such as Dos Passos and Hemingway.

[4] Mitchell gives a similar overview of the critical situation on film and literature (22).

[5] See the supporting remarks of Spiegel (124-30). For a brief comparison between Robbe-Grillet and Cabrera Infante, see Ferguson 150-52.

[6] See the concurring view of Rodríguez Monegal in "Myth Exploded" 64.

[7] Hazera ("Cinematic" 45), referring to *Tres tristes tigres*, makes a similar point:

Since Cabrera Infante's main preoccupation in *Three Trapped Tigers* is the nature of language and its possibilities for constructing an autonomous verbal reality, the influence of film is diffused.... (my ellipsis)

[8] For the process of "mitificación" (and its contrary) in *Tres tristes tigres*, as well as the origin of my reference to the "Cuban middle and upper classes," see Giordano 163-70.

[9] I owe the notion of cinematic mythos to Professor Lanin Gyurko. See Parker Tyler, *Magic and Myth of the Movies* and *The Hollywood Hallucination*, for stimulating remarks on film and myth.

[10] Alvarez-Borland, "El cine documental"; Nelson, "*Tres tristes tigres*."

A Cinematic Background

HE BACKGROUND OF Guillermo Cabrera Infante in the cinema is extensive, both as a film enthusiast and as a professional film critic and screenwriter. Although his cultural background, encompassing literature, painting, and music as well as film, can hardly be said to be narrowly "cinematic," Cabrera Infante is nevertheless deeply imbued with a sense of the history of film, of its theoretical evolution, and of its power to entertain and absorb the viewer through, in the words of Parker Tyler, its "magic and myth" (in *Magic and Myth of the Movies*). Due to the difficulty in assessing the relative importance of cinematic and of literary culture in the work of Cabrera Infante, his case is particularly interesting to the critic.

The author states quite straightforwardly in an interview with Rita Guibert that

> ... mis primeros recuerdos están asociados con imágenes sobre una pantalla, sobre una pared: las luces y sombras del cine. Recuerdo películas que vi cuando tenía, no podía tener más de tres años. ... podía leer en el cine antes que en los libros. (*Siete voces* 410; my ellipsis)

Referring to his viewing of films in 1932 or 1933, in his early childhood, he establishes a connection between the film, in its early sound or "talking" form, and his sensorial education—as he says in the same context, "'Para mí el cine, efectivamente, ha sido más que una escuela, ha sido una educación.'" Such a statement as his reference to his ability to "'leer en el cine antes que en los libros'" can perhaps be understood in a not quite literal sense; that is, Cabrera

Infante is perhaps not seriously referring to the titles or credits on films, which might have taught him to read, but rather to his development of a capacity to "read" film, to interpret its visual and auditory language, to be "film literate"—versed in visual and sonic imagery before learning to read the alphabet and to deal with strictly verbal expression. Actually, he says, he "'learned to read'" from "'the funnies'":

> As a child I watched anything and everything that moved. And even things that didn't move—the funnies. Incidentally, it was the comic strips that bridged the gap between pictures and words for me because I learned to read by deciphering the words in the little balloons. (Cabrera Infante, "Art" 177)

His background in films can thus be seen to have far-reaching implications for his later literary work, possibly contributing to his marked tendency for spatial redistribution of language, a penchant exemplified by his fascination with the "portmanteau" word as cultivated by Lewis Carroll (Cabrera Infante, O 106-07).[1] The influence of the cinema on Cabrera Infante is also evident with regard to his strong visual sensibility and finely developed visual memory, crucial to his narrative reconstructions of La Habana.[2]

Film has represented much more than a simple escape or entertainment for Cabrera Infante. His interest in film extends to virtually all its areas and periods, concentrating especially on the great era of Hollywood films in the 1930s and 1940s and on the period of Italian neorealism and the French New Wave, extending from the mid-1940s to the early 1960s. He was born at a most propitious time for the development of such a lifelong interest in the cinema: 1929, the year of his birth, was, he states, the beginning of "'Esa Edad de Oro del cine, que comenzó en 1929 con la instalación del cine hablado...'" (*Siete voces* 410). His childhood film experience encompassed the great era of the Hollywood star system—the 1930s—which saw such luminaries as Carole Lombard, Cary Grant, Katharine Hepburn, and Spencer Tracy, either at or growing into the peak of their powers. His adolescence and young adulthood occurred during the period of the *film noir* in Hollywood, of the New Wave in France, and of neorealism in Italy.

It is significant that Cabrera Infante emphasizes two years—1929, his birthdate, and 1949, his twentieth year—as peaks in film history.

These years respectively represent, according to Cabrera Infante, the coming of age of film and its apogee. He identifies his true interest in film completely with the output of Hollywood: "'El único para mí ha sido el cine sinfónico de Hollywood'" (*Siete voces* 410). This "'cine sinfónico,'" as he states in the same interview, had its true beginning "'en 1929 con la instalación del cine hablado,'" a year which saw the release of some of his personal favorites as well as some milestones in movie history:

> ... ese [sic] es el año de *Broadway Melody*, del nacimiento de Mickey en *Steamboat Willie*, de *All Quiet on the Western Front*, de *Morocco* conteniendo a la Dietrich y a su mito, cuando Garbo habló por primera vez y, por supuesto, de *Little Caesar*.... (410)

He also identifies his first film experience with the year 1929:

> La primera vez que fui al cine tenía 29 días de nacido, que me llevó mi madre, una loca por el cine, cuyo lema, cuando yo era niño, era "cine o sardina." Es decir, comíamos o ahorrábamos el dinero para el cine. Por supuesto que no tengo ningún recuerdo de esa primera película que vi, que fue la reprise [sic] de *Los cuatro jinetes del Apocalipsis*, en que reaparecía entre mis sueños ese inmortal, Rodolfo Valentino. (410)

The "Golden Age" of Hollywood, whose birth is fixed by Cabrera Infante as contemporaneous with his own, ended for him in 1949,

> en que se hicieron o comenzaron o estrenaron *Letter from an Unknown Woman*, *A Double Life*, *On the Town*, *An American in Paris*, *The Set-up* [sic], todas para mí cintas de mitología privada y, por supuesto, *Asphalt Jungle*, donde apareció ese mito de todos, Marilyn Monroe. El resto es la agonía de Hollywood, la decadencia al mismo tiempo de un gran arte popular y de la industria que lo hizo posible. (410)

During the decade following 1949, when Hollywood was indeed in a period of decline, Cabrera Infante began his serious work in film criticism.

From 1954 until 1960, Cabrera Infante, as he says of himself, "'...me ganaba la vida escribiendo sobre el cine'" (Cabrera Infante, *Siete voces* 410). He worked most extensively for the magazine *Carteles*. He writes, referring to this stage in his career, that:

> Su antiguo jefe es nombrado director de *Carteles*, la segunda revista

de Cuba. Todavía usando su nombre de capa y espada—*G. Caín*—, comienza a escribir una columna semanal sobre cine que se hace notoria en Cuba y en el área del Caribe. (Pereda 243; original emphasis)

His work for *Carteles* and, after 1959, for *"Lunes,* suplemento literario de *Revolución"* (Pereda 245), was contemporary to the latter part of the vogue of Italian neorealism, to the blacklisting in the United States of numerous liberal filmmakers due to the activities of HUAC,[3] and most especially to the rise of the *politique des auteurs* in France with the work of the critics of *Cahiers du cinéma.* His career as a critic ended with the banning by the Castro government of "un breve film de 25 minutos llamado *P.M."* by "su hermano Sabá Cabrera" because of its concentration on "ciertas *formas de vida* del pasado pre-revolucionario sentenciadas a desaparecer" by the régime (Jiménez 37-38; original emphasis). The furor over this government action resulted in the closing of the magazine and in the decisions by Cabrera Infante not to write film criticism and eventually to leave Cuba.[4]

The film criticism of Cabrera Infante, while quite personal and independently thought out, does show a great influence from the *politique des auteurs,* or *"auteur* theory," which can be loosely defined as a critical stance or approach which stresses the importance of the director as the author of the film on which he works (Graham 135-36). Some of the contributors to *Cahiers du cinéma,* in which the *politique* was expounded and popularized, were André Bazin, Alexandre Astruc, François Truffaut, and Jean-Luc Godard (Graham 7-8). The cinema criticism of Cabrera Infante, which seems to owe much to the work of these writers, will be dealt with more extensively in a later chapter; for the present, it is enough to note that his criticism, more significantly than the juvenilia to which he refers (Pereda 243), served for Cabrera Infante both as a livelihood and as a valuable literary effort. He was also a forceful and engaging spokesman for many of the ideas and causes championed by the French film critics.

Cabrera Infante later collected much of his criticism and published it in *Un oficio del Siglo 20* (1963). He also published a collection of his lectures on directors in *Arcadia todas las noches* (1978), in which he deepened his focus on some of the preoccupations found in his critical columns.[5] The title *Arcadia todas las noches* is indicative of this view of film "'...como un sustituto serio de la religión para un pagano primitivo como yo'" (*Siete voces* 411). His fascination with film as myth, as we will see, relates closely to certain aspects of his fiction. In general, his film criticism exhibits many of the same points of view and much of the same imagery as can be found in his work in fiction and in other prose efforts like *Holy Smoke*. The influence of the films which he saw as a youth and as a young adult can be seen at many points in his fictional work, sometimes quite patently; and his opinion of and approach to the films as aesthetic objects can be gleaned through a study of his critical columns and essays.

In response to a question by Rita Guibert about cinematic impact on his work, he has claimed the "'influencia'" of film on his writing to be a curiously indirect one: "'No en mi escritura, que es una excrescencia: en mí, que la contengo. Nací con una pantalla de plata en la boca'" (438). His remarks seem more than a mock disclaimer; rather, they suggest one of the problems, alluded to by Andrew Sarris ("Rerunning" 47), in studying the relationship of film to the work of Cabrera Infante: many cultural influences, including that of the cinema, have been filtered through his perceptions and sensitivities. Concerning his cultural background, he has stated that:

> Mi música—swing, jazz y comedias musicales—venía de USA, sonando sincopada, y de Europa en suaves sinfonías. Mis lecturas fueron las imágenes de vértigo del cine, los *comics*, las confusas novelas de Faulkner: artes americanas, y después Conrad y Carroll.... ("Salsa" 22)

Allusions to music, painting, literature, and the film abound in his work to such an extent that evaluating the relative importance of each area is often difficult.[6]

Furthermore, Cabrera Infante does not differentiate between the aesthetic value of popular films or fiction and that of well-established "serious" literature.[7] Such an attitude, a refreshing one, runs counter to the notions held by many literary critics. Cabrera Infante seems to suggest that the line of influence on his work is not a direct or simply evaluated one but must be understood by reference to his living experiences, an important part of which has revolved around film and film culture.

Although Cabrera Infante has clouded the issue with regard to the influence of film on his work, he has also made some very clear statements about the same question. He has said to Regina M. Janes that "'...I don't know about influences. I can't say that any given author had an influence on me when I started. It was all movies, more than books'" (34). Such statements suggest that film is the benchmark against which he would measure the other aesthetic content which has influenced him; in essence, his aesthetic lenses would be those of film. The impetus of his absorption of aesthetic stimulation is still in the direction of the cinema, although he is somewhat less clear about this point. When Janes asks him if it is "'still true'" that films are more influential on him than books, he responds: "'In a way. I see a lot of movies, and I read very few books'" (34).

Clearly, any account of the work of Cabrera Infante which shunts film to one side while concentrating directly on literary background or analogies will be seriously skewed. The chiefly literary approach is, not surprisingly, the one which has been adopted by most critics of his work. Those critics, such as Ardis Nelson and Isabel Alvarez-Borland, who have worked with the relationship between cinema and the literary production of Cabrera Infante have not yet undertaken extensive studies concerning the question. While literary influence is certainly important to his creative work, the impact of film on his career needs to be properly presented and evaluated.

Unquestionably, Cabrera Infante has invested much effort in work directly concerning the film. His reviews for *Carteles* and *Lunes de Revolución* are extensive—*Un oficio del Siglo 20* is but a selection, albeit a large one, of the total—and his essays in *Arcadia todas las noches*, largely ignored by critics of his work, are important not only for their intrinsic literary worth and in understanding his work but also in evaluating the production of the directors upon whom he comments.[8] Although he no longer writes film criticism on any regular basis, having stopped his critical work in 1960 because, as he says to Eligio García Márquez, "'La situación política de Cuba impedía ejercer la crítica y no me interesaba más como forma literaria la crónica de revista o diario'" (183), he does write occasional articles on film and television as well as creating his own filmscripts. Two of his scripts, for *Vanishing Point* and *Wonderwall*, have been filmed, the latter with indifferent results apparently due largely to inept direction,[9] while other scripts, such as his adaptations of *Under the Volcano* by Malcolm Lowry and of "La autopista del sur," a Julio Cortázar story, as well as a collaborative effort called *El Máximo*, have never been produced ("Guillermo Cabrera Infante" 183-84, 213-14). He is still deeply involved in movies, mainly as a spectator. He tells Eligio García Márquez that, with the exception of a wish to see his script for *Under the Volcano* produced, " 'No tengo proyectos inmediatos para el cine . . . . Me gustaría tener un argumento original para el cine, pero estoy concentrando todas mis fuerzas en la literatura' " (184; my ellipsis). Nevertheless, he says that he sees many films: " 'Ahora veo más cine que nunca, con la televisión inglesa permitiéndome recobrar películas perdidas, de los años treintas, cuando iba a menudo al cine pero por ser demasiado niño no he retenido su recuerdo o se ha torcido...' " (208; my ellipsis).

Given the heavy immersion of Cabrera Infante in the film, both as spectator and critic and as creator, to study his literary work and to ignore or gloss over the area of film is not only to present an inadequate portrait of his literary enterprise, but also to fail to distinguish one of the major reasons for his individuality in the large field of Latin-American writers. No other Latin-American writer of major stature, except Manuel Puig, has shown a primary interest in film to rival that of Cabrera Infante. Like Puig, Cabrera Infante is thus understandably difficult to classify. By first analyzing the concept of film held by Cabrera Infante, a readjustment of the critical perspective on his work can perhaps be initiated.[10]

NOTES

[1] Sarris ("Rerunning" 46) also refers to his use of "vaguely derisive portmanteau effects"; see also Acosta Cruz 19, 98.

[2] I owe the notion of memory (and its somewhat "creative inaccuracy") in Cabrera Infante's reconstructions of La Habana to Eliana Rivero, according to her close reading of *La Habana para un Infante Difunto.*

[3] See Gordon Kahn, *Hollywood on Trial;* Victor S. Navasky, *Naming Names,* for information on this period.

[4] See also Gallagher, "Guillermo" 51-58, 68-69. For remarks by Cabrera Infante on the subject, see, e.g., Cabrera Infante, Interview with Montaner 167.

[5] See the brief summary of works by Cabrera Infante and "varios motivos de importancia" found in them in Alvarez-Borland, *Discontinuidad* 17-20.

[6] Sarris ("Rerunning" 47) expresses a similar idea when he writes of "Cabrera Infante's anarchic temperament."

[7] Cabrera Infante spoke along these lines during an interview with me.

[8] Néstor Almendros has said of him: " 'He is, without doubt, the greatest film critic Cuba ever produced, and also one of the greatest film critics in the whole of America...' " ("Photography" 128; my ellipsis).

⁹ In an interview with me, Cabrera Infante spoke of the problematic realization of *Vanishing Point* and referred to *Wonderwall* as "un desastre."

¹⁰ Mitchell refers to the broad literary background of Cabrera Infante and says that his attribution of more influence to film than to books "may be an oversimplification" (23).

2

Cabrera Infante as Critic:
His Concept of Film

ABRERA INFANTE ESSENTIALLY conceives of film as a visual presentation of contemporary myths, or of modern versions of older myths. The director, actors, and other personnel involved in the making of a film are engaged in producing and creating myths. Sometimes the actors, and less frequently the directors, themselves become mythic figures: the process of filmmaking is then a self-generating mythification. The mythification of actors, and of directors, through film provides a corpus of myths upon which Cabrera Infante draws in his creative writing. His focus on films as mythic force, as a system linked to the mystery and the rite,[1] is closely connected to his neoromantic vision of the director as "un poeta" (*Oficio* 377) and of the star or actor as mythic hero. An important source of his emphasis on the artistic role of the director is to be found in the auteurist criticism of *Cahiers du cinéma*, while his view of mythic patterns in the careers of stars is strongly reminiscent of the seminal views of Erwin Panofsky.

Cabrera Infante, working as a film critic during the period of the rise to influence of *Cahiers du cinéma* in the 1950s, could hardly have remained neutral or indifferent to the work of André Bazin, the most famous critic to contribute to the magazine, or to the *politique des auteurs* espoused in its pages. His approach to film during this period is quite close to the line taken by *Cahiers du cinéma*. In fact, he says, he consciously followed the auteurist line: "'En *Arcadia* sostuve la teoría cinemática, copiada de Bazin y Truffaut, de que existen los *autores* cinematográficos, los directores de cine tan creadores únicos como los escritores'" (Cabrera Infante, "Viaje" 68; original emphasis). He favors an emphasis on the director as creative force in the process of filmmaking, admits a "transcendental"[2] aspect of film, and qualitatively differentiates its pursuit from that of literature. He even favors some of the directors typically praised by the *Cahiers* critics: Howard Hawks, Otto Preminger, Alfred Hitchcock, and Orson Welles are examples.

For a fuller comprehension of the historical importance of *Cahiers du cinéma* and of Cabrera Infante in film criticism, a brief review of trends in film theory will be helpful.[3] As J. Dudley Andrew notes, two major and generally opposed strains have flowed through film theory and its application in the form of serious criticism: the "formalist" trend, represented particularly by theorists such as Rudolf Arnheim, Erwin Panofsky, and Sergei Eisenstein; and the "realist" approach, defended by theorists such as Siegfried Kracauer and André Bazin. The two trends, while basically opposed, are sometimes merged in the work of one critic, such as André Bazin, who defended realist principles while arguing that the film should present the mystery of reality through subtle artistry.

The formalist view of film, as Andrew suggests, might also be termed "non-representationalist"; for such a theorist as Arnheim, the "cinematic" is that which does not represent or imitate reality. A film is more cinematic if the filmmaker twists the real, using the power of the camera to, as Andrew says, "transform" reality as we usually experience it into an artistic construct. The camera is not a device for making carbon copies of the world but a tool for presenting an artistic view of it. Arnheim especially favored the silent film because of its power of abstraction. He felt that the use of sound would destroy the illusion of an art removed from everyday reality.

The transformationalism of the theory proposed by Arnheim is extended and developed in the work of Sergei Eisenstein. Eisenstein developed his famous theory of montage along lines similar to those of the argument presented by Arnheim, with, of course, the important qualification that the cinema of Eisenstein was oriented towards Marxist didacticism.

Eisenstein also falls within the climate of Russian formalist theory, which was being extended to film at the time of his work (Eagle ix).

His theories, suggests Eagle, should be understood within this climate:

> The concepts advanced in *Poètika kino* [defined by Eagle as "the title of the early Formalist volumes on literary theory"] would seem not only to relate to but also to have influenced at least the formulation of the works on montage published two years later by Lev Kulešov and Sergei Eisenstein. Of course, Kulešov and Eisenstein began expressing their respective ideas about montage much earlier, but Kulešov's *Iskusstvo kino* (*The Art of Cinema*) was not published until 1929 [two years after "*Poètika kino* (*Poetics of Cinema*) was published in the spring of 1927," as Eagle says] and Eisenstein's famous polemical articles on montage began appearing in that same year.... (ix; see also 29-36)

For Eisenstein, montage—the joining together of images to provoke a shock in the viewer—thus changing his perceptions, was a method of reorganizing reality artistically in order to educate the spectator into a dialectical view of the world. His conception of montage is a restatement, or a close relation, of the notion of "singularización" presented by Victor Shklovski, one of the Formalist theorists:

> La automatización devora los objetos, los hábitos, los muebles, la mujer y el miedo a la guerra.... La finalidad del arte es dar una sensación del objeto como visión y no como reconocimiento; los procedimientos del arte son el de la singularización de los objetos, y el que consiste en oscurecer la forma, en aumentar la dificultad y la duración de la percepción... En arte, la liberación del objeto del automatismo perceptivo se logra por diferentes medios... L. Tolstoi...según la opinión de Mereikovski, parece presentar los objetos tal como los ve; los ve en sí mismos, sin deformarlos. (Todorov 60-61; my ellipsis)[4]

Directly opposed to such transformationalism is the realist trend in film theory, whose most forceful champion was Siegfried Kracauer. He proposed a "content-oriented" cinema, one which would perform its proper function of presenting reality, or the outside world, to the viewer, thus helping him to discover hidden connections in its structures. Rather than transform reality, Kracauer would intensify and concentrate the content of the world through the recording powers of the camera. He often opposed abstract experimental films because of their distortion of phenomena.

Less doctrinaire than the foregoing theorists in his approach to film was André Bazin, one of the founders of *Cahiers du cinéma*. Bazin, despite his strong defense of realist tenets, set a high value on the capacity of the cinema to induce in the viewer a perception of the "mystery" and "ambiguity" of the world. He stressed the need for heightened realism in film, but in a most peculiar and paradoxical fashion: the filmmaker should not structure or break up reality for the viewer, as the montage theorist would advise. He should efface himself from the work, hiding behind the camera, as it were, presenting reality as a surface to be interpreted by the viewer.

Bazin thus championed the use of "depth of field" or deep focus by directors such as Jean Renoir, William Wyler, and especially Orson Welles because of its ability to present a scene—a piece of reality—without undue analysis of the relationships between the characters and objects presented there. Rather than cut the scene into fragments by the use of montage, the director should strive for a unified presentation of events.[5] The ambiguity of the world will thus present itself to the viewer, since the director does not clarify or limit the picture by means of excessive editing.

The theories of Bazin were finding wide circulation at the time during which Cabrera Infante began his work for *Carteles*. The stance taken by Cabrera Infante at the time generally identifies him as close to the critical positions of Bazin. Although Cabrera Infante was not one of the *Cahiers* critics, and thus was not formally associated with the development and popularization of Bazin's ideas which was effected in that magazine,[6] he did read the magazine rather closely, as his citations from it suggest. He has in fact stated with reference to Bazin that "... éste es uno de los pocos críticos de cine que.... yo he estudiado desde que empecé a escribir crítica de cine" (Interview with author; my ellipsis). He drew much inspiration from the ideas in the columns of *Cahiers*; his later criticism, in the form of the essays of *Arcadia todas las noches*, shows him reacting against positions, such as the *politique des auteurs*, which he once held himself (*Arcadia* 142).

The general approach to film criticism taken by Cabrera Infante is indeed akin to that of André Bazin. Like Bazin, Cabrera Infante praises ambiguity, seeing it as essential to the creation of art. He is characteristically flippant about his preference for ambiguity in film, saying that "Si estoy por la ambigüedad es por simple razón de economía" (*Arcadia* 27). He nevertheless develops the idea of "economía" into an interesting statement regarding the necessity of ambiguity in art. This position is less comprehensive than the statements of Bazin, stressing the usefulness of ambiguity in giving meaning to the works of artists like Orson Welles who have produced a limited corpus.

In developing his idea of ambiguity, Cabrera Infante creates an arithmetic of aesthetic value. He states that "Es solamente la multiplicación lo que hace del gesto de los panes y los peces un milagro..."; the creation of "un pan y un pez" would be only "un acto de magia, un truco de prestidigitación, un escamoteo brillante, pero nunca un milagro." Art, like miracles, follows the principle of multiplication: "Si tenemos una obra de arte, ¿qué nos hará ricos en obras de arte? Muchas obras de arte, está claro. Y si un autor tiene sólo una obra maestra, ¿cómo conseguirse el número, la muchedumbre, la multiplicación?" (*Arcadia* 27-28). The answer which Cabrera Infante gives to his self-proposed question is that the work of art reveals its nature by the good offices of criticism: "Es la exégesis la que al referirse a *uno*, parece hablar de *muchos*: así, tenemos el *Hamlet* de Laurence Olivier y el *Hamlet* de Madariaga y el *Hamlet* de Eliot..." (*Arcadia* 28; original emphasis).

Here Cabrera Infante reformulates an idea which has long been the subject of debate and which is basically a Platonic question: does the work of art have an independent existence as an "Idea," or is its existence determined by the subjective perception of the reader who experiences it? That is, does interpretation create an entirely new work of art each time, or does the work of art maintain its objective character regardless of interpretation?

Roman Ingarden, in *The Literary Work of Art*, provided an elegant solution to the problem by postulating a "stratum of schematized aspects" (see esp. 255-75), "held in readiness" for a "concretization" by the act of reading (see, e.g., 269, 346). Thus, the literary work of art has a certain *"individuality"* which is "expressed" throughout its "life" in the hands of readers; it is therefore, so to speak, one work and many works (346; original emphasis):

If we observe that a literary work can undergo change, only on condition that it be expressed in a concretization, one can speak of its "life" in a twofold and, in both cases, figurative sense: (1) the literary work "lives" while *it is expressed in a manifold of concretizations;* (2) the literary work "lives" while it *undergoes changes as a result* of ever new concretizations appropriately formed by conscious subjects. (346-47; original emphasis)

The more complex the "stratum of schematized aspects," the more varied will be the "concretizations" of the work. Cabrera Infante expresses a similar concept with regard to the work of art, but, of course, in a less rigorous form than does Ingarden.

The work, for Cabrera Infante, must above all other qualities possess ambiguity:[7] like *Citizen Kane*—or, one might add, *Tres tristes tigres*—, the artistic creation must not be entirely transparent:

> Una obra cualquiera—mal escrita, peor compuesta, técnicamente perversa—que diera lugar a la duda, que dejase ver que 2 y 2 son 5 en este libro, que sustituyera con el gris al blanco y negro groseros, tendría intérpretes, porque admitiría interpretaciones. Es de esta duplicidad, de lo que yo quiero llamar ambigüedad, que se nutre la historia del arte... El ciudadano [*Citizen Kane*] es un paradigma de esta ambigüedad creadora.... (*Arcadia* 28; my ellipsis)

The remarks of Cabrera Infante about film and literature are similar to the views of Bazin regarding reality, summarized in the following way by Andrew: "Nature has many senses and can be said to speak to us 'ambiguously.'" For Bazin such ambiguity is a value and cinema should preserve it, making us aware of its possibilities" (*Major Film Theories* 158). The comments of Cabrera Infante not only help to connect him to the ideas of Bazin but also illuminate his approach to the novel, in which, particularly in *Tres tristes tigres*, he tries to achieve complexity through the use of neologisms and other "neobaroque" devices.[8]

From his defense of ambiguity, a concept close to that of mystery, another idea dear to Bazin, Cabrera Infante segues into a discussion of the film as mythic force as exemplified in the figure of Orson Welles (*Arcadia* 30-33). He asserts that "No es extraño que el cine, arte del siglo, haya producido todos los mitos del siglo: en el pasado ese mismo papel lo llenaron la literatura, la poesía, la pintura" (31). Art, whose chief contemporary manifestation is arguably the film, is placed at the service of myth. The mythic corpus of film has provided Cabrera Infante with the aforementioned "'sustituto serio de la religión para un pagano primitivo como yo'" (*Siete voces* 411). The mission of film for Cabrera Infante is to manufacture myths for a society which has ceased to believe in its structures of religion.

Myth, Joseph Campbell explains in *The Hero with a Thousand Faces*, is a means for the revelation of another reality—thus, the central importance of the hero who returns from "the other shore" (23) bringing knowledge of "something forgotten not only by ourselves but by our whole generation or our entire civilization..." (17). The adventures of the hero, "a superior man, a born king" (173), are typically larger than life. According to Campbell, mythic narrative which exhibits such exaggeration "can readily be interpreted" in terms of childish "fantasies" of "indestructibility" (173-92). Myth is an adult version of "all the magic of childhood" and therefore holds within its structure the "golden seeds" of "all the life-potentialities that we never managed to bring to adult realization..." (17).

Cabrera Infante expresses a rather similar point of view when he characterizes a myth as "una realidad mayor que la realidad" (*Arcadia* 31). He says that "...una bestia con cuerpo de caballo y busto y cabeza de hombre es un animal que está por encima del hombre y del caballo porque está en posesión de una realidad mayor: la doble realidad del hombre y la bestia..." (31).

The function of film, for Cabrera Infante, relates here to the loss by modern man of the capacity for openly expressing "fantasy" as did the ancients. Through cultural repression, the exteriorized fantasies of the ancients, expressed in myths, have become increasingly interiorized:

> Para los antiguos la realidad fue siempre mayor que la realidad y no era raro que se refirieran amables encuentros con un unicornio o combates feroces con un dragón: la fantasía era la mayor realidad. Para nosotros, más sabios o más torpes, la fantasía ha quedado reducida a los sueños, a la imaginación, a la incómoda estrechez de la realidad imaginativa y fantástica de un libro. Pero el hombre ha sabido siempre cómo procurarse sueños cuando está despierto: es esto lo que está en el fondo de las drogas, de la bebida, de la literatura; y en nuestro siglo de fábricas ha creado una "fábrica de sueños" ... el cine es una enorme fábrica que produce sueños en serie, fantasías a granel, y vende estas invenciones al por mayor. (31; my ellipsis)

Another aspect of the capacity for open expression of fantasy possessed by the ancients was their indulgence in rite and "mysteries." Fantasy was a structured, institutionalized part of social intercourse. Much of the external structure of religion has now been lost or secularized, and the drama, for the Greeks the center of much ritual, has lost its religious function. The film, Cabrera Infante suggests, has taken over much of the function of the old rites, though in a much less hieratic fashion; and openly expressed fantasy has been sublimated into aesthetic response and internalized or hidden in dreams and imagination.

Here Cabrera Infante is, like Joseph Campbell, very close to Freud, who explained religious feelings as the internalization of explicit myths—stories—which in turn rationalize repressed guilt arising from actual incidents (see Merrim, "Through the Film"). Freud treats monotheism, for example, as an institutional rationalization of the actual tribal murder of the father (*Moses* 129-30; see also 43-49).

Cabrera Infante also hews close to Bazin, who " . . . posed a goal for cinema which is outside the realm of our usual conception of art: cinema as a 'sesame' to universes unknown; cinema as a new sense, reliable like our natural senses, giving us knowledge of empirical reality otherwise unavailable" (Andrew, *Major Film Theories* 145), and to the expressionist movement, which, according to Andrew, tried not only to communicate a deeper or greater reality but to "transform daily life" (13). Cabrera Infante offers a simple analogy to the "greater reality" of myth which is expressed through cinema: the actual physical medium of film, with its "imágenes ampliadas" and "voz amplificada," represents an important aspect of its larger-than-life quality (*Arcadia* 31).

Film, like its heroes, is thus for Cabrera Infante a reality subjected to magnification. The effect of the film image is not that reality is mirrored, as in the Kracauer theory, but that it is enlarged, made grandiloquent through spatial and thematic exaggeration.

The mythic figures fitting the Hollywood type were not only physically enlarged on the screen—any film image is so enlarged—or closely scrutinized by the camera. They were also products of the public relations mechanism of the Hollywood studios, a system which included physical glamorization of the actors so that they came to seem godlike (see Morin, *The Stars*). Although such treatment is still given to the actor today, the effect is not so pervasive because the method is not as systematized as before and because audiences seem to have become more perceptive of the public relations "hype" behind such glamorization.

One typically mythic figure in the movies is, according to Cabrera Infante, the historical or legendary hero who has acquired godlike characteristics. Alexander Nevsky and Billy the Kid, on the screen,

> ... son gigantescos comparados con los modelos de la realidad: Nevsky, el guerrero, nunca pudo tener, exceptuada la leyenda, el tamaño de Alejandro Nevsky, su facsímil del film; Billy the Kid, el asesino, jamás soñó ser el héroe trágico de todos los films que llevan su nombre. (*Arcadia* 32)

The process of mythic expansion mentioned here by Cabrera Infante is exemplified in his own work by the figure of La Estrella in *Tres tristes tigres*, who, as he has pointed out on more than one occasion (e.g., *Siete voces*, quoted in Jiménez 57; Interview with author), is an exaggerated version of a singer in Cuba.

Cabrera Infante speaks in *Arcadia todas las noches* of two other types of myths in connection with the cinema. The figures of "la vampiresa, el galán audaz en el amor y en la vida, los villanos muertos en el último rollo" (32) recall the classifications of Erwin Panofsky, who traced the survival of melodramatic icons like the Vamp, the Straight Girl, and the Family Man in the early cinema and their progress into more contemporary films ("Style" 162-63). These so-called "myths" actually seem closer to Plautine stock-figures, summarized by his successor Terence as "'a running slave, virtuous wives and dishonest courtesans, greedy spongers and braggart soldiers' (*The Eunuch*, 36-38)" (Radice, Introduction 15), than to the idea of myth as involving "heroic saga" (Graves 2: 12) which Cabrera Infante develops with respect to Nevsky and Billy the Kid. The other type of myth to which Cabrera Infante alludes is more precisely a subtype of the "heroic saga" variety. He speaks of "mitos particulares, que se ponen de moda, declinan y desaparecen tras el horizonte del olvido" (*Arcadia* 32). These myths or fads—such as, perhaps, Valentino or the "It" Girl—are related by Cabrera Infante to older myths which have also been forgotten or subsumed under the category of a larger mythic system, as for instance, the posited merging of the local god Yahweh with the Egyptian god Aton which resulted in the Old Testament figure of God.[9]

For Cabrera Infante, the myth has a precise form: "Los fantasmas—imprecisos, informes, ectoplasmáticos—no son un mito." In his discussion of this idea, he offers examples of mythical figures: "Sin embargo es un mito la sirena—cuerpo de mujer, cola de pescado—, la esfinge—busto de mujer, garras de león, alas de águila, cola de toro—es un mito, y el minotauro, mitad toro y mitad hombre, es también otro mito milenario" (*Arcadia* 32). The quality which these figures cited by Cabrera Infante share is their appearance of physical reality—their phenomenal clarity and distinctness. They are distinguished from less "precise" "phantasms" because they have taken on a clear form; they exist in sharp relief. Not only do they awaken a mental image in us because of their clarity, but they also exhibit a striking quality. They are composed of conflicting or incongruous elements, like those of the neologisms created by Cabrera Infante or one of the images created by Eisenstein by means of the montage process. In fact, the mythical figures adduced by Cabrera Infante all evince cinematic qualities. They are myths, according to him, because of their "horror de la vaguedad" (32), being precise, clear, and complete images formed through a process of montage.

The concept of the equivalence of myth with the film image is extended by Cabrera Infante into the medium of film itself. He says that "...la luz se descompone en el mito del arco iris" (*Arcadia* 32). Here he offers, perhaps, a subtle metaphor for the approach of Vsevolod Pudovkin to film editing, a process of breaking up reality, or the image of reality, into components, so as to impress the viewer with a greater significance when the elements are reassembled.[10]

The new image of the rainbow in the example cited by Cabrera Infante has a very particular significance. Sunlight, broken into its components and forming a rainbow, finds a mythical incarnation in the figure of Iris, the Greek "messenger of the gods" (Zimmerman 140). Greta Garbo or Jean Harlow, as mythical figures formed by the action of "la luz" of cinema on the real persons who were Greta Gustafsson and Harlean Carpenter (Katz, *Film* 464, 534), represent for Cabrera Infante incarnations like Iris. These incarnations have themselves undergone, or perhaps suffered, "nuevas encarnaciones":

> Los mismos mitos del siglo (nacidos a la oscuridad del cine) crecen con la luz: Greta Garbo se convirtió en un mito cuando dejamos de verla actuar sobre la realidad desde el cine. El mito del sexo rubio y exhibido, que tomó cuerpo en Jean Harlow, creció después de su muerte, y así hemos tenido nuevas encarnaciones del mito (Marilyn Monroe, Jane [sic] Mansfield), siempre humilladas por la analogía: son las nuevas Jean Harlow, Jean Harlow de nuevo. (*Arcadia* 32)

On a more sociologically oriented plane, film, or the institution of film, is for Cabrera Infante the carrier of "valores ecuménicos" for the modern public (*Arcadia* 181). Here he echoes Parker Tyler, who, rather more disparagingly than Cabrera Infante, speaks of the powers of "magic and myth" which have been appropriated by the film. Like Bustrófedon in *Tres tristes tigres*, the director or the powerfully talented star becomes for Cabrera Infante a mythmaker, a magician who transforms reality with his talismanic tools: editing, camera placement, or perhaps even "method-acting."

Cabrera Infante repeatedly uses such terms as "milagro" and "mágico" (*Arcadia* 181) to refer to the effects of film. He sounds like a surrealist critic speaking about the magical workings of the word on reality. The poet and the filmmaker, as Cabrera Infante might argue, share the characteristics of the shaman, who has the alleged power to transform reality and who incarnates and expresses the "ecumenical values" of his culture.[11] The reference by Ortega y Gasset to film as "'mágico'" and as allowing an audience to "visit" other locales while watching a movie in their neighborhood, quoted in *Arcadia todas las noches* (181), recalls the wonderment of Joseph Campbell at the universality of myths: "Why is mythology everywhere the same, beneath its varieties of costume?" (*Hero* 4).

For Cabrera Infante, film has become as universal in modern experience as the practice of religion was for an earlier age. Here can be found much of the "magic" of film—its ability to speak ecumenically to people of the modern age (*Arcadia* 181). Cabrera Infante accordingly locates the film experience on a seemingly banal, because everyday, axis: the temporal plane of local film showings, which occur in most places "todas las noches." Thus, the filmgoer can experience—or live in—"Arcadia todas las noches": "...digo si hay una ocasión mágica, si hay un momento en que el juego se hace religión, ese milagro ocurre todas las noches y se llama cine, *le cinéma, the movies*" (*Arcadia* 181).

The use of the phrase "todas las noches" as well as the reference to "dream" as the essence and function of film which is found in "la exacta frase de Lebovici" quoted by Cabrera Infante in the essay on Vincente Minnelli in *Arcadia todas las noches* to the effect that "'El cine es un sueño...que nos hace soñar'" (162; original spaced periods) point to a possibly deeper significance in the phrase "Arcadia todas las noches." Following the interpretation made by Campbell of the heroic quest, one could state that, like Theseus conquering the Minotaur, the person who goes to see a film undergoes a rite of passage. He journeys through the realm of dream and confronts his inward fantasies:

> The passage of the mythological hero may be overground, incidentally; fundamentally it is inward—into depths where obscure resistances are overcome, and long lost, forgotten powers are revivified, to be made available for the transfiguration of the world. This deed accomplished, life no longer suffers hopelessly under the terrible mutilations of ubiquitous disaster, battered by time, hideous throughout space; but with its horror visible still, its cries of anguish still tumultuous, it becomes penetrated by an all-suffusing, all-sustaining love, and a knowledge of its own unconquered power. Something of the light that blazes invisible within the abysses of its normally opaque materiality breaks forth, with an increasing uproar. The dreadful mutilations are then seen as shadows, only, of an immanent, imperishable eternity.... (Hero 29)

Such revelations are perhaps available to the moviegoer who shares the sensitivity of Cabrera Infante to the power of the film to release him from the confines of his "normally opaque materiality." Cabrera Infante indeed ascribes such power to films such as Vertigo and Citizen Kane. The "inward" journeys of some of the characters in his books, such as Arsenio in Tres tristes tigres and the narrator of La Habana para un Infante Difunto, seem to reflect the same preoccupation, although neither the mock death of Arsenio Cué nor the erotic initiation of the narrator liberates the characters from the isolation in which they live.[12]

From the foregoing discussion of the views of Cabrera Infante on the function of film, one would expect his film preferences to lean in the direction of movies which help to transform the ontological vision of man, a concept expressed in the following terms by Luis Buñuel:

> What I mean is that through books, newspapers, and our experiences we come to know an external and objective reality. Film, through its technique opens up a little window onto the extension of this reality. My wish, as a film viewer, is that a film make me discover something new. (Buñuel 96)

Cabrera Infante would seek in a film a value similar to the quality which fascinates him in literature: the characteristics of a writer like Lewis Carroll, who surprises the reader into new viewpoints by juggling linguistic reality. By the same token, Cabrera Infante would tend to eschew such trends as socialist realism, or the Nazi "realism" of Leni Riefenstahl, tendencies which subordinate the investigation of the mythic aspects of reality to the presentation of an ideological viewpoint. The key to the power of film, for Cabrera Infante, is not that it mirrors reality in the impersonal fashion of a neorealist film but rather that it has the capacity to entertain and enchant the viewer through an appeal to the capacity for fantasy.[13] Film, as we have seen, has in the judgment of Cabrera Infante replaced the more open and simpler expression of fantasy, the imaginative faculty of man, which was possible in earlier ages through rite or even just in everyday discourse.

A film need not be a "fantasy," in the sense in which that term is commonly used to refer to a film or a story bearing little or no relation to everyday reality, like, for example, *Frankenstein*, or, on another level, *Orphée*, in order to possess the power of "miracle" to which Cabrera Infante refers. He in fact tends to favor the great genres of the Hollywood cinema, all of which are not "fantastic," in the particular way in which that designation applies to horror movies or "fantasy" films, but which do have the crucial element often lost in more "serious" attempts at filmmaking, a great power to entertain the audience. These genres thus have the quality of fantasy to which Cabrera Infante refers without necessarily belonging to the category of "fantasy movies."

The Cabrera Infante of *Carteles* and *Lunes de Revolución* is not a coldly intellectual critic. His strong personal interest in movies is evidenced in his enthusiastic investigations of the genres of musicals, comedies, Westerns, and detective or gangster films. He also shows some interest in the documentary film, although certainly not with the fervor of an apologist for that form such as John Grierson (see Lindgren 215-20). Some of the reviews in *Un oficio del Siglo 20* reveal a strong social conscience, with Cabrera Infante defending directors like Elia Kazan and attacking documentaries like *Mau-Mau*, which he accuses of misrepresenting a just revolutionary cause.

Generally, however, the social concerns of Cabrera Infante are subordinated to a Bazin-like humanism, a concern for the universal human condition. His stance is similar to the "Personalism" followed by Bazin. Personalism, according to Hugh Gray, was central to the thought of Bazin and was derived from the work of Emmanuel Mounier (1905-1950) (Gray 3-5, 11-15). Personalism was not unlike existentialism in its less pessimistic forms.[14] The "basis" of Personalism, according to Gray, "was the affirmation of the existence of free and creative persons and it introduces into the structure of its thought the idea of the unforeseen which naturally rules out any desire for definitive systematization" (3).

Such a philosophy, as will be seen from the following presentation of the views of Cabrera Infante on directors and genres, expresses an important aspect of his own philosophical standpoint. Nevertheless, his emphasis on the power of nostalgia and memory in determining one's preferences in film and literature, as well as, perhaps, one's predilections in work and companionship, implies a facet of his viewpoint which seems at best tangential to the humanist defense of freedom and creativity. In his fascination with nostalgia, memory, and dream, Cabrera Infante borders on a Proustian pessimism, a determinism less of the Zola variety than of the Pascalian. The creativity of man, his employment of fantasy and its harnessing through the rational faculty, is both spurred and bound by his nature, by the memories of his childhood which connect with his archetypal memories and his sense of collective myth. The work of Cabrera Infante, then, exhibits a double-action quality, on the one hand a drive towards a humanistic idealism not unlike the thought of Bazin and on the other, a tendency towards a psychological or spiritual negativism such as one might find in the work of Orson Welles or in the writing of John Dos Passos.[15]

With regard to the concern of Cabrera Infante for nostalgia, it is useful to point out that his literary memories are expressed in highly visual terms, paralleling his emphasis on the same power in film. His extensive recall of La Habana is a visual one; the narrator of *La Habana para un Infante Difunto* helps the reader to "see" the city: "...desde el balcón se podía ver el tráfico habanero bajando la cuesta donde la Avenida de los Presidentes encuentra su monumento ..." (240).

In his film criticism as well as in his fiction, Cabrera Infante emphasizes the visual. He values the capacity of, for example, the film *Moby Dick* for conveying "una grandeza visual que el libro no alcanza con la furiosa prosa barroca de Melville..." (*Oficio* 143). His evaluations of movies often stress their visual texture. Although he deals at times with the shot breakdown or the use of, for instance, deep focus in a film, he tends to emphasize the presence and the effectiveness of Technicolor, Cinemascope, Eastmancolor and other technical processes which lend a striking visual quality to the films in which they are used. The cinematographer and even the credit designer are, for Cabrera Infante, important to the process of filmmaking; here, he differs from a strict auteurist, who cleaves to the policy of the director as the sole important creative force. The distance from a critic with such visual concerns to the observant narrator of *La Habana para un Infante Difunto* is not a very great one.

The interest shown by Cabrera Infante in the musical partakes strongly of his fascination with the visual. The American musical film in its highest form, such as the work of Fred Astaire and Gene Kelly as performers and interpreters and of Busby Berkeley, Vincente Minnelli, and Stanley Donen as directors, is a strongly visual art. The three directors mentioned here are especially interested in visual creativity, in original staging to create striking effects.

The musicals of these creators show a remarkable range of expression. The geometric designs and patterns created by Berkeley, with the female form as their basis,[16] have never been surpassed. Minnelli creates rich, colorful settings for his dancers, who move in a stylized world of backdrops, a trend also seen in the work of Donen and Kelly. Settings such as those in the park scene in *The Band Wagon*, where Astaire and Cyd Charisse dance a rehearsal which is unmistakably intimate, are closely related to the tradition summarized in the term "Arcadia," which, as a dwelling place for the god Pan and other mythical figures, "was adopted by the poets [of antiquity] as a symbol of quiet rustic life" and was closely associated, through Theocritus, with "The pastoral tradition in literature" (Zimmerman 28). The "Arcadia" which is the metaphor for film in *Arcadia todas las noches* can be found in musical films from *Footlight Parade* to *An American in Paris* and *On the Town*.

Cabrera Infante is quite interested in the field of music, as his article "Salsa para una ensalada" demonstrates. His fascination with music is strongly evident in *Tres tristes tigres*, in which one of the major characters is a bongo player and another important figure, La Estrella, is an enormous mulatto woman who sings *boleros*. The importance of music to the work of Cabrera Infante is an area which has, as Eliana

Rivero once noted in conversation, been even less studied than that of film.[17] Within the limits of the present study, the great significance of music, both "popular" and "serious," to his work is shown by his preference for musical films such as *On the Town*, *Brigadoon*, *Meet Me in St. Louis*, and *Funny Face*, a taste to which he refers when speaking of his musical background: "Mi música—swing, jazz y comedias musicales—venía de USA, sonando sincopada, y de Europa en suaves sinfonías" ("Salsa" 22).

The typical setting of the American musical forms a chief component of the subject of these films, many of which are set in the city, especially in New York. Some musicals do not center around the city. In *Brigadoon*, for instance, New York is the setting that frames the central part of the story, which occurs in a mythical village. Even in this case, however, the work gains its poignancy from the contrast between urban and rural settings. *Meet Me in St. Louis*, also by Minnelli, is a case in point: St. Louis, although a large enough town, is presented as the receptacle of traditional values, an alternative to urban, foreign New York.

Such oppositions, as well as the exalted presentations of the big city which also occur in many musical films, like *The Band Wagon* and *On the Town*, help to explain the interest of Cabrera Infante, whose subject is typically the city, in the musical. Perhaps the great myth of the city, the dream world of American capitalism, invoked in the musical, captured his imagination and helped to propel him towards the evocation of La Habana which is the center of his later work. In any case, the concentration in the musical of mythic energy around the city, and dialectically around the country, which, in a musical such as *Meet Me in St. Louis*, by its contrasting values effectively demythifies the city, connects smoothly with the interest of Cabrera Infante in the city as a kind of *locus amoenus*, as a place of initial innocence which gradually, with adulthood, becomes corrupted and distorted by the twin engines of sex and intellectual awakening, as in the case of the narrator of *La Habana para un Infante Difunto*.

The city is also the center of one of the other great generic interests of Cabrera Infante, the gangster film, to which the detective and police films are related (see Cavell 55-60). Cabrera Infante, like Robert Warshow, views the "classical" gangster tragically, as an individualist who, like Rocco in *Key Largo*, is defeated by a society with which he cannot or will not compromise. Warshow speaks of the "tragic error" of the gangster in terms which bring to mind the self-imposed situation of Macbeth:[18]

> But the gangster's loneliness and melancholy are not "authentic"; like everything else that belongs to him, they are not honestly come by: he is lonely and melancholy not because life ultimately demands such feelings but because he has put himself in a position where everybody wants to kill him and eventually somebody will. He is wide open and defenseless, incomplete because unable to accept any limits or come to terms with his own nature, fearful, loveless. And the story of his career is a nightmare inversion of the values of ambition and opportunity. (136-37)

Compare the declaration by Cabrera Infante to Rita Guibert that " 'No hay línea más trágica en toda la tragedia moderna que su exclamación [la de Edward G. Robinson] al final de *Little Caesar*: *"Mother of God, is this the end of Rico?"*, se pregunta incrédulo antes de morir este Maquiavelo de Chicago' " (414; original emphasis).

Warshow fixes the " 'classical' " gangster as a creature of the city: "The gangster movie, which no longer exists in its 'classical' form, is a story of enterprise and success ending in precipitate failure. Success is conceived as an increasing power to work injury, it belongs to the city ... (135; my ellipsis). He highlights the adaptation of the gangster to his milieu, calling him " ... graceful, moving like a dancer among the crowded dangers of the city" (136). Certainly, as Carlos Clarens points out in *Crime Movies* (13), the description fits the protagonists of *Little Caesar* and *Scarface*, but what about such films as *Bonnie and Clyde*, which occur in a more or less rural setting?

The answer is similar to one which could be given to the same type of question about "rural" musicals such as *Meet Me in St. Louis*. A film such as *Dillinger* or *Bonnie and Clyde* seems rather out of step, as if the characters belonged elsewhere, their careers alluding to those of big-city gangsters but their temperaments betraying a different kind of self-reliance. Perhaps such films are not gangster movies at all but rather offshoots of the Western.[19] The gangster can only be understood in relation to the urban environment which has produced him; here the attention of Cabrera Infante would seem to revolve around a point similar to the axis of his predilection for the musical: the issue of the mythification of the city.

Thus, in *Little Caesar* the city acquires a mythical status through the struggle of the hero of the movie. Rico evinces a *hubris* on the order of Heracles shooting arrows at the sun. At the same time, the city of this film is no *locus amoenus*, having been corrupted by money and power. Somewhat like the Cabrera Infante protagonists, Rico Bandello comes from humble beginnings to prominence in the big city and loses in the process whatever innocence or naveté which he may once have had. While the energy and bustle of the city in such films lends it some mythical status, the impression is rather of a trend towards demythification in the form of social criticism.

Significantly, the gangster or detective films cited by Cabrera Infante in *Un oficio del Siglo 20* do not include those examples such as *You Only Live Once*, *Dillinger*, or *They Live by Night* which seem to derive from and comment on the Western. He typically refers to movies such as *The Asphalt Jungle*, *The Killing*, *The Naked City*, and *Scarface*, all set in an urban milieu. The heroes of these urban films are usually set off against a crime "machine" or organization, either opposing it or attempting to lead it. A strong feeling of oppression and soiling by the corruption is often present. The milieu is not unlike the darker side of the urban portraits in the fiction of Cabrera Infante, with their seamy, noisy night spots and gallery of appropriate characters. Films like *They Live by Night* and *Dillinger*, while undoubtedly of much interest to Cabrera Infante,[20] find less resonance in his work, perhaps because of their relatively pastoral emphasis and the tendency of their heroes to flee, not to seek, the city.

Within the realm of the gangster film in an urban setting, a certain development of the gangster character has taken place as the genre has progressed. The progression from the "expansive and noisy" "'classical'" gangster, exemplified by Rico Bandello from *Little Caesar* or Tony Camonte from the Howard Hawks *Scarface* (Warshow 136) towards a character like the Richard Conte gangster in *Cry of the City* (see Clarens 217), who, like Sam Spade on "the other side" of the law, typifies the "introverted" "Dandy" figure, seems inevitable if the gangster figure is to survive in a hostile society.

To a reader of *Tres tristes tigres*, the terms in which Baudelaire speaks of the "dandy" figure should seem familiar enough:

> [The] dandy does not make love his special aim.... [He is] free from the need to follow any profession.... For the true dandy ...[personal appearance and material elegance] are ...symbols of the

aristocratic superiority of his personality.... What then is this ruling passion...? It is, above all, a burning need to acquire originality, within the apparent bounds of convention.... It is the delight in causing astonishment, and the proud satisfaction of never oneself being astonished.... The characteristic beauty of the dandy consists, above all, in his air of reserve, which in turn arises from his unshakeable resolve not to feel any emotion.... (quoted in Cavell 55. Original internal ellipsis and brackets)

The "tigres," despite their less than elegant qualities, are variants of or commentaries on this basic pattern. They "'delight in causing astonishment'" but remain introverted and marginal to the concerns of society. One senses a rootlessness in *Tres tristes tigres* which is similar to the ambience of *film noir*, a development of the gangster film. Although some of the antecedents to the alienated quality of *Tres tristes tigres* are certainly literary, the fact remains that Cabrera Infante himself points to movies as a primary influence on his writing. Cué and Silvestre, who cover up their emptiness by banter and parodic use of movie-style dialogue,[21] may not be far from the tragicomic Cain and Abel of *Scarface*, the blustering Tony Camonte and the sardonic and dandified Guino Rinaldo, who also indulge in competitiveness over women.

While such questions are difficult to answer definitively, still it is necessary to stress the importance of film models to the literary development of Cabrera Infante, if only to correct the underemphasis on his filmic sensitivity. The gangster film and the musical are not the only film genres which have left their mark on him. At least as important to his literary consciousness is the Hollywood comedy film and its European, particularly French, counterpart.

Cabrera Infante is usually, and rightly, considered a comic writer. His comedy, like that of the great film comedians, has a serious underside, just as the tragic demise of Rico has its comic and grotesque obverse. Cabrera Infante has even said that he wanted to be "'a stand-up comic'" ("Memories of an Invented City") but that he could not achieve his goal. He stressed the importance of the comic aspects of his writing in an interview with the author of the present study. Furthermore, he stated to Rita Guibert that:

Nada más cercano a mis objetivos en *TTT* que la filosofía de la vida como la expresaron los Marx en sus películas, ¡y en Jill Levine [the translator] mis tres tigres marxistas habían encontrado su Margaret Dumont! (421)[22]

The thematics of American film comedy are tightly woven into the texture of his fiction, and the *métier* of comedian holds more than academic interest for him.

The influence of the comedy film on the work of Cabrera Infante is a clear and strong one. Even among the literary antecedents to his work about which Cabrera Infante is explicit, comic or satiric works and authors predominate. Ardis Nelson, in her book on Cabrera Infante and the traditions of Menippean satire, has emphasized his great debt to this ancient comic form as well as to the *Satyricon* of Petronius Arbiter, *Tristram Shandy* of Laurence Sterne, and the works of Lewis Carroll.

While these influences have clearly been powerful, his debt to comic film is equally apparent. He once considered Charles Chaplin to be *"el mayor genio del cine"* (*Oficio* 247; original emphasis) and enthusiastically praises Jacques Tati, the Marx Brothers, and the work of Billy Wilder. His preferences in the area of film comedy line up along the axes of satire and parody. All the aforementioned comic artists of film derive their animus from sophisticated social satire, from the parody of established institutions and ideas. Some, like Chaplin and Wilder, have overt pretensions to social commentary, while others, like the Marxes and Tati, do not tend to preachiness, letting their comedy speak for itself.

The feature of social satire is common to film comedy and to the "Menippean tradition," which, as Nelson says, was a form of satire without "moralistic end" (*Cabrera Infante* xxiii, 5), not too harsh in its approach, but effective nonetheless in deflating sacred cows. Once again, the interests of Cabrera Infante in literature and film can be seen to dovetail nicely. To neglect the films is to eliminate the possibility of discerning certain patterns in his writing.

These patterns, though often subtly concealed, are possible to distinguish. Following the lead given by Cabrera Infante himself, one can easily see that the repartée between Silvestre and Cué, in *Tres tristes tigres*, is redolent of the banter between Abbott and Costello. In reading the following section of dialogue, one is reminded of a classic routine by the two comics about a baseball game, with its absurd questions and answers:

  —¿Qué vas a cantar?
  —A petición, voy a decir Tres Palabras.
  —Lindo título—dije.

—Ese no es el título—dijo Cué.

—¿Es otra canción?

—No. Es la misma canción....

—¿Y cuál es el título?

—No lo recuerdo, pero te puedo decir cómo se llama ella.

—¿Cómo se llama?

—Reina.

—Esa es la canción. La conozco. Preciosa.

—No, no es la canción. Es el nombre propio de una amiga....

—¿Cuál es entonces la canción?

—La que voy a decir.

—¿Qué vas a decir?

—Tres Palabras.

—¡Esa es la canción!

—No, ese [sic] es el título. La canción es lo que viene debajo del título.

—¿Qué viene debajo del título?

—El subtítulo.

—¿Y debajo?

—El sub-subtítulo.

—Pero entonces, demonio, ¿cuál es la canción?

—Mi nombre es Arsenio, señor mío.

—¿CUÁL ES LA CANCIÓN? (389-90; my ellipsis)

Compare the above dialogue to a selection from the Abbott and Costello routine:[23]

BUD: Let's see, on the team, we have: Who's on First, What's on Second, I Don't Know's on Third....

LOU: You the manager?

BUD: Yes.

LOU: You know the guys' names?

BUD: I should.

LOU: Then tell me the guys' names.

BUD: I say, Who's on First, What's on Second, I Don't Know's on Third....

LOU: I'm asking you, who's on First?

BUD: That's it!

LOU: Well, go ahead and tell me.

BUD: Who.

LOU: The guy on First!
BUD: That's it.
LOU: What's the guy's name on First?
BUD: No. What's on Second.
LOU: I'm not asking you who's on Second!
BUD: Who's on First.... (*Abbott and Costello Live*; my ellipsis)

Somewhat less obvious is the appearance of a motif which could be called the "masquerade." The formula applied to Cué, that "'En cada actor hay escondido [sic] una actriz'" (308),[24] so that Cué becomes an actor hiding his feminine qualities and masquerading as a totally masculine figure, reverses the pattern of *Some Like It Hot*, in which Curtis and Lemmon play musicians disguised as women.[25] Masquerade motifs of different valences—the false blonde, the dark glasses used by Cué, from *Tres tristes tigres*, and the pseudonymous Violeta del Valle from *La Habana para un Infante Difunto*, are common in the writing of Cabrera Infante, suggesting that the true identities of his characters are placed in doubt. Such masquerades are frequent elements of the Hollywood comedy. *Duck Soup*, *To Be or Not to Be*, and *Gentlemen Prefer Blondes* are just three movies which contain the device.

The heritage of the comedy film, then, provides a clear analogy to and a probable influence on the writing of Cabrera Infante. The confluence of themes and motifs from film, from literature, and from other arts such as music and painting in his work helps to account for the difficulty in classifying that work. *Tres tristes tigres* and *La Habana para un Infante Difunto* seem at times like novels, in the traditionally accepted sense of that term, at other times like critical experiments, and at still others like sustained exercises in allusiveness. The allusion is not solely to films, music, and books by title or with reference to characters but also involves references to styles, such as in the section with the parodies of the literary styles which are used to narrate the story of the assassination of Trotsky. Film style is also mentioned, as in the case of the reference to the "'momento en que el viejo Hitch cortaría para insertar inter-cut de fuegos artificiales'" (*Tres tristes tigres* 166).

Some of the more obvious stylistic allusion in *Tres tristes tigres* centers around the Western (see 373-74).[26] Cué and Silvestre, who imitate the speech patterns of a Western hero, only formally resemble the heroes portrayed by Gary Cooper and John Wayne. They mimic the speech of the Westerner but cannot attain to his self-possessed "completeness," in the terminology of Robert Warshow (137-38). The pose adopted by Cué and Silvestre, with its overtones of masculine competitiveness and conflict with women, is arguably a sustained allusion or parallel to a classic Western situation best expressed in the work of Howard Hawks.

Like Cué and Silvestre, the heroes in Hawks films frequently displayed their skills in open competition, usually in rivalry over a woman. In *Tres tristes tigres*, of course, the irony is that the competition on the surface level, and not with reference to Laura, is empty, since the men are trying to impress not one woman but two prostitutes who fail to be amused. The sustained attempt by the men to entertain the women is an ironic reversal of the statement by Warshow that "...the West, lacking the graces of civilization, is the place 'where men are men'; in Western movies, men have the deeper wisdom and the women are children." It is precisely the "feminine" culture and "civilization" of the two men which fail to amuse the two prostitutes, who, like some rough Western heroes, simply cannot understand the sophisticated wit of their companions. This reversal of the typical Western pattern as elucidated by Warshow (138) is only part of the network of allusions to the Western to be found in the work of Cabrera Infante.

Cabrera Infante also shows some interest in the documentary. A small but significant percentage of his reviews in *Un oficio del Siglo 20* concerns films such as *Mau-Mau* and *The World of Silence*. Here his social conscience is visible, in particular with respect to films such as *Mau-Mau* (183-84), of which he speaks as distorting the Mau-Mau movement for "imperialistic" reasons. Such criticisms belie the oft-repeated attacks on Cabrera Infante as a writer who is not "involved" politically and who lacks social conscience. More correctly, one could say that Cabrera Infante feels that political statement should not be allowed to detract from artistic integrity.

The other documentaries, such as the Cousteau film *The World of Silence* or the semi-documentary film *Torero*, which interest Cabrera Infante are notable for their re-creation of the external world. In such cases, his links to the realist film tradition are apparent. He also demonstrates his interest in varied fields of endeavor such as bullfighting.

The predilection of Cabrera Infante for genre criticism relates closely to his view of film as myth. As Cavell argues (36), "...there are movie cycles," and these cycles or genres such as "prison movies,

Civil War movies, horror movies, etc...." have engendered character "types" which have in turn "ramified into individualities as various and subtle, as far-reaching in their capacities to inflict mood and release fantasy, as any set of characters who inhabited the great theaters of our world." Cycles of heroes from myth and legend, of representative types which have acquired individuality, are familiar to any student of medieval or classical literature. Hollywood has supplanted the ancient cycle as carrier and creator of new mythical personalities.[27] The idea expressed by Cabrera Infante as a borrowing of film genres from "*literatura de pacotilla*" (*Oficio* 244; original emphasis) and their "*conversión*" "*en arte a golpes de intuición poética*" is put rather differently and more precisely by Cavell: "For a cycle is a genre...and a genre is a medium" (36; my ellipsis). A cinematic means of artistic expression and mythic generation was formed out of popular elements for admittedly commercial reasons (36). The shaping of the medium of expression was a creative effort to which many people contributed, among them certain directors, who became influential because of technical skill, force of personality, and artistic talent.

Some of these directors, among them Hitchcock, Minnelli, and Huston, became the favorites of the *auteur* school. As Peter Graham notes, however, the auteurists have tended to abuse the limits of the "theory":

> The term politique des auteurs *(literally 'the policy of authors') is a vague one, and has been used to encompass a number of widely differing attitudes. Understood in the sense of a faithfulness to certain directors and a willingness to champion them through the thick and thin of their inspiration, it is a term which applies more accurately to the critics of* Positif *than of* Cahiers. Positif's *favourite directors (Buñuel, Welles, Ford, Huston, Minnelli, Antonioni, to mention but a few) have remained more or less constant. But* Cahiers *has a long record of fickle tastes: first there were the grotesquely styled 'hitchcockhawksiens', then the worshippers of Lang, Losey, Sirk, and Walsh, then the fanatics who swore by Edgar G. Ulmer and Riccardo Freda, and so on.* (The New Wave *135-36; original emphasis)*

Bazin makes a similar point when he comments that "So it is that Hitchcock, Renoir, Rossellini, Lang, Hawks, or Nicholas Ray, to judge from the pages of *Cahiers*, appear as almost infallible directors who could never make a bad film" ("*La Politique*" 137-38).

Cabrera Infante differs with the *auteur* theory. In *Arcadia todas las noches,* he cites the well-put defense by Néstor Almendros of the role of the actor in filmmaking (142) and notes the importance of other artists and technicians such as cinematographers and screenwriters in the creative process.[28] He recently summed up his opinions on the theory:

> Yo creo... que [la teoría] estaba fundamentalmente equivocada, y que uno se dejó llevar por esa habilidad extraordinaria que tienen los franceses para verbalizar cualquier pensamiento. Entonces, ellos hicieron un cuerpo coherente de ideas acerca del cine, pero, una vez que entraron en el cine, no nos dijeron qué pasaba cuando un crítico se hace autor... la idea del autor en el cine es una idea imposible... ¿cómo es posible que John Huston debe sus películas a que otro las edite, sin preocuparse siquiera de ver el resultado final? Eso no puede ocurrir con un... autor de... ficción—jamás ocurre. Es decir, ese autor vigila hasta el último momento posible lo que va a ocurrir con su libro.
>
> Así que yo creo que la *politique des auteurs* estaba acertada en algunas cosas, es decir, en llamar la atención acerca de la importancia, por ejemplo, de Howard Hawks...y estaba equivocado [sic] en atribuir autoría a directores que realmente no la merecían o negar autoría a directores como Mitchell Leisen.... (Interview with author; my ellipsis)

Clear from the foregoing is the conclusion that the reactions of Cabrera Infante to the *auteur* concept are ambivalent. His corpus of criticism, as we have noted, reflects considerable auteurist influence. He particularly favors directors with mythmaking qualities, men whom he sees as fulfilling to varying degrees his prescription that "...la anotación directa de lo cotidiano no [es] suficiente [   ] para hacer un creador: un autor de películas tiene que ser también—y más que nada—un poeta" (*Oficio* 377; my ellipsis).

These directors include Howard Hawks, Orson Welles, Vincente Minnelli, John Huston (with reservations), Charles Chaplin, Billy Wilder, John Ford, and Jacques Tati. The list is not exhaustive but does illustrate his eclecticism with regard to genre. Directors who chiefly cultivate one genre, such as Chaplin, are included as well as directors who favor different genres as part of their *oeuvre*, such as Hawks, who worked as effectively in comedy as he did in Westerns.[29] Several genres are represented (comedy, the Western, the detective film) as well as films which do not easily fall into a generic category, such as some of the work of Welles.

Cabrera Infante, then, does not link himself to one school of film—neorealist over expressionist, surrealist over documentary. His eclecticism is as apparent in his movie tastes as in other areas of his aesthetic preference and often shows an engaging idiosyncracy. The work of each director strikes a responsive chord in his aesthetic sensibilities, which are finely and importantly tuned to film. His literary work clearly reflects his awareness of and sensitivity to film themes, motifs, and styles as expressed through the work of his preferred directors.

A brief and partial summary of thematic reflection and parallelism with the work of these directors in his own art is indicative of the range of their impact on him. Thus, the fiction of Cabrera Infante reflects themes and techniques from Hawks ("male comradeship," in the phrase of Stanley Cavell [48], and especially "visual geometry"[30]), Hitchcock ("vertigo" or metaphysical rootlessness, nightmares, the importance of dreams), Welles (baroque expression, the role of memory, pessimism), Minnelli (the love triangle, dance and music as mythic vehicles, the emptiness of parties, the mythified or debunked city), Chaplin (moral pessimism, misogyny[31]), and Wilder (the parody of institutions, the debunking of show business, nostalgia). Styles and themes from the films of other directors have also found resonance in the work of Cabrera Infante or can be seen to parallel it. He has of course, given his own artistic talent, assimilated and improved upon any influences, integrating them into his writing so naturally that they have frequently avoided detection by critics unfamiliar with or uninterested in the films from which the motifs or themes may echo or from which they may have originally been derived.

The derivation or paralleling of themes and styles from the work of directors does not prevent Cabrera Infante from a tendency towards glorification of the star. Here, he takes a position in line with his romantically humanist point of view. His stance clearly opposes "the rejection of the star concept" that, according to Bazin in "An Aesthetic of Reality" (23), is "the hallmark of social realism" and neorealism. The auteurists, with whom Cabrera Infante also disagrees, tended to substitute worship of the director for worship of the star, while the neorealists in Italy after World War II were understandably reacting strongly against the idea of the personality cult.

The cult of personality in Hollywood, whose chief manifestation was the manufacture of star personalities and the construction of a mythology with them as its heroes, tended to ignore the ordinary person, or at least the unsentimental presentation of the life situations of ordinary men and women. Even everyday people in Hollywood films tended to be mythified or made into political or social abstractions. Compare, for example, the presentation of "typical" Americans in *High Sierra*, directed by Raoul Walsh, or the Frank Capra film *Mr. Smith Goes to Washington*, with the relatively objective portrait of ordinary Italians in *Ladri di biciclette*, the famous work by Vittorio de Sica. Certainly such a reaction against the Hollywood system as was carried out by the neorealists was understandable and salutary. The work of Paddy Chayevsky or of Elia Kazan, so admired by Cabrera Infante, seems unthinkable without the precedent of the neorealist critique. Nevertheless, like any critique carried to its logical conclusion, neorealism ended in destroying the attraction of its films for the public, who well understood, as Cabrera Infante says in making this point, "la importancia del actor en el cine" (*Arcadia* 142).[32]

Cabrera Infante adopts a position more in line with the viewpoint of the average moviegoer, with whom he shares an interest in being entertained. One is reminded of the remark by James Agee, which, notably, forms part of the epigraph of *Un oficio del Siglo 20*, concerning his point of departure as a film critic and directed to his readers:

> I suspect that I am, far more than not, in your own situation: deeply interested in moving pictures, considerably experienced from childhood on in watching them and thinking and talking about them, and totally, or almost totally, without experience or even second-hand knowledge of how they are made.... It is my business to conduct one end of a conversation, as an amateur critic among amateur critics. (22; my ellipsis)

The reaction of Cabrera Infante against neorealism in *Arcadia todas las noches* and against "'El cine de cámara'" and the New Wave with its *politique des auteurs*, in his interview with Guibert (410, 415), is in effect an attack on the intellectualizing of criticism and the appropriation by self-proclaimed critics of the capacity to understand and enjoy films.[33] A similar spirit is seen in the parodies of overly revered literary styles in *Tres tristes tigres*, in the deliberate use of scurrilous language and situations in *La Habana para un Infante Difunto*, and in his remarks to Guibert concerning his approach to the reader:

Si el lector comprende lo que digo, bien. Si no lo comprende, también me parece bien. No le brindo otra cosa que la posibilidad de comunicación en igualdad de condiciones. Mi ideal es una absoluta identidad entre el lector y el escritor. Si ésta no es posible totalmente, acepto una gradación pero nunca una degradación de uno o del otro. (414)

His predilection for Petronius and Sterne and his professed aesthetic line up neatly with his taste for the decidedly unpretentious Marx Brothers and W. C. Fields as well as for one of the most "popular" of film genres, the musical.

Cabrera Infante, then, values film both as the carrier and creator of modern myths and for its great worth as a popular entertainment. His fiction can only be fully understood by investigating the extent and importance of his sensitivity to the history and myths of film, to which his characters tend to turn for analogies to their situations or for categorizations of their fellow characters and of their experience. The work of several directors and stars, as well as varied examples of films according to genre, form an important subtext to the fiction of Cabrera Infante. Clues to the many allusions to movies in his fiction can be gleaned from an investigation of his film criticism. The analysis which follows will attempt to elucidate the basis of his interest in those films, directors, and stars upon whose thematics, style, and myths he has drawn so heavily in his literary career.

NOTES

[1] My reference to "rite" follows Graves (1: 12).

[2] See Andrew, *Major Film Theories* ch. 2.

[3] I follow Andrew, *Major Film Theories*, throughout the theoretical overview presented below.

[4] Eagle also connects the montage theory of Eisenstein directly to the "deautomatization" of Shklovski (34).

[5] See Cavell (158-59) for remarks on the criticisms by Bazin of the position held by the montage theorists.

[6] See Andrew, *Major Film Theories* 177-78, for the origin of my remarks on the popularization of the theories of Bazin.

[7] He later modified this view, placing other aspects of the work above that of ambiguity. He also attributed his "'teoría de la ambigüedad'" to William Empson and "'varios estetas'" ("Viaje" 68).

[8] My use of the term "neobaroque" derives from Acosta Cruz, *The Discourse of Excess*. Acosta says of "neobaroque" that "This term currently

characterizes contemporary Latin American literature" and attributes her "study's focus" to "Severo Sarduy's theory of the neobaroque" (Abstract). She states that "The two main texts where Sarduy's theory appears are: an article from 1972 called 'El barroco y el neobarroco' and a book from 1974 called simply *Barroco*" (11). Acosta Cruz quotes Linda Hutcheon as saying that:

> What Sarduy calls contemporary neobaroque still uses the technical devices of the baroque—that is, linguistic artifice, inter- and intratextuality, and narrative mirroring. The change in the present usage of these techniques is in intention; the baroque search for consonance is replaced by a willed neobaroque lack of harmony and homogeneity which is literally and figuratively revolutionary in its transgressions of contemporary literary and linguistic norms (27). (34-35)

(34-35). Acosta Cruz offers a summary of some of the "devices" used by neobaroque authors: '

> Of all the neobaroque characteristics studied here a few can be said to be imperative and constitutive of that type of literature. Most of these elements are the ones defined by Sarduy in his theory. On the level of the expression there are the three mechanisms: substitution, condensation and proliferation.... On the level of content the neobaroque relies on different elements that are based mostly on parody.... One important character-istic of neobaroque writing is its emphasis on purely ludic elements such as the intra-textual category of graphic-phonetic grammes. (200; my ellipsis)

She says that:

> of the three mechanisms...condensation is the one used in TTT [sic]...Working alongside with puns, condensation in TTT follows the line established by Lewis Carroll and Joyce. Examples of condensation are: "víboa" (p. 108)—a condensation of víbora and boa; "curiocosa" (p. 219)— which brings together cosa and curiosa.... (98; my ellipsis)

Her definition of condensation refers to it as a "direct descendant of the portmanteau work (frequently associated with puns) [which] appears in the neobaroque not as a summary of related terms but as confrontation and interaction of the components" (19).

⁹ The ideas expressed in this sentence derive from Freud, *Moses*. See esp. 72-82.

¹⁰ See Pudovkin 72-74 for an explanation of the technique.

¹¹ I derive my remarks on shamanism from Campbell, *Hero* 98-101.

¹² See, however, the remarks of Ferguson on the analogy between *Tres tristes tigres* and games ("*TTT* is similar to a board quiz game, particularly one currently popular, *Trivial Pursuit*."). She states earlier in the same paragraph that "Board games, hopscotch, or quiz games are the hero myth and the search for the self made concrete" (131; see also her Introduction [1-21]). She also connects Cabrera Infante with minotaur imagery through Bustrófedon

and La Estrella: "With the deaths of Bustrófedon and La Estrella, the creative power is trapped in the unconscious like the minotaur in the maze" (130). For the minotaur, see also 131, 135, 138. Mazes and labyrinths are discussed through much of the chapter.

[13] Rodríguez-Luis notes this tendency in connection with *Tres tristes tigres*:

El cine que mejor conoce y que más atrae a Cabrera Infante...es el norteamericano; sin embargo, la imitación del cine en *TTT* no se propone, como continúa sucediendo en general en el cine, la reproducción de la realidad social y psicológica, sino muy modernamente, subrayar cómo la literatura de ficción debe evitar el análisis psicológico, la caracterización, la pintura social tradicionalmente característicos de aquélla; de modo que se intentará aquí la reproducción de conversaciones e imágenes...mas teniendo buen cuidado de no someter las tomas al tipo de montaje que organizaría la película en un todo coherente desde el punto de vista realista. (89; my ellipsis)

See also Merrim ("Through the Film") and Rodríguez Monegal ("Estructura" 337-38).

[14] See Andrew, *Major Film Theories* 172, for remarks on the existentialism of Bazin and his view of "'the human condition.'" See also the remarks Cabrera Infante, "Cantando" 11, on the importance of "'cada hombre.'"

[15] Magny writes of the "profound negativism" of Dos Passos (139). For her discussion of this author and cinematic technique, see esp. 105-43.

[16] I owe the notion of "geometric patterns" based on the female form in the work of Berkeley to Dr. Ron Stottlemyer.

[17] See, however, Scheybeler 13-16.

[18] I owe the concept of "tragic error" to Dr. Richard Hosley.

[19] For a similar view with some qualifications, see Solomon 26-29. See also the discussion of the forms in McArthur 17-21. McArthur, in a formulation similar to mine, says that "There is within the gangster film a sub-genre beginning with *Dillinger* (1945) and culminating in *Bonnie and Clyde* (1967) in which the action does not take place in the city, but in the small towns of the rural mid-West" (28 n; see also 49).

[20] During the interview in Wellesley, he expressed interest in the John Milius *Dillinger*, which he had only recently seen.

[21] Jiménez (73-74) concurs with my observation about movie-style dialogue.

[22] Perhaps the remarks of Bakhtin on laughter in the Renaissance (*Rabelais* 66-67) would be apropos here:

The Renaissance conception of laughter can be roughly described as follows: Laughter has a deep philosophical meaning, it is one of the essential forms of the truth concerning the world as a whole, concerning history and man; it is a peculiar point of view relative to the world; the world is seen anew, no less (and perhaps more) profoundly than when seen from the serious standpoint. Therefore, laughter is just as admissible in great literature, posing universal problems, as seriousness. Certain essential aspects of the world are accessible only to laughter. (66-67)

Nelson (*Cabrera Infante*) suggested to me the relevance of Bakhtin for Cabrera Infante.

23 In the citation, "Bud" refers to Bud Abbott and "Lou" to Lou Costello.

24 Quoted in Nelson, "Betrayal" 158. Nelson observes that this remark "is an indirect way of Silvestre's telling him [Cué] that he knows the story of Cué's having loved and lost Laura" (158).

25 See Siemens, *Worlds* 144, for reference to the imputation of homosexuality to Arsenio.

26 Jiménez also notes the imitation of "actores de la ficción cinematográfica" and quotes the dialogue referred to above in reference to the Western (73-74). He notes other parallels, including those with Abbott and Costello and Fred Astaire.

27 Cabrera Infante expresses a similar idea in *Arcadia* 29-32.

28 For a similar argument, and one which may have influenced Almendros, see "Six Characters in Search of *auteurs* [sic]," in Hillier (31-46; see esp. 37).

29 For the origin of this view of Hawks, see Robin Wood, *Howard Hawks*, and Donald C. Willis, *The Films of Howard Hawks*.

30 The "visual geometry" was noted by Cabrera Infante himself at Wellesley.

31 For remarks related to the issue of misogyny, see Rivero, esp. 282-88.

32 Manuel Puig influenced me in this connection. See "Síntesis" 484-85.

33 Like Cabrera Infante, Cyril Connolly, an author whom he cites repeatedly, treated such elitism disdainfully, calling such writers or critics perpetuators of the "mandarin style" (*Enemies* 12-13).

3

The Film Criticism of
Cabrera Infante:
Un oficio del Siglo 20

 N OFICIO DEL SIGLO 20 (1963) is the most ample
evidence concerning the film interests of Cabre-
ra Infante. The book is cast in terms familiar to
readers of André Gide, with the author causing
one of his personae, in this case the narrator of
the pages printed in italics and the annotator of
the collected articles, to comment upon and crit-
icize the work of an earlier persona of the
author, the critic G. Caín.[1] The collection is quite valuable as an index
to the ideas of Cabrera Infante on film prior to his termination as
editor of *Lunes de Revolución* and to the launching of his career in fiction.
Despite the humorous, Sterne-like tactics of the book, the general
concept of the cinema as myth and of the director or the star as
mythmaker is fleshed out and detailed in the many reviews included.
By examining a selection of the reviews, many influences on the
literary works of Cabrera Infante can be discovered, demonstrating
the close relationship of the creativity of the author to his involvement with the cinema.

The film reviews compiled here by Cabrera Infante are extensive
and ecumenical in their scope and interest. The catalogue by the
author of film genres, cited earlier in this book, is found in the section
of *Un oficio del Siglo 20* entitled "Manuscrito encontrado en una botella...de leche" (229-48; original spaced periods), one of the chapters

which serves chiefly as authorial commentary.[2] The genres mentioned are all represented in the collection, with comedies and thrillers predominating. The reviews were selected by Cabrera Infante, with the expressed intention

> ... *de corregir el estrabismo, si no la miopía crítica de Caín: cuando una crónica me ha parecido larga sin remedio o por gusto, la he cortado; ... cuando una película importante ha tenido una crítica indigna de su talla, la he eliminado.* (*Oficio* 41; original emphasis; my ellipsis)

As it stands, then, the selection of articles not only reflects some aesthetic hindsight by Cabrera Infante regarding his film tastes, but also represents his earlier interests, allowing the general tendencies of the reviews to become evident. Thus, Italian cinema of the 1950s, generally in the neorealist vein, is well represented, though not always favorably. Hitchcock, Minnelli, Welles, Chaplin, and Aldrich are all well-documented here, reflecting the liking of Cabrera Infante for these directors as well as for others such as Hawks. While French films are frequently reviewed, films from other countries such as Japan, Sweden, Germany, and Great Britain are less significant in the collection. The strongest concentration of the book, as one would expect, is on the Hollywood film.

American movies, in the form of comedies, dramas, and thrillers, then, predominate in *Un oficio del Siglo 20*. The movies reviewed are not uniform as to their nature beyond these broad categories. For instance, the dramatic films reviewed here by Cabrera Infante (or Caín) range from tearjerkers like *I'll Cry Tomorrow* to purely dramatic movies like *12 Angry Men* and *Paths of Glory* or tragicomedies like *La strada*. Cabrera Infante tends to mix his evaluative focus, finding the comic elements within the dramatic and vice versa. His sense of tragedy is shown to be as keen as his feel for comedy, foreshadowing the hybrid quality of *Tres tristes tigres*.

A useful point of departure for studying the collection in terms of the filmic concept of Cabrera Infante is the statement of cinematic preferences which is provided by him, under the "authorship" of G. Caín, in "Manuscrito encontrado en una botella... de leche" (242-47). Here, he offers a kind of film manifesto which includes "'*una lista de las "mejores películas de todos los tiempos"*'"[3] as well as the genre summary mentioned above.

The manifesto, or statement of critical position, is consistent not only with the distribution and nature of the reviews in the book but also with the later statements by the author to interviewers such as Janes and Guibert. Thus, Caín, or the critical persona of Cabrera Infante in the 1950s and the very early part of the 1960s, values the sound film much more highly than the silent one. As Caín says:

> Considero que el cine—el cine-para-mí, esto es: si no sería otra persona quien haría estas consideraciones [—] empezó con el cine sonoro: el resto es prehistoria, pinturas en una caverna, hachas de sílice. (242)

Such a position, because of its emphasis on the oral, fits well with the feeling of Cabrera Infante for language.[4]

The importance of the visual component in the cinema is certainly not ignored by Cabrera Infante, since he sees film as fully realized only through a felicitous merging of sound and image, not through the undue dominance of one over the other:

> El cine silente ponía el énfasis en la imagen por defecto, no por cálculo estético, de la misma manera que los gestos de una conversación detrás de una vidriera adquieren un sentido diverso: a ambos les falta el sonido: esto es, la realidad completa. (242)[5]

The point made here by Cabrera Infante, concerning the unity of sound and image into "'la realidad completa,'" can better be understood with some historical perspective on the debate over visuals and sound.

The controversy over silence and sound in film has been heated at certain times, especially when sound films first appeared commercially with *The Jazz Singer* in 1929 (see Lindgren 127). The debate has, in broad terms, focused on the question of how artistic the film can and should be. In other words, the issue raised is similar to the disagreements between "realists" and the proponents of fantasy or abstract art, although one must keep in mind that the distinctions are not always clear.

Thus, Rudolf Arnheim and like-minded critics hotly defended the silent film, with its artistic tradition, against what they considered "a technical novelty that did not lie on the path the best film artists were pursuing" (Arnheim, "The Complete Film" 27). As Lindgren explains, the early sound film "... had little artistic merit and fell far below the standards of even the moderately good silent film" (128).

For such critics, the silent film had been paramount because of its emphasis on the visual, or the image on the screen. Sound was for them of little account, given the power of the image, and could well be a liability by detracting from the images or vitiating the inventiveness of the director, leading to films in which "much of the freedom with which the visual image had been used in the silent film was suddenly lost" (Lindgren 128). Arnheim expressed the virtue of the silent film, in terms of its power, in an interesting manner:

> Because of sound film, in the future it will be possible only with great difficulty to show speech in a silent way. Yet this is a most effective artistic device. For if a man is heard speaking, his gestures and facial expression only appear as an accompaniment to underline the sense of what is said. But if one does not hear what is said, the meaning becomes indirectly clear and is artistically interpreted by muscles of the face, of the limbs, of the body.... Silent laughter is often more effective than if the sound is actually heard. The gaping of the open mouth gives a vivid, highly artistic interpretation of the phenomenon "laughter." If, however, the sound is also heard, the opening of the mouth appears obvious and its value as a means of expression is almost entirely lost. ("The Making of a Film" 202-03; my ellipsis)

Other critics, including the director and theorist Sergei Eisenstein, have accepted and defended sound as a necessary and useful complement to the visual image. Eisenstein formulated a stimulating theory on "contrapuntal" film, in which sound and image cooperate dialectically (see *The Film Sense* 70-107). Lindgren comments that "Sound added a new dimension to film, a new extension of realism" (127); here can be seen a point similar to that made by Cabrera Infante.

Among the defenders of innovation, of which sound was once an example, is Charles Barr, who, in an article on Cinemascope, is close to the tone and thrust of Cabrera Infante (Barr, "Cinemascope: Before and After," in Mast and Cohen 120-46). He quotes the opinion of Arnheim on laughter and subjects it to ironic comment because of its alleged silliness:

> Arnheim also wrote, and I am not making it up: "Silent laughter is often more effective than if the sound is actually heard...." But I don't know that this argument against sound is any more unconvincing than that against Scope—the logic is identical. (129 n; my ellipsis)

Cabrera Infante sounds rather similarly deprecating when writing of the "nostalgia" of critics who defend silent film:

> Siempre me ha intrigado saber por qué los críticos de cine (y me refiero a los críticos mayores de edad) defienden con un amor insensato al cine silente—en definitiva, una muestra imperfecta del arte del cine...y tienden a comparar cada obra maestra del cine actual con una supuesta obra maestra superior de los años veinte. Creo que no se trata de un juicio crítico sino de un sentimiento nostálgico, y hay que relacionar cada película silente con momentos estelares o simplemente inolvidables de la juventud o de la niñez del crítico. (*Arcadia* 88)

For Cabrera Infante, then, those critics who worship the silent film are confusing sentiment with theoretical rigor.

Cabrera Infante admits openly his indulgence in nostalgia with respect to movies (*Arcadia* 88-89) as well as his feeling for them as occasions for entertainment. His attitude towards silent films exemplifies his view of cinema as vibrant and entertaining, a perspective which will also make itself clear in his comments about films in the reviews in the collection: "'*Por otra parte, siempre me he sentido como en el museo cuando veo películas silentes—y el cine es precisamente lo contrario de los museos*'" (*Oficio* 243). Caín does mention "'*tres grandes films silentes*' "—*The Great Train Robbery*, *Potemkin*, and *Un Chien andalou* (245-46), as well as several others, of which he says, "'*a pesar de la ausencia de sonido me han conmovido siempre que los he visto*'" (246-47).

The film lists "presented" by Caín to Cabrera Infante, as the narrative device of the book would have it, closely follow the pattern of interest established in the earlier chapters of this study. The sound films are strikingly of the mythic, ambiguous variety. Documentaries are virtually absent. *Tabu* does find a place, but that film, significantly, deals with religion or cultural myth. *Citizen Kane*, of which Cabrera Infante says in *Arcadia todas las noches* that:

> si me dieran—con la espada de Damocles sobre mi cuello, porque de otra manera no lo haría—un solo film para que quedara entre los restos de una debacle atómica, éste, sin una sola duda, sería *El ciudadano*, (29)

as well as *Vertigo*, *Ugetsu*, and *Ivan the Terrible*, are strongly mythopoeic. They either concentrate twentieth-century experience into mythological areas, like *Citizen Kane* and its fictional treatment of William Randolph Hearst, poeticize experience, or reach into older myth and legend, as do *Ivan the Terrible* and *Ugetsu*.

Tribute is paid in particular to Chaplin, Welles, Murnau, Hawks, Griffith, and Minnelli. Several of these directors, as well as others such as Hitchcock, will be prominently represented in the reviews in the book. Although Cabrera Infante does not adhere strictly to the *auteur* line here, the *auteur* approach will be apparent in the emphasis of the book on directors as well as in some of the themes and preoccupations shared by Caín with the critics of *Cahiers du cinéma*.

While directors highlight the book, an important feature is its emphasis on genre. By approaching the collection from a generic point of view, one can see its disparate materials as a more thematically unified whole. This approach is also helpful because it demonstrates the especial interests of Cabrera Infante in certain genres and those directors and stars who have excelled in them and elucidates the formal and thematic nature of the role of film in his fiction.

Caín devotes several major reviews to works of the comic cinema. The comedies reviewed, excluding the musicals, which will receive separate treatment in this chapter, range from slapstick and farce, like *Les Vacances de M. Hulot* and *The Trouble with Harry*, to social satire of the most biting sort, like *Some Like It Hot* and *A Face in the Crowd*. Here many of the stylistic and aesthetic preferences of the literary Cabrera Infante appear in a more clearly stated form than in his fiction.

Jacques Tati is a major figure for Cabrera Infante. Both as a director-writer and as an actor, Tati has created several films which exhibit a highly individual comic style. The essay on Tati by Cabrera Infante shows a sure grasp of comic film history as well as a deep interest in the general area of comedy as an art form. His interest in Tati also reflects his general agreement with the *Cahiers* critics, who were also eager to promote Tati.[6]

Cabrera Infante connects Tati with Chaplin, the focus of his greatest interest in cinema at the time.[7] Both directors, he says, are keen observers of life:

> Como Chaplin—a quien Tati debe más de lo que muchos creen, pero no precisamente por lo que muchos piensan—, Jacques Tati es un observador del hombre, un francotirador de la vida, que dispara precisos retratos a las situaciones del individuo deambulando por su medio particular. (*Oficio* 103)

He speaks of *Hulot* as "un tratado de sociología" (103).

The quality of observation, which implies the marginality of the observer, is central to the fiction of Cabrera Infante as well as to the work of Tati and Chaplin. Códac, in *Tres tristes tigres*, is the observer by definition, the photographer (named for Kodak) who watches with a bemused eye the progress of, for example, a wild house party (120-26). The rather voyeuristic position of Códac recalls not only M. Hulot but also the photojournalist of the Hitchcock film *Rear Window*.

The cacophony of the party in *Tres tristes tigres*, with the competing sounds created by the drumming of Eribó, by the record player, and by several conversations, is reminiscent of the ambience of the beach house in *Hulot*, where people also become isolated into coteries, unmindful of each other because of their absorption in pastimes. The boy in *Hulot*, for instance, who plays the record player so loudly that he disturbs the other guests, is only obeying the ritual of the party as conceived by Tati, in which people try to absorb themselves totally by escaping their daily routines and thus become oblivious to the concerns of others. Like the party or the bar scenes in *Tres tristes tigres*, and similarly to the ubiquitous parties in the films of Minnelli,[8] the beach in *Hulot* "es la escapada fuera del tiempo, una huida hacia un breve espacio confinado entre los dos períodos de tiempo de la vida antes y después, que no significa nada" (*Oficio* 103). Cabrera Infante adds that, despite his attempt to escape from himself, man reveals his true nature in such situations: "En ese ambiente—como en otra fiesta cualquiera, el carnaval, por ejemplo—el hombre trata de ser otro y no logra más que ser él mismo con énfasis" (103). The Minnelli film *Bells are Ringing* makes a similar point, with the heroine (Judy Holliday) comically revealing her plebeian tastes amid a bevy of pseudo-intellectuals of the New York theater scene.

The comedy which Tati sees and presents in the party environment at the beach is characterized, Cabrera Infante says, by his use of the "gag," or "el viejo recurso cómico del chiste visual, la broma de situación" (*Oficio* 105). In *Les Vacances de M. Hulot*, the gag reaches a high level of sophistication, resulting in a deflation of solemnity or in the "deautomatization" of the normal and everyday.[9] Tati, like the surrealists of whom Cabrera Infante writes with evident familiarity (see *Oficio* 366-67), sabotages ordinary ritual and routine. His treatment of a funeral, with its tire which becomes a wreath,[10] is surrealist in a manner similar to the *Viridiana* of Buñuel, with its crucifix which becomes a pocketknife. The mechanism of deautomatization is the same, although performed on different levels: Tati deflates the solemn content of a symbol perceived as humanly inspired, while Buñuel directly attacks the sacred. Nevertheless, the gag or "visual joke" is used by Tati, as well as by Buñuel and Chaplin, to great comic effect. The work of Cabrera Infante also contains fine examples of the gag, as in *Tres tristes tigres*, with the story told by Mr. Campbell, containing the cane-switching episode, and the incident in which Ingrid Bérgamo, to whom, as Silvestre says, "'le dimos ese apodo porque así es como ella pronuncia el nombre de Ingrid Bergman,'" reveals her true nature as a "'calva,'" certainly quite different from the real Ingrid Bergman, by losing her wig (165-67).

Cabrera Infante also reveals his interest in film as a visual and sonic art in the essay on Tati. One of the infrequent theoretical references to film to be found in the criticism of Cabrera Infante, the statement that *"Hulot* es cine puro" because of "La utilización que hace de la imagen como vehículo de la risa y la poesía...el ritmo tan cinemático de la acción, el empleo del sonido y de la música" (*Oficio* 102-03; my ellipsis), exemplifies his view that the visual and the auditory have approximate equivalence in film. Cinematic, or for that matter, literary purity does not stand out as one of the primary concerns of Cabrera Infante. As Feal notes (29), "...he does not see clear dividing lines between literary genres...." His list of film genres seems clearly enough divided; but he avoids theoretical rigidity, taking issue with purism such as that of Arnheim, who, as noted above, defended the silent film as the highest form of cinema. Despite his greater sympathy for the sound film, however, Cabrera Infante tends towards the view of James Agee with respect to film comedy. For Agee, comedy reached its peak in the silent era (see Agee 2-19). Both Agee and Cabrera Infante are rather conservative on this point, although Agee is much more backward-looking than the Cuban critic. The two are definitely in agreement on the status of Charles Chaplin in the history of the comic cinema. For the author of *Un oficio del Siglo 20*, Chaplin is "'el mayor genio del cine'" (247; my emphasis).

The approach taken by Cabrera Infante to Chaplin in *Un oficio del Siglo 20* demonstrates his concept of comedy as a frequent vehicle of pathos. Although Cabrera Infante is certainly not a foe of light comedy like that of Danny Kaye, he often gravitates towards the rather saddening comedy which is so prevalent in *Tres tristes tigres*.[11]

The comedy surrounding La Estrella, for instance, is made mournful by her tragicomic demise and the fate of her reputation, which becomes that of an object of pornography (*Tres tristes tigres* 287). The resolution of such pathetic conflicts in otherwise comic situations is, for Cabrera Infante, a primary contributory factor in the greatness of Chaplin. In the Tramp films, the pathetic aspects of the character and his situations form a layer subordinated to, but not obscured by, the catharsis through laughter which the character provokes.

Once again, the humanism which finds expression in the views of Cabrera Infante on film as a mythic system which can speak to anyone, regardless of academic qualifications, is evident. The conception surfaces in the essay on Chaplin and his career in *Un oficio del Siglo 20*. He remarks of Chaplin that "Si hay algún drama en su vida, es el del hombre bueno..." (177-78). The appeal of Chaplin is universal because of his sympathy for the underdog. Cabrera extends the idea of humanistic universality by referring to the words of Chaplin himself:

> Chaplin, que ha dicho: "No he procurado adular a los espectadores, pero tampoco he pretendido nunca imponerles silencio", dosifica las lecciones de filosofía, la crítica de costumbres, y llena el film de carcajadas, confundida la dulce saliva de la risa con alguna sal de lágrimas. (*Oficio* 178)

The strongly moral grounding of the work of Chaplin[12] strikes a responsive chord in the sensibility of Cabrera Infante, for whom the comic often performs a critical function, deflating the pretensions of society and exposing the shibboleths of prevalent institutions.

The Chaplin hero has a mythic status, appropriate to the interests of Cabrera Infante. He takes upon himself, as Cabrera Infante suggests, the resolution of conflicts, journeying, however unwillingly, into dangerous regions or situations in order to reestablish justice, usually with reference to himself, as one of the downtrodden. The comedy lies to a great degree in the weakness of the Tramp, in his paradoxically powerful exploitation of his debility in order to conquer or sidestep the forces of evil or adverse fortune:

> Pero los elementos están de parte del débil [in *The Gold Rush*]: un viento atroz impide que Chaplin se mueva de su sitio. Por mucho que él quiera no logra avanzar en su intención—forzada por las circunstancias de un hombre fuerte—de abandonar la cabaña.

Cuando ya todo está perdido, los elementos vencidos por el mal, llega el azar vengador. Otro hombre grande, pero de buen corazón, se instala en la cabaña y el pequeño queda con él, las dos fuerzas opuestas, el bien y el mal, neutralizadas, el equilibrio conseguido. (*Oficio* 178)

The Gold Rush, as presented by Cabrera Infante, is a mock epic, with a seemingly unappealing or at least unheroic hero who triumphs with the aid of chance, native craftiness, and friendly support. The same character is to be found in other Chaplin films such as *City Lights* and *The Great Dictator*.

A similar mock-epic quality is apparent in *La Habana para un Infante Difunto*, in which the erotic misadventures of the narrator seem like hyperbolic cousins of the sentimental adventures of the Tramp. Both figures rely heavily on the intervention of chance: the liaisons of the narrator are often motivated by random encounters at school, on the subway, and on city streets. The narrator, with his lack of allegiance to his petty-bourgeois background, despite his tugging nostalgia for it,[13] and his meandering search for the ideal woman, seems almost as much like the Chaplin Tramp as like the Encolpius of *The Satyricon*, a self-admitted influence on Cabrera Infante.[14] Certainly the basic innocence, morality, and sensitivity of the narrator place him further from Petronius, or from Fielding, than from Chaplin. The sketch of the Tramp made by Cabrera Infante in *Un oficio del Siglo 20* could easily be applied to the narrator of *La Habana para un Infante Difunto*, with the important qualification of a more ironic and cynical attitude to be found in the narrator:

Chaplin no hace más que repetir en todo el film, cada vez que menciona a Canillitas, *the poor little fellow*, esto es: el pobre hombrecito. En esa frase no hay nada despectivo, ni irónico, ni reconveniente, cuando más un lejano sentido perdonavidas, que le impulsa a seguir dejar viviendo a su personaje a pesar de la inclemencia del tiempo, de la época y de los hombres. Es esto lo que separa definitivamente a Canillitas de Don Quijote—y lo acerca a los *déclassés* del siglo XX, a los remanentes del viejo mundo en un bravo mundo nuevo, a un emigrado de la moral victoriana y las costumbres burguesas, a un personaje de otro Charles, Charles Dickens. (181)

The Tramp figure later yields, as Agee points out (256), to other characters, such as Monsieur Verdoux, the hero of the eponymous film, listed by Caín as one of his "twelve best." It illuminates, in exaggerated form, the fear of personal involvement with women which leads the narrator of *La Habana para un Infante Difunto* to search for an ideal woman. The narrator, in fact, bears some biographical resemblance to Chaplin himself in this respect; for, as Molly Haskell says, Chaplin was both repelled by and obsessed with women and could never be satisfied in his quest for the ideal:

> The biographies of Swift, Strindberg, and Chaplin reveal that all were continuously attracted to, obsessed with, and even adored by, women. In the abuse he took from women in life, Chaplin seems more justified in his misogyny than Swift and Strindberg do in theirs, but Chaplin, like the others, and in a peculiar mixture of arrogance and obsequiousness, was driven to seek out the very woman, the "ideal," who would end by disappointing him and destroying his illusions. (69)

The misogynistic strain of *Monsieur Verdoux* finds a parallel in the extreme distrust felt for women by the males in the fiction of Cabrera Infante. The women in these works are generally either idealized, like Violeta del Valle in *La Habana para un Infante Difunto*, or debased, like Ingrid Bérgamo or one of the whores in *Tres tristes tigres*. The narrator of *La Habana para un Infante Difunto* does not run from human relationships to the degree of Verdoux, but he does exemplify the tendency of the Cabrera Infante protagonist to approach women as sexual objects, however idealized, and to fear their power.[15] The dilemma of Verdoux seems of a more philosophically serious nature than that of the Cabrera Infante protagonists, since, as Agee says, he deals with "the bare problem of surviving at all in such a world as this" (256). The characters of Cabrera Infante are less singleminded, more hedonistic than Verdoux. All share, nevertheless, an inability to relate normally to women (see Rivero 282-86).

The combination of serious intent and comic treatment which is present in the work of Tati and Chaplin also suffuses the films of Billy Wilder. His *Some Like It Hot* is a key work in the cinema mythology of Cabrera Infante. He cites it in *Un oficio del Siglo 20* (244) as one of the chief representatives of the comedy genre and draws on its structure and iconography for literary inspiration in *Tres tristes tigres*.

Some Like It Hot is important to the work of Cabrera Infante for several reasons. Its pairing of Jack Lemmon and Tony Curtis as well as their rivalry and comradeship are similar in spirit to the pairing of Cué and Silvestre in *Tres tristes tigres,* and the comment made about Cué by Silvestre that "'En cada actor hay escondido [sic] una actriz'" (308) finds an obvious concretization or parallel in the transformation of the Jack Lemmon character into an almost believable woman, a figure which is, as Cabrera Infante says in *Un oficio del Siglo 20,* a powerful "caricatura":

> Pero Jack Lemmon hace algo más: crea un personaje. Su fingida, precaria mujer, vestida en perenne coqueteo con el ridículo, larga, desgarbada, con postizos renuentes a mantener la posición correcta, con un maquillaje—como el de las mujeres feas—que convierte su cara en una máscara grotesca, y por entre la peluca, el oficio de permanecer vivo y la camaradería, brota, dolorosa, la real situación de los transformistas meros trasvestidistas que han hecho de su perversión un arte y una forma de ganarse el pan: como ellos, Jack Lemmon es una patética caricatura de una mujer.... (347)

Caricatures and parodies are frequent in the work of Cabrera Infante,[16] and his characters often indulge in masquerades or burlesques of Hollywood figures. Thus, Silvestre adopts a Cary Grant-like persona to try to seduce Bérgamo in a scene which not only recalls the Cary Grant imitation sustained by the Tony Curtis hero throughout several scenes of *Some Like It Hot* in his pursuit of the girl (Marilyn Monroe) but also parodies *To Catch a Thief* as well as *Notorious,* with its hotel room love scene between the protagonists, played by Grant and Bergman (*Tres tristes tigres* 164-68).

Some Like It Hot is also one of the chief sources for the mystique of Marilyn Monroe, an actress whom Cabrera Infante calls "'ese mito de todos'" (*Siete voces* 410) and "la definitiva sustituta de Carole Lombard en la comedia americana..." (*Oficio* 347). The presence of Monroe in the film adds to its mythic quality, as does its mock-nostalgic treatment of several genres, such as the gangster film, the romance, and the burlesque.[17]

The film exemplifies the tendency of Wilder to treat Hollywood legends in an ambivalent fashion. As Parker Tyler notes in *The Three Faces of the Film* (90-93), the debunking of Hollywood myth in *Sunset Boulevard* actually conceals a tendency towards the reinstatement and glorification of that myth. Similarly, the parodies of genre in *Some Like*

It Hot, epitomized by the mock-epic treatment of the St. Valentine's Day Massacre, suggest a mannerist ambivalence in the work of Wilder. His witty, brittle revisionism suggests the notion of mannerism which, according to Wylie Sypher, came to be widely accepted among art critics, for whom "mannerism came to mean a kind of facile learning, an abused ingenuity, a witty affectation, a knowing pose, a distorting through preciosity, or a play with conventional proportions, images, and attitudes" (109). One might say that the treatment by Wilder of Hollywood myths, like the adaptation of classical myths or legend by Shakespeare in the mannerist play *Troilus and Cressida*,[18] often seems intellectualized or reliant on "ingenuity."

Just as *Some Like It Hot* borrows from Hollywood myth, so too does it recall *The Amphitryon* in its use of disguise and masquerade for the comic presentation of amorous situations. Cabrera Infante does not establish this connection directly but alludes to the similarity of the film to a mythically inspired comedy when he says that:

> Tony y Jack no son maricas sino músicos . . . a quienes los dioses— como a Aquiles o Changó—convierten en mujeres momentáneas, pese a su virilidad permanente; y, como Ulises, han de viajar y navegar de tropiezo en tropiezo, antes de volver al hogar; entre ellos, cada noche, Marilyn, una Penélope demasiado frecuente, teje su tela de sueños eróticos *ad perpetuum*. (*Oficio* 347; my ellipsis)

The tendency of Cabrera Infante to see comedy as a dialectic of humor and pathos is again evident here, as he says, concerning the mythic underpinnings of the film, that "Es esto lo que sitúa a *Algunos prefieren quemarse* por encima del vodevil, de Mack Sennett y de todas las parodias y le da cierto sentido trágico entre el fragor de la carcajada" (347). The mixture of seriousness and humor noted in the Wilder movie by Cabrera Infante is paralleled in the treatment of the figure of La Estrella in *Tres tristes tigres*. While she is certainly a character of Rabelaisian comic dimensions, she ends pathetically, with her talent hardly understood by many more than a small circle of friends.

The motif of the masquerade or of shifting identity, seen at the center of *Some Like It Hot*, is also crucial to the fiction of Cabrera Infante. His characters, especially those of *Tres tristes tigres*, are often unsure of their orientation in society. Cué, Silvestre, Códac and, to a lesser extent, Eribó, frequently seem to merge into one another.[19]

The narrator of *La Habana para un Infante Difunto*, deeply unsure of his personal identity, wants to determine his orientation through the power of a woman. As Feal points out, the grammatical subject of the first-person narrative of the book is mixed with the plural "we"; this is a further example of what she also calls a tendency towards "masquerade" in the fiction of the Cuban writer (see *Novel Lives* 33-61). The blending of Caín and Cabrera Infante, as Feal also suggests, is another example of the difficulty of ascribing precise identity to the characters in his work.[20]

The protagonists of *Some Like It Hot* are perfect existential analogues of such a "confusion of the narrative person" (Feal, *Novel Lives* 35), since they undergo a mock transformation into women. The Lemmon character even becomes confused about his masculine identity. The mention by Cabrera Infante of Ulysses in connection with the film is interesting, since Ulysses was a master of masquerade, changing his appearance or voice in order to escape from peril or to further his designs. The Penelope figure in the movie, Marilyn Monroe, could serve as a parody of the ideal of female constancy for which the narrator of *La Habana para un Infante Difunto* searches. While the film is indeed a carrier of modern myth, its revisionist, mannerist treatment of Hollywood genre and theme suggests the type of satiric approach to values about love which so pervades the fiction of Cabrera Infante.

The parodic approach to genre in *Some Like It Hot* is also seen by Cabrera Infante to apply to *Love in the Afternoon*, another Wilder film which starred Gary Cooper and Audrey Hepburn. Cooper is an important mythic figure for Cabrera Infante, as the apparent parodies of his style, or of a Western style very similar to that which Cooper greatly helped to establish, by Cué and Silvestre in *Tres tristes tigres* (372-74)[21] and the remark by Cabrera Infante in *Un oficio del Siglo 20* to the effect that Cooper is "...este decano de la comedia americana y, sin duda, uno de los verdaderos creadores de Hollywood..." (270) suggest. The film is like an ironic version of the Prince Charming myth, with Hepburn as a most appealing "ugly duckling" who pretends to be a *femme fatale* in a comic attempt to outmatch the Don Juan of Gary Cooper and thereby to make him jealous of her imaginary lovers. Like *Some Like It Hot* this movie, as Cabrera Infante suggests, satirizes romantic conventions and clichés, exhibiting an ironic thrust similar to that of *La Habana para un Infante Difunto*:

"Audrey Hepburn...es la imagen exacta de lo que el film quiere ser: la crónica romántica del amor agridulce de un viejo verde y una jovencita inmadura" (*Oficio* 270; my ellipsis).

Love in the Afternoon falls, for Cabrera Infante, into a truly comic category. Even the use of myths has an ironic thrust: the Hepburn character, an "immature young girl," "se inventa una vida emocionante, única y depravada: la verdadera vampiresa moderna" (*Oficio* 272). Her name, Ariane, recalls Ariadne, who led Theseus out of the labyrinth, perhaps, in this case, the maze of deceit and bedevilment practiced by Cooper on the women seduced by him. The film, despite—or, given its subject matter concerning adultery, because of—its general irony, has a fairy-tale ending which completes and comments on the Prince Charming structure which forms its basis. The ending contributes greatly, for Cabrera Infante, to the status of the film as a genuine comedy:

> Este final feliz le ha sido reprochado al film (por otra parte, muy poco comprendido y bastante maltratado), pero es la razón de ser de la cinta, al fin y al cabo una comedia: bien está lo que bien acaba. ¿No es ésta la esencia de la comedia, la felicidad momentánea de los espectadores a través de la felicidad eterna de los personajes? (*Oficio* 272)

The admiration of Cabrera Infante for Gary Cooper, whose forté was the Western hero (Jordan 41-42, 50), is paralleled by his praise for John Wayne and the American mythic figure which he came to represent. In the characters typically played by Wayne, one can see the self-possessed, confident figure to which Robert Warshow alludes:

> The Western hero...is a figure of repose. He resembles the gangster in being lonely and to some degree melancholy. But his melancholy comes from the "simple" recognition that life is unavoidably serious, not from the disproportions of his own temperament. And his loneliness is organic, not imposed on him by his situation but belonging to him intimately and testifying to his completeness. The gangster must reject others violently or draw them violently to him. The Westerner is not thus compelled to seek love; he is prepared to accept it, perhaps, but he never asks of it more than it [can] give, and we see him constantly in situations where love is at best an irrelevance. (137; my ellipsis)

Rio Bravo shows Wayne to excellent effect, as Cabrera Infante suggests (*Oficio* 357), and is considered by the critic to be "una obra maestra del género [del oeste]..." (359). Unlike Wilder, Hawks does not approach his material ironically or campily, satirizing and intellectualizing myth, legend, or genre in order to make a moral statement or simply as an exercise in mannerist aesthetic commentary. Much to the contrary, Hawks is a fairly wide-eyed humanist who extends and solidifies the mythic structure of the Western, with its powerful, self-confident hero who, in a masculine society, protects the values of civilization.[22] *Rio Bravo* fits squarely into the concept held by Cabrera Infante of the film as mythic text and also into the philosophy of humanistic idealism which is an important part of his worldview.[23]

The humanism of Cabrera Infante is stimulated by the values of friendship, particularly of male friendship, which are at the moral center of *Rio Bravo*. The renewed friendship offered to the alcoholic Dude (Dean Martin) by John T. Chance, the Wayne hero, which takes the form of a refusal by Chance to participate in the self-pity indulged in by Dude, is in sharp contrast to the rather resentful and superficial "friendship" of Cué and Silvestre. The "tigers" have substituted intellectual dilettantism for true human friendship.[24]

The strong relationship between the self-sufficient Western hero, Chance, and his distorted image, the once competent but lately degenerate Dude, is paralleled by the frequent "double" motifs in the works of Cabrera Infante as well as by such structures in other films reviewed by Caín, including *A Face in the Crowd* and *Vertigo*, or used by Cabrera Infante in his fiction, such as *Dr. Jekyll and Mr. Hyde*. The doubling in *Rio Bravo* is not dissimilar to the central motif of *Un oficio del Siglo 20*, the fictive relationship between Cabrera Infante and G. Caín, his film critic persona. Much as Dude represents either a potential version of Chance, or perhaps even mirrors an actual phase in the life of the now confident sheriff, so "Caín," as Nelson says,[25] "se proyecta ya como íntimo conocido del autor, representando seguramente *otro* aspecto esencial del ser del escritor: el amor por el cine" ("El doble" 510; original emphasis).

The Cain motif is not only important to *Un oficio del Siglo 20* as a book but also to the film *East of Eden*, reviewed in the collection. In this film, adapted by Elia Kazan from the John Steinbeck novel, a regenerative process not unlike that of *Rio Bravo* is depicted in a modern version of the Cain/Abel myth.[26] The myth is carried past its classical conclusion, with the Cain character, played by James Dean, finding redemption in the eyes of his father, the Yahweh-like Raymond Massey, after having driven away his brother, the Abel figure. The pattern of regeneration is present in the moral schemes of both films, although the treatment by Hawks is vitally different from the heavy-handedness of Kazan and Steinbeck.[27]

Rio Bravo is an epic of character, with a strange surface covering its structural tension: the suspense of the film, as Cabrera Infante notes, is in the "espera" in the jail for the arrival of the marshal who will resolve the legal conflict (357). It is curious that Cabrera Infante should find the "wait" so interesting and make it the basis of his defense of the film—apparently a minority opinion at the time of the review (see Oficio 355)—since one of the outstanding motifs of his own fiction could be called "the wait," a situation which, like the one in Rio Bravo, is typically "larga, enriquecida por los incidentes menos previstos..." (357). Consider, as examples, the time-killing represented by the conversations of Cué and Silvestre; the feeling of entrapment or vertigo which one obtains from reading the descriptions of parties in Tres tristes tigres; or the long waiting period for sexual experience which is much of the focus of La Habana para un Infante Difunto.

The general feeling of waiting and searching is very pronounced in the fiction of Cabrera Infante. His characters, like those in the films of Hawks, are not static or futile figures like those of Samuel Beckett, or, in a somewhat different manner, of Buñuel or Bergman; but they do participate either in time-killing, in aimless partying, or, on the other hand, in goal-oriented action which is temporally extended through prose devices like the parentheses in La Habana para un Infante Difunto.[28]

Small wonder, then, that central to the film work and the fiction of Cabrera Infante are inspirations from quest films such as Moby Dick, Vertigo, and Citizen Kane, as well as, with respect to the related motif of waiting, from the films of Minnelli, which typically include a chaotic and subjectively boring party scene as a moralizing or satiric set-piece. The difference between a work like Rio Bravo and, for example, Tres tristes tigres is that the waiting in the novel is hollow, a mere postponement of reality, as in the parties of Minnelli, while Rio Bravo centers on an Aristotelian process of character discovery. The characters of Cabrera Infante are largely deprived of the kind of moral growth and regeneration experienced by Dude. The views of Cabrera Infante on film, then, highlight an important facet of his fiction.

While Westerns are not heavily represented in *Un oficio del Siglo 20*, thrillers and detective or gangster films are notably present. The interest of Cabrera Infante in the thriller film illuminates the mannerism of his work, a tendency whose highest point is probably reached in the strained, thin narrative of *Así en la paz como en la guerra* (1968) and *Vista del amanecer en el trópico* (1974) but whose traces remain in his more baroque novels and in *Vanishing Point* (1969-70). His evaluations of films such as *Brute Force*, *Kiss Me Deadly*, *Vertigo*, and *The Killing* reveal the pessimism and fatalism which contrast so sharply with the congeniality and idealistic humanism to which he responds in musicals, especially those of Minnelli, in many comedies, and in the Western.

The interest of Cabrera Infante in stylistic economy is shown in some of his reviews on the thriller or gangster film, suggesting that, as William Siemens argues (*Language and Creativity* esp. ch. 5-6 [79-172]), the apparent chaos of *Tres tristes tigres* is not chaos at all but highly disciplined and polished, if opulent, narrative. Study of the reviews on thriller films in *Un oficio del Siglo 20* can help to illuminate some pronounced organizational traits of the work of Cabrera Infante, as well as some aspects of his mythic approach to film.

The Killing is an important film for Cabrera Infante. Not only does it relate closely, as he says, to one of the films in his "'mitología privada,'" *The Asphalt Jungle* (*Siete voces* 410), but it also contains in concentrated form some of his chief preoccupations: the pressure of time on the individual, the difficulty of successful human cooperation, and a romantic attraction towards fictional extralegal activities, an attraction which is transmuted into the view of tragedy which he applies to movies such as *Little Caesar* and *Scarface*. The film, with its "cronometrismo" and its fatalism (*Oficio* 157), is also a possible source for the film *Vanishing Point*, which focuses on a one-man car race ending in death.

The Killing, a 1957 movie directed by Stanley Kubrick, was, like *The Asphalt Jungle*, a "caper picture."[29] The professionalism of the criminals in both films recalls that of the characters in many Hawks movies, but the two films exhibit none of the back-slapping geniality of that director. These two movies, with their "tonos sombríos,"[30] are of a mannerist stamp where Hawks is more properly (within this context) tied to the Renaissance. His style is more harmoniously linear; while those of Kubrick and Huston, at least in these films, are closer to the "'troubled' and 'obscure,' if not 'illogical'" qualities applied by Sypher to "Mannerist art" (108).

Cabrera Infante assigns the tag of "tragedia" to *The Killing* and speaks of the "cronometrismo" of the burglary (*Oficio* 157). Rational planning fails, as in the Huston film, because of a chance element. The tragedy is one of circumstance and hints throughout at the *hubris* motif common to Greek drama and the Biblical tradition. As with *Vertigo*, the interest of Cabrera Infante in the film can be attributed in large part to its anti-rationalist, fatalist concentration on the "presencia del destino inexorable..." (157).

The concentration of Cabrera Infante on the tragic nature of the Kubrick film leads him to accord it mythic treatment. He ties it to Greek tragedy with his mention of the "narrador," whose "...voz es también el coro fatal de la tragedia, al par que avisa al público que la compleja máquina del asalto se ha echado a andar." The indication by the critic that, if the audience, like the criminals, "pierde el hilo de las horas, está perdido" (157), suggests an allusion to the need for Theseus not to lose the thread which will show him the way out of the Labyrinth.

The Minotaur myth is one of the favorites of Cabrera Infante, who devotes a chapter to it in *Exorcismos de esti(l)o* (67-84) and makes repeated reference to it in the script for *Vanishing Point*; and here he seems to suggest that the power of *The Killing* depends in part on that myth. The result of the "time thread" device is to cause the audience to merge its perspective with those of the protagonists, a function similar to that performed by classical tragedy, as a religious rite, and to the ideal of communication between author and reader which is espoused by Cabrera Infante with respect to his own work (see Cabrera Infante, *Siete voces* 414). The tendency of Cabrera Infante to place cinema on a mythological plane is quite apparent here, as in other sections of the book and especially in *Arcadia todas las noches*.

The mythic status accorded *The Killing* and the emphasis placed by Cabrera Infante on time in the film are closely interrelated, since the time indicated in this movie becomes frozen or eternalized on film. The relationship between a myth and time established here is continued in *Vanishing Point*, written by Cabrera Infante under the pseudonym "'G. Cain'" (*Siete voces* 412). In *Vanishing Point*, the headlong rush to death of the iconoclast racer Kowalski is measured, to borrow the expression of Cabrera Infante relative to *The Killing*, "con la escrupulosidad de un *timekeeper*" (*Oficio* 157). Kowalski, unlike the protagonists of *The Killing*, does not exactly form part of a team, although, like Orphée in the Cocteau film which bears his name, he does receive messages over the car radio. The messages come from his partner or, to use the terminology of Nelson, his "double," a disc jockey. Like the criminals in the Kubrick and Huston films, he undertakes a seemingly impossible venture, a drive from Colorado to San Francisco in a very limited time. The similarities of *Vanishing Point* to "caper pictures" are evident, despite the apparently motiveless nature of the enterprise of Kowalski, and demonstrate the manner in which Cabrera Infante tends to abstract qualities from films and rework them to fit his own creative scheme.

Like Kowalski in *Vanishing Point*, the Mike Hammer character in *Kiss Me Deadly*[31] is an iconoclast, with little respect for established authority. *Kiss Me Deadly* seems to prefigure not only *Vanishing Point* but also *La Habana para un Infante Difunto*, with its phantasmagoric and apocalyptic ending,[32] in which the genre is stretched beyond its limits. The apocalyptic ending of *Kiss Me Deadly* seems closer to that of a 1950s science fiction film about atomic radiation than to a hard-boiled detective movie.

Here the flexibility of Cabrera Infante with respect to genre can be readily seen. *Kiss Me Deadly* shares such generic flexibility not only with *La Habana para un Infante Difunto*, with its Bulgakov-like ending of a figurative journey into the underworld (Nelson, "*La Habana*" 218), but also with *Vanishing Point*, which is not a simple racing film or melodrama, due to its mythic overtones.[33] In all three works, the conventions of genre are teased and stretched to a significant degree.

Kiss Me Deadly is characterized by Cabrera Infante as "gótico moderno" and is seen by him as therefore a stylistic sequel to *The Lady from Shanghai* by Orson Welles (*Oficio* 86). Once again the taste of Cabrera Infante for "barroquismo" is evident. The "neobaroque," as Acosta Cruz says in *The Discourse of Excess*, is very important to Cuban writers of the generation of Cabrera Infante. The employment of the techniques either of mannerist or of "neobaroque" art is not exclusively due to the "'elitismo'" referred to by Alvarez-Borland

(*Discontinuidad* 125) in connection with the interest of Cabrera Infante in Wellesian mannerism, although this perspective is certainly present in Cabrera Infante as in Sarduy or Lezama Lima. More precisely, Cabrera Infante believes in not patronizing his readers while still writing for his own enjoyment:

> I write for myself. To read what I've written I must then retype my material. I read myself again and the matter could rest there. I publish for the rest of you out there. Yes, you out there on the other side of the page. For you and for you and for you. For all of you: to let you share with me the pleasure of my company ... What I really hate is not for my readers not to know how to read me but that they might feel I am boring them. (Cabrera Infante, "A Portrait" xviii; my ellipsis)

His "barroquismo" or "manierismo" is no more nor less elitist than that of Welles or Aldrich. Like Cabrera Infante, "Welles," as Pauline Kael says, "has the approach of a *popular* artist: he glories in both verbal and visual rhetoric" ("Orson Welles" 244; original emphasis).

Cabrera Infante and Welles both try to reach their audiences precisely by not patronizing them and, on the other hand, by not exalting them unrealistically. As Kael says of Welles, he "is always being attacked for not having fulfilled his prodigious promise"; nevertheless, "What makes movies a great popular art form is that certain artists"—including, as she says, Welles,—"can, at moments in their lives, reach out and unify the audience—educated and uneducated—in a shared response" (240). Although the baroque or "mannerist" style of Welles has alienated certain supersophisticated critics and audiences—as Kael also states, "His work is often referred to as flashy and spectacular as if this also meant cheap and counterfeit"—, he has acquired a steady following among moviegoers who are willing to appreciate his style (244). Much the same can be said of the career of Cabrera Infante, who can easily but superficially be criticized for his exhibition of verbal virtuosity and often outrageous humor by those who fail to appreciate the special power of his style.

Among directors heavily influenced by the style of Welles is Robert Aldrich, the director of, for example, *Kiss Me Deadly* and *The Big Knife*, and a filmmaker to whom a baroque style is attributed by Cabrera Infante, who calls him "el último creador de Hollywood,..."

at least of the Hollywood of 1955 (*Oficio* 85-86). His expressionism and humorous style of the grotesque, with its low- and high-angle shots, indeed constitute, as Cabrera Infante notes, a "poesía macabra" (85). Again Cabrera Infante shows himself to be attracted to a mythical motif, since *Kiss Me Deadly* involves a clear reference to Pandora's Box, in this instance a leaden case containing radioactive material. The film is also a modernized, revisionist version of the gangster genre in which the critic shows such interest.

If *Kiss Me Deadly* is for Cabrera Infante a fascinating exercise in the "gothic" and closely related to the work of Welles (*Oficio* 86), *Touch of Evil* represents for the critic a great exercise in style by Welles as well as a development of an important theme in the work of Cabrera Infante: the nostalgic "remembrance of things past."[34] Sheriff Hank Quinlan, played by Welles, is a baroque figure of decay and corruption who reminisces with a prostitute, played by Marlene Dietrich, about past happiness. Like La Estrella, the black singer in *Tres tristes tigres*, who was converted into a figure of cheap pornography after her death from overeating (286-87), Quinlan "'was,'" as the Dietrich character says, "'some kind of a man....'"[35] The fate of La Estrella, incidentally, recalls the characterization of Welles by Cabrera Infante as "un glotón" (*Arcadia* 36-37) and, like La Estrella, a "'ballena'" who is directly associated with Moby Dick[36] (*Tres tristes tigres* 64, 123).

The interest of Cabrera Infante in nostalgia as a theme is perhaps also the reason for his admitted fascination with *Letter from an Unknown Woman*, in which the antiheroic lead character, a pianist gone to seed because of his playboy dissolution, finds within himself a means of redemption through the memory of a woman (Joan Fontaine) who died because of love for and loyalty to him. She refused wealth and security to follow him, and he, satyr-like, never remembered her until reading a letter written to him from her deathbed. Fleeing from a duel at the beginning of the film, he is inspired by her letter to go to the duel and thereby to achieve personal redemption.

This pattern of dissolution and redemption through memory is to be contrasted to the failure of the narrator in *La Habana para un Infante Difunto* to redeem himself through memory; he cannot form a relationship with Violeta del Valle. Unlike the Jourdan character in *Letter from an Unknown Woman* and, in a similar fashion, the Orson Welles character in *Touch of Evil*, the narrator's situation reflects no real moral decline, since he is an essentially defective person. Thus, he cannot utilize his recall of his once considerable talent and charm (like Jourdan) or of his former moral strength and professional ability (like Welles) to lead him towards some dignity at the threshold of death.

Cabrera Infante writes more fully of the elements of "nostalgia" in *Touch of Evil* in *Arcadia todas las noches*, tying the memories of Quinlan about Tana (Dietrich) to those of Welles about Dietrich and Dolores del Río (42-43). The tendency of the author towards autobiographical fiction, studied by Rosemary Feal, is extended here into his criticism in a manner somewhat different from that in *Un oficio del Siglo 20*, in which the identity of the author is confused by means of techniques like those of Gide.[37] In *Arcadia todas las noches*, the life of Welles is subjected to a treatment which links its biographical reality with the characters in his films.

The perspective of Cabrera Infante on *Touch of Evil* is not of one piece, since it does not concentrate exclusively on the seriousness or sadness of the film but also on its humor (42). Humor is a quality usually found in films and books which attract Cabrera Infante as well as, to a very large degree, in works of his own such as *Tres tristes tigres* and *La Habana para un Infante Difunto*.

Occasionally, however, he gives high marks to a film which conspicuously lacks the quality of humor. A film on the margin of the thriller genre which seems almost totally humorless, as he says, is *Vertigo*, which is nevertheless one of the central films in his mythology of cinema. The film is extremely serious in its approach, and, as Cabrera Infante notes, any humor present in it "se transforma en una sonrisa amarga y aplastada por lo desconocido—y dado [sic] rienda suelta a todos los misterios" (*Oficio* 371).[38]

Vertigo, a 1959 film directed by Alfred Hitchcock and starring James Stewart and Kim Novak, receives perhaps the highest, most unqualified praise of any of the films reviewed in *Un oficio del Siglo 20*.[39] Cabrera Infante responds strongly to its "surrealism" and mythic nature, seeing Scottie (Stewart) as a modern-day Orpheus who descends into the underworld of his vertigo and insanity to try to retrieve or to re-create his Eurydice, Madeleine (Novak). He sees the camera style of Hitchcock, closer to that of Welles than to that of a montage-oriented director like Eisenstein, as perfectly suited in its fluidity to the theme of the film (*Oficio* 364-72). The style does in fact create a sensation akin to vertigo by means of dizzying zig-zags and slow tracking shots.

Much as Hitchcock crystalizes the sensation of vertigo through his style, Cabrera Infante attempts in *Tres tristes tigres* and especially in his book of styles, *Exorcismos de esti(l)o* (1976), to create and even to prescribe verbal equivalents of sensations, giving plastic qualities to words.[40] Style or mode of narrative is a critical concern for both artists.

As with the Aldrich film *Kiss Me Deadly*, the qualities of *Vertigo* which seem to stand in highest relief for Cabrera Infante are its "misterio" and gothicism (*Oficio* 371). One begins to understand what Cabrera Infante sees in "baroque" films: the veiling and unveiling of essentials through an emphasis on appearances and surfaces, a well-known convention of mannerist art such as *Hamlet*.[41] His fascination with the mannerism of Welles, for instance, revolves around its affectation and rhetoric, though not only, or not at all, in the shallow or pejorative sense with which those terms are usually employed. The stylistic affectation marking the work of Welles has a deeper meaning, being an artistic convention to which Kael refers as "theatrical" and not, she says, a vulgar attempt at artistry:

> His work is often referred to as flashy and spectacular as if this also meant cheap and counterfeit. Welles is unabashedly theatrical in a period when much of the educated audience thinks theatrical flair vulgar, artistry intellectually respectable only when subtle, hidden.... He uses film *theatrically*—not stagily, but with rhetorical bravado...there's life in that kind of display: it's part of an earlier theatrical tradition that Welles carries over into film, it's what the theatre has lost, and it's what brought people to the movies. ("Orson Welles" 244; my ellipsis)

The style of Welles, like that of Hitchcock, is intended at least in part to convey the truth behind surfaces,[42] not to hide it behind veils of rationality as would an ordinary Hollywood film.

Metaphysical investigation is in fact so pronounced in the work of Alfred Hitchcock, or at least, as Cabrera Infante notes, in *Vertigo*, that he is properly to be called "un presocrático" (*Oficio* 371). Like the Presocratics, Hitchcock, according to Cabrera Infante, has "una mentalidad mucho más rica que la religiosa: el temperamento mágico." He adds that "Un hombre que propone características—las macabras —más allá de la realidad a un objeto cotidiano como un huevo, es un presocrático" (370-71).

These qualities, at their most visible in *Vertigo*, which fittingly deals with the Orphic myth, a source of occult mysteries, make of Hitchcock an exponent of myths. A penetrator of surface impressions, who awakens "El asombro...ante la insistencia de la irrealidad" (371; my ellipsis), Hitchcock is indeed "el director quien más le atrae y fascina [a Cabrera Infante]" (Alvarez-Borland, *Discontinuidad* 126). *Vertigo* is central to the views of Cabrera Infante on film because of its mythic character and its emphasis on mysteries and rite. Scottie, like Cabrera Infante with film, has found in his worship of Madeleine "a pagan substitute for religion." The film is a paradigm for the more metaphysical side of the concept of cinema espoused by Cabrera Infante.

Cabrera Infante can even be seen to have developed a literary style with much kinship to the beautiful, "flowing" camera movement of *Vertigo*. He speaks in *Un oficio del Siglo 20* of the camera style of the film:

> ...ese ritmo fluyente y refluyente, de ola y resaca, de vaivén del tiempo sobre el espacio, de fluir etéreo, que es el exacto vocabulario sensual y mágico para esta película tan atrayente, tan obsesiva y fatal como la mirada que se tiende al abismo bajo los pies. (371)

One of the most immediate impressions given by *La Habana para un Infante Difunto* is of flowing prose with extended parenthetical interventions contrasting with and commenting on the words of the narrator, resulting in a rhythm of "ola y resaca."[43] The text of the novel, with its fluid rhythms, does have musical analogies, the most obvious being the *Pavane pour une infante défunte* of Ravel;[44] but the possibility of influence by the camera style of *Vertigo* should not be discounted. The film has certainly influenced *Tres tristes tigres*, as we will later discover in examining that book.

The preoccupations which appear prominently in the essay on *Vertigo*, namely an interest in metaphysical questions, are supplemented by a strong ethical focus in the reviews in *Un oficio del Siglo 20* on films belonging to a genre not specifically enumerated in the genre compendium which appears in the book. This genre is the drama, or more properly in some cases, the melodrama. Many of the movies reviewed by Cabrera Infante in the collection fall into this category. Furthermore, many of them have an allegorical quality. *Journal d'un curé de campagne*, *Moby Dick*, and *La strada* are just three of the films towards which Cabrera Infante consistently leans because of their spiritual significance or because of his tendency to attribute to them a cluster of meanings which centers around the humanist, rather Personalist philosophy which he espouses from time to time.

The double-action philosophy of Cabrera Infante, of optimistic humanism on the one hand and pessimism on the other, is not unusual, since a humanist is bound to encounter disappointments or contradictions to his philosophy leading to pessimistic attitudes: consider, for example, Ibsen, Tolstoy, or Faulkner. The negativism of Cabrera Infante cuts deeper than a mere attitudinal pessimism, however. He often seems emotionally attracted to themes such as that of *Vertigo* and to somber films like those of Robert Bresson. Nevertheless, he wishes morally to defend the kind of optimism which often appears in the Hollywood cinema and which is carried to extremes in films such as the musical *Gigi* by Vincente Minnelli. Cabrera Infante does not completely eschew, as Alvarez-Borland suggests, the philosophy of Minnelli. She argues "que a Cabrera Infante le interesa muy poco el cine de este director con su filosofía idealista, simple y romántica..." (*Discontinuidad* 127). On the contrary, his attitude towards the Hollywood entertainment film demonstrates the closeness of his position to the optimism of Minnelli, despite his intellectual rejection of that position in *Arcadia todas las noches* (183-84).[45] Even in his reviews of films such as those of Bresson, *Vertigo*, or the works of Buñuel, he tends to stress the importance of human endeavor and aspiration, placing him well within the existentialist viewpoint and highlighting his pronounced streak of idealism.

The films of Robert Bresson are represented in the collection by two reviews which are among the more fervent of Cabrera Infante's essays. The Cuban critic bestows very high praise on *Journal d'un curé de campagne* and *Un Condamné à mort s'est échappé*, two films with a mystical or at least an existentially Catholic viewpoint. He takes some care to secularize his remarks, saying that to him "...importan bien poco la trascendencia del alma, la gracia divina y la mano de Dios" (*Oficio* 304). Pointing out instead the importance, in *Un Condamné à mort s'est échappé*, of the striving by the hero to escape and the self-knowledge brought to him by his endeavor, Cabrera Infante veers away from a Christian emphasis and strikes one of his familiar chords, paganism. The philosophy of Bresson is cast by the critic in Stoic terms, recalling his remarks on *Vertigo* and foreshadowing the mock-Stoic viewpoint of the narrator of *La Habana para un Infante Difunto*:

...el azar puede ser artículo de fe. El subtítulo del film [*Un Condamné*]...convierte la mano que dirige los pasos de Fontaine, los azares que facilitan su fuga, en una mano divina. Por supuesto, que se tropieza casi con la herejía: con el azar, que es un dios pagano. (*Oficio* 303; my ellipsis)

The chord of paganism is amplified by a subtle implication of mythic status for "la prisión, con su figuración del laberinto..." (303), a formulation recalling once again the image of the Minotaur.

In his critical response to the work of Bresson, Cabrera Infante demonstrates more spiritual depth than may be readily apparent from his major fictional works and from his usual ironic pose. He also shows his remarkable sensitivity to cinematic artistry, that is, to predominantly visual depiction, by statements such as, referring to *Journal d'un curé de campagne*:

Es curioso que la cinta resulte tan lúcida, tan acogedora para quien— como el cronista—no ha sentido nunca inclinación por la teología y a quien los problemas de la trascendencia espiritual son tan ajenos y distantes como las estrellas. ¿Por qué? Porque *El diario de un cura rural* ha dejado de hablar un idioma filosófico particular para expresarse en el idioma universal del arte. (*Oficio* 75)

The notion of the process of trying to achieve a goal and of growing spiritually through that process, studied with great seriousness by Bresson, is rather more lightly or campily treated in *Vanishing Point*. Kowalski, moreover, does not seem to grow much through his experience, as do the priest and his ex-seminary friend from *Journal d'un curé de campagne* (see *Oficio* 73).

One of the more heavily allegorical and existential of the dramatic films reviewed in the collection is the John Huston film *Moby Dick*. Like *Vertigo*, this movie is important to the allusive and thematic structure of the work of Cabrera Infante. Not only do direct allusions to the film—perhaps, of course, to the Melville novel itself—appear in the form of puns in *Tres tristes tigres*, for instance the pun "Caulme Ishmael" (268); but one of the central characters in the novel is La Estrella, "'La Ballena Negra,'" a comic version in negative of the "Great White Whale," who is pursued by Códac, or, more precisely, seems to pursue him (64-70, 82-85, 160-63).[46]

The motif of the quest or search is again present in this film, as it is in numerous others reviewed by the critic and in both his novels. In addition to the mythic resonance gained by the central presence of such a motif, the film is placed on a level of contemporary allegory, as is *Kiss Me Deadly*, with its reference to atomic power. *Moby Dick* is also connected by Cabrera Infante to atomic power because Huston used the island of Bikini as a site for the last scenes of the film. This island, as Cabrera Infante notes, was "el sitio" of United States atomic testing, "donde las fuerzas físicas, morales y espirituales del universo han encontrado su Némesis..." (*Oficio* 143-44).

Such references by Cabrera Infante show at least a minimal amount of social concern as well as a significant interest in apocalyptic imagery of the type found at the end of *La Habana para un Infante Difunto*. The film, like *Vertigo* with its water images of death and resurrection, is of still further interest because of its prefiguration of "la abundancia de imágenes marítimas en *TTT*...."[47]

Characteristically, Cabrera Infante seems to relate the imagery of the Huston *Moby Dick* to that of another film, *20,000 Leagues under the Sea*. As a result of the striking visuals of the film, he says, "la ballena cobra un aspecto hermético, más allá de la razón, rápida y mortal como el Nautilus, el submarino malvado del capitán Nemo, otro marino demente, ella misma una máquina infernal" (*Oficio* 143). The whale is a grandiose, hyperbolic image which well fits the definition of the mythic offered by Cabrera Infante as "Una realidad mayor que la realidad..." (*Arcadia* 31).

At times Cabrera Infante focuses on cinema as a somewhat more prosaic vehicle which is mythic chiefly in terms of reducing modern experience to a paradigm or a narrative document. Such films as *La Grande illusion*, *A Face in the Crowd*, *Paths of Glory*, and *The Quiet American* are examples of social, political, or ethical "documentos" of the modern era (*Oficio* 254) and generally, with the important exception of *La Grande illusion*, rank lower on the scale of mythical, mysterious, or magical values than do works such as *Vertigo*, *Moby Dick*, or *La strada*.

His reviews of such socially oriented films, in whose company can be included the examples of neorealism appearing in the collection, generally show him in a more declamatory, less poetic vein, attacking fascism, imperialism, warmongering, and the public relations "culto a la personalidad depravada" (254) which has so corrupted mass culture, particularly in the United States. These reviews, with some exceptions, are rather less informative, and less entertaining to read, with respect to the later literary enterprises of Cabrera Infante than are reviews such as the one on *Kiss Me Deadly*. Nevertheless some of the reviews help to place the Cuban writer with regard to social, political, and cultural points of view, demonstrating that his stance is not purely aesthetic. As *Tres tristes tigres* will reveal, Cabrera Infante carries his political concerns into his fiction, transferring the aversion which he shows towards British and American imperialism in some of the reviews of *Un oficio del Siglo 20* to a "distaste for the route that the Cuban Revolution was following by the mid-1960's."[48]

The review of *The Quiet American* allows Cabrera Infante to comment on American "imperialism" in Vietnam. The most significant passage in the review concerns the transformation of the American from "la inocencia malvada" of the Graham Greene novel, the basis for the movie, into the character of "inocente inocente" in the film and the consequent shifting of blame for the bomb attack which is the subject of the film to "un mestizo de indio y español llamado Domínguez," a man who is "el único personaje del libro que recuerda la bondad de Gandhi..." (308). The sympathy for the *mestizo* as well as the generalized anti-imperialist thrust of the review show Cabrera Infante, in this stage of his career as well as subsequently, to possess the ambivalent "actitud" towards Cuba and America which, as Jaime Giordano suggests (163-70), is present in *Tres tristes tigres* in "complementary" halves (167). One aspect of the stance of Cabrera Infante is the "glorificación del cine" of the United States, with the consequent "devaluación del mundo local e inmediato"; while, on the other hand, a character, like Códac, may also undergo "un ataque de patriotismo" with a concomitant "aceptación del valor inferior de lo local como 'superior,' por el sólo [sic] hecho de ser verdadero, auténtico" (166-69).

Overt political statement is relatively rare in the writing of Cabrera Infante, but he does devote some space to such concerns in two important reviews. *Paths of Glory* and *La Grande illusion* are for Cabrera Infante two powerful pacifist statements with which he places himself in agreement.

Like the film, the review of *Paths of Glory* is strongly anti-war. Cabrera Infante sees war as lying along coordinates of unreality; and for him, the film by Stanley Kubrick gives this image to the viewer: "En fin, que [Kubrick] ha rodado el film de guerra ideal: aquél que ayuda a conseguir que las guerras sean lo que siempre debieron ser: no una visión premonitoria, sino un mal sueño, una pesadilla que se olvida, una película" (*Oficio* 299). His review is straightforward, avoiding the metaphysical language and romantic analogies of an essay like the one on *Vertigo*. Nevertheless, the essay on *Paths of Glory* is strangely prophetic. The predilection for verbal irony so prevalent throughout the work of Cabrera Infante seems here to yield to an unconscious dramatic irony when he refers to the banning of the film by the French government (298). A similar incident, the banning of *P.M.* by the Castro régime, was to lead to the silencing of Cabrera Infante as a film critic in Cuba.

The other important pacifist manifesto reviewed by Cabrera Infante is *La Grande illusion*, the magnificent film by Jean Renoir. Here the issue revolves around a critical reassessment performed by Cabrera Infante on the film. He accords it the status of "una obra maestra" (*Oficio* 403), while before he had seen it as stupidly idealistic given its milieu, the year 1938, not long before the Second World War (399). He refers to its use of the camera, tying it to the technique of Hitchcock and Rossellini and recalling the defense of Renoir and Welles by Bazin as opposed to the rigid montage theorists (401).

The interest of Cabrera Infante in *Paths of Glory* and *La Grande illusion* is also related to his view of the cinema as speaking "ecumenically" to people of the modern era. He calls *Paths of Glory* "un arma de la paz" (295) and the Renoir film "una obra individualista, un canto a la 'solidaridad humana por encima de las fronteras'..." (401). Presumably the fact of the power of film, through its wide diffusion and magical nature, would help to effect what political rhetoric cannot.

While *Paths of Glory* and *La Grande illusion* are seen by Cabrera Infante to attack the evils of war, films such as *A Face in the Crowd* and *The Goddess* are cited by him as examples of the necessary debunking of the myths of popularity, the star system, and Hollywood itself—in short, of the American success story. Elements of a similar attack, carried out by Cabrera Infante himself, are present in *Tres tristes tigres* in the early chapters dealing with Cuba Venegas, a starlet who is prostituted and spiritually hollowed out by her quest for success, and in the story of La Estrella, whose pathetic story parodies the already sordid success story of Cuba Venegas.

Again in the review of *A Face in the Crowd* Cabrera Infante elevates the documentary or recording aspects of a film above its qualities of entertainment or myth.[49] At least, he speaks of documenting an epoch, with his introductory remarks about "una 'bala al futuro'" (254). The context of his references, however, makes the remarks seem somewhat less than ingenuous.

One of the films which, according to the critic, should have gone into the "'bala,'" or "time capsule," buried "Por los últimos años treinta,..." was *Citizen Kane* (254). This film was hardly a documentary or an objective biography of William Randolph Hearst, but rather a complex mixture of social commentary, mythic deflation, and tribute to the image of American greatness (Thomson 155-56). Kane, apart from being the central figure in a film whose "...screenplay is a scathing commentary on America and on the domineering charm of Welles himself" and a thinly veiled portrait of Hearst, "is a version of the grotesque spiral of American success, but...also a picture of any man trying to transcend himself and reach others" (155-56; my ellipsis). Thomson adds that "*Citizen Kane* is a study of the intellectual isolation of an intelligent, sensitive, enterprising man, a man whose career has helped dilute meaning with style and presentation" (156). All this hardly adds up to a documentary like *Nanook of the North* or *Tabu*, seeming closer to a euhemerism, though with negative aspects, of a figure who was already for the public of the time an ambivalent version of the Horatio Alger myth.

Cabrera Infante puts the Hearst/Kane myth into a typically baroque, Quevedesque formula: "el coloso era un hombre infeliz, el poder era la concha de una ostra, la armadura de un guerrero de museo: dentro no había más que soledad y vacío. Aquél era el documento del todopoderoso devenido polvo y ceniza y silencio" (*Oficio* 255). From the foregoing presentation, it is clear that Cabrera Infante is not completely literal when speaking of social "documentation." He appears more to intend the sort of anthropological documentation of a culture which is accomplished by its mythology.

A Face in the Crowd is, Cabrera Infante suggests, the "reverse" of the Kane myth, since the protagonist of the Kazan film, Lonesome Rhodes, "'vendería' una soledad que jamás padeció" (*Oficio* 255). Here, incidentally, the myths proposed are closer to types, being variations on or relatives of the kinds of character typology proposed for film by Panofsky. Lonesome Rhodes—an overtly symbolic name—is the other side of the Kane coin: "...el arribista, el nadie convertido en un dictador de la opinión pública..." (255).

As Cabrera Infante says, however, "No es casualidad que el héroe del film no sea el demagogo, sino el intelectual" (258). From the point of view of Cabrera Infante, who is not only a novelist but also a screenwriter, the film has perhaps some personal relevance. He says that "Kazan ha declarado...que es el escritor quien ha de salvar a Hollywood..." (258; my ellipsis). Certainly, such an anti-commercial, and, incidentally, anti-directorial, message would appeal to a writer such as Cabrera Infante.

Another film critical of Hollywood is *The Goddess*, to which Cabrera Infante devotes one of his longer reviews. Despite the critical nature of the movie, its thrust is not characterized by Cabrera Infante as one of absolute demythification. Rather, he suggests, the film illuminates the true nature of the "goddess" (Venus) by employing another, more mannerist myth: "Durante dos horas muestra a un público acostumbrado a adorar a una deidad, que es en realidad la versión de Jano Bifronte: por delante la imagen dorada del éxito, por detrás toda la sordidez que esconde la existencia" (*Oficio* 333). The John Cromwell film, similar in subject matter to *A Face in the Crowd*, to *Sunset Boulevard*, and to *A Star Is Born*, differs somewhat from the other films in following a three-part scheme (334) which contains a "history" of the goddess or heroine and which recalls in ironic fashion "the myth of the birth and death of the hero" as set forth by Otto Rank in his book of that name and developed by Joseph Campbell in *The Hero with a Thousand Faces*.

Cabrera Infante does not blink at sharply criticizing Hollywood, referring to its "falsa arquitectura" (335). Despite his almost religious attitude towards movies, he is clear-eyed enough about the commercialism and hollowness of much of American cinema. The goddess of the title, he says, is "La fama" (336); again, one sees his leaning towards Stoicism in his emphasis on such a theme. *The Goddess* is one of the writing efforts of Paddy Chayevsky, in whom Cabrera Infante shows considerable interest in the collection.

The criticisms of Hollywood contained in such films as *The Goddess* and the commentaries made on these movies by Cabrera Infante relate closely to his attitude of opposition to corporate enforcement of conformism and to his defense of the individual against oppression or repression of any sort. Thus, his point of view concerning Hollywood and the distortion of personality involved in the star myth is of a piece with the attitudes which lead him to evaluate positively such creations as *La strada*, *Les Sorcières de Salem*, *12 Angry Men*, and *Et Dieu créa la femme*. In his reviews of these productions, and the list is not exhaustive of the films of this type reviewed in the collection, a recurrent libertarian position is evident.

The relationship of such a position to his antinomic fiction is apparent, although he does not present the individualism of his characters or their maverick lifestyles without irony. Cué and Silvestre are hardly examples of attractively self-sufficient, free-thinking men; the narrator of *La Habana para un Infante Difunto* confuses sexual pursuit with philosophical liberation, much as the Jack Warden character in *The Bachelor Party* searches for freedom or escape in the same activity; and, in the area of screenwriting, Kowalski in *Vanishing Point* is even more ironically presented. The truth about the hero Kowalski is actually rather sordid, just as the exterior of the "goddess" conceals unsavory reality. Nevertheless, the fact of a striving for individuality seems central to the work of Cabrera Infante, even if, stoically, he ironizes the quest of his characters.

La strada, one of the most highly praised films in the book, has a rather ironically presented hero and heroine, a circus strongman and his lover. The strongman, Zampano (Anthony Quinn), refuses to compromise with society, becoming a belligerent loner who relies on his brawn to carry him through life (*Oficio* 131-32).

The tendency of Cabrera Infante to cast his criticism in terms of myth is apparent here, since he says that "El hombre se llama Zampanó, pero se podía llamar de otra manera, incluso Adán" (131). The connection with Adam rests on the structure of the relationship between Zampano and his "wife" Gelsomina (Giulietta Masina). Gelsomina is given knowledge by a rather benevolent Satan figure, "The Fool," a tightrope artist played by Richard Basehart. He tells her of her importance to Zampano, enlightening her as to the purpose of all things.[50] Given this knowledge, she returns to Zampano and feebly tries to enlighten him or just to support him; but he kills "The Fool" in a fit of angry vengeance, and the paradise of innocence or of ignorance enjoyed by Zampano and Gelsomina ends with his abandonment of her and her eventual death. Losing his innocent bestiality, Zampano "Llora: por primera vez en su vida demuestra que es un ser humano" (*Oficio* 134). In presenting the ethical structure of the film, Cabrera Infante comes close to a Christian set of ideals but can probably better be seen as espousing his humanist views. A notable aspect of the review is his placing of almost equal emphasis on the highly touted director-author, Federico Fellini, and on his actors.

As is evident from the reviews studied here, Cabrera Infante expresses many of his major themes in the areas of drama, comedy, and thriller films. Musicals, for all their importance to his work, are less well-represented in the collection.

One of the few musicals studied in the book is *Funny Face*, directed by Stanley Donen. As in the retrospective on *The Red Shoes* elsewhere in the collection (220-24), Cabrera Infante stresses visual values. Much of the review of the Donen film is devoted to its visual texture, deriving from designs by Richard Avedon (208).

Cabrera Infante distinguishes sharply here between cinematic and graphic qualities; despite his interest in the visual in film, he feels that the visual or the graphic does not of itself constitute the cinematic (209). This point of view seems consonant with his criticism of the silent cinema as deficient in technical terms. His major objection to the overuse of visuals in *Funny Face* does not, however, center on the lack of sound, but on the relative lack of "movimiento" in the film:

> ...los éxitos de *Cenicienta* son casi todos plásticos: el director Stanley Donen se ha dejado llevar de la mano por la maestría de Avedon y ha rendido cautivado homenaje al arte de la fotografía en colores, olvidándose del arte de la fotografía en movimiento. (209)

The film interests of Cabrera Infante can be clearly discerned by reference to the reviews of *Un oficio del Siglo 20*, with some allowance for changes in his points of view over the years since the pieces were written and the collection put together. His view of film as contributory to modern myths, as well as some of the allusive structures which he builds around that concept, are well illustrated in the book. His critical position, weighted towards auteurism but not falling unequivocally into that camp, is also evident. An even sharper concentration and elucidation of some of his then current preferences, approaches to, and views of film is to be found in *Arcadia todas las noches*, composed in 1962.[51]

NOTES

[1] Cabrera Infante says to Montaner that "'—El prólogo, intermedio y epílogo de *Un oficio del siglo XX* no son otra cosa que el intento del autor por desembarazarse de su *alter ego*, de alejar a ese otro yo alienado por el oficio del crítico de cine'" (167).

[2] Alvarez-Borland expresses similar ideas (*Discontinuidad* 119-21).

[3] *Oficio* 242. The quotations which follow from this section of the book all have original emphasis. See also Pereda 124-30 for an extended listing by Cabrera Infante, with commentary, of some of the films personally important to him.

[4] See Hazera, "Cinematic" 44-46 for comments on the preoccupation of Cabrera Infante (and Caín) with language in written and cinematic terms.

[5] The image of the silent film as "'*una conversación detrás de una vidriera*'" is

comically repeated in *La Habana para un Infante Difunto* (407-08), with reference to the "boring" quality of voyeurism without sound.

⁶ Jim Hillier, writing of the 1954 Truffaut essay "Une Certaine Tendance du cinéma français" (21), says:

> The names Truffaut cites in arguing for a French cinema of *auteurs* are Renoir, Bresson, Cocteau, Becker, Gance, Ophuls, Tati, Leenhardt (which more or less exhausts *Cahiers'* French *auteurs* before the *nouvelle vague*).... (22; my ellipsis)

⁷ Cabrera Infante recently said that he was highly interested in Chaplin "En una época" (Interview with the author).

⁸ The importance of parties in the work of Minnelli is pointed out by Cabrera in *Arcadia* 164-65, 174.

⁹ For the term "deautomatization" as used by Victor Shklovski and as applicable to Eisenstein, see Eagle 34-35.

¹⁰ I owe this insight into the film to Gilliatt (35).

¹¹ This quality of the book has also been noted by critics such as Scheybeler (59) and Sousa ("Rev. of *La Habana*" 97).

¹² The moral seriousness of Chaplin was clarified for me by Agee, who speaks of the ethical purpose of Chaplin in his reviews of *Monsieur Verdoux* (252-62).

¹³ See Feal, *Novel Lives* 62-72 for discussion of the attitude of the narrator towards his mother and its importance for his "sexual initiation."

¹⁴ For a summary of the influence of Petronius on Cabrera Infante and *Tres tristes tigres*, see Nelson, "Betrayal," esp. 153.

¹⁵ For similar ideas regarding the narrator, see Feal, *Novel Lives* 62-72.

¹⁶ See Nelson, "Betrayal" 154, for a connection between "Menippean satire," which included "'parody,'" and Cabrera Infante.

¹⁷ The debt of the film to "burlesco" was suggested to me by Cabrera Infante (*Oficio* 346).

¹⁸ I owe the idea of the mannerist nature of *Troilus and Cressida* to Professor Richard Hosley.

¹⁹ Sarris expresses a similar idea, which may have contributed to my point here, when he says that "Cabrera Infante's sensibility spills all over his characters until they dissolve into a series of stylistic options" ("Rerunning"47).

²⁰ Siemens, for example, sees Cué and Silvestre as two aspects of one personality:

> Silvestre's fate is closely tied to that of Cué, not only in his awareness of riding in the "death seat" of the speeding Mercury, but in some rather remarkable ways as well. It becomes evident that he and Cué, once referred to as "Silvestre Ycué" (p. 222 [of the English translation]), are Cabrera Infante's dual representation of Lewis Carroll,... in the two aspects of his love of play, the verbal and the mathematical. (*Worlds* 148).

²¹ Jiménez (73-74) quotes from the "Western" dialogue of the two characters and notes their imitation of "actores." Cué is explicitly compared to

Cooper by Silvestre (379-80). For the Western métier of Cooper, see Jordan 41-42, 50.

²² For the origin of this idea on the Westerner, see Warshow 138-43. The notion of Hawks as espousing human values is important to the study *Howard Hawks* by Robin Wood, contributory to my work.

²³ A film like *Sunset Boulevard* or, to a lesser degree, *Love in the Afternoon*, feeds rather into the pessimistic, mannerist ambivalence which is also found in the work of Cabrera Infante and which finds a deep cinematic echo in the films of Orson Welles.

²⁴ I am indebted for the idea of the superficiality in the friendship of the "tigres" to Bonnie K. Frederick (25-26).

²⁵ In "El doble, el recuerdo y la muerte," Nelson develops and summarizes both the importance of the Caín motif in *Un oficio del Siglo 20* and that of the double motif in more general terms in the work of Cabrera Infante.

²⁶ This idea was suggested and developed by Cabrera Infante in *Oficio* 76-77.

²⁷ Heavy-handedness is attributed to the Steinbeck work by Cabrera Infante in *Oficio* 76.

²⁸ I owe the concept of "temporal extension" to Bordwell and Thompson 162.

²⁹ The term is that of Clarens (*Crime Movies* 202).

³⁰ The phrase is actually applied to *The Killing* by Cabrera Infante. He seeks to contrast the film with *The Asphalt Jungle*, whose contribution to its plot he also notes; but the terms could fit both movies (*Oficio* 156-57).

³¹ This film, adapted from the Mickey Spillane novel, was directed by Robert Aldrich, a "creador" praised by Cabrera Infante (*Oficio* 85). The review by Bitsch (see p. 43) was a likely influence on Cabrera Infante here.

³² This notion of the ending of the book was suggested to me by Nelson, who deals with it in mythic terms ("*La Habana*" 217-18).

³³ These overtones are not absent from the movie, despite its mutilation of the mythic structure in the script.

³⁴ See *Arcadia* 42-43 for a discussion of "nostalgia" and *Touch of Evil*.

³⁵ Quoted in Kael, "Orson Welles" 454. She treats the film along lines very similar to those followed by Cabrera Infante, even calling Quinlan "a dead whale." See 454-55.

³⁶ This epithet for Welles, and its connection to *Moby Dick*, is attributed by Cabrera Infante to Welles himself (*Arcadia* 49-50).

³⁷ See Alvarez-Borland, *Discontinuidad* 120-21, for a brief treatment of the identity game in the work.

³⁸ Gilberto Gómez aided me in clarifying this passage.

³⁹ Cabrera Infante, in an interview with me, almost deprecated his reviews of the film. He indicated, however, that his impression of it had changed somewhat due to a more recent viewing. His remarks should thus be understood within a context of hindsight:

Bueno, *Vértigo* fue una película muy importante para mí, en el sentido en que... el crítico de cine regresó a una etapa anterior y se proyectó frente a la película más como un fanático de cine... como un espectador de cine que alguien que va directamente a criticar la película. Inclusive las dos críticas que Vd. debe de conocer, la de... *Un oficio del Siglo 20*—la doble crítica en *Un oficio del Siglo 20* y la crítica en *Arcadia*—son *raves* más que... verdaderas .anotaciones críticas.... (My ellipsis)

40 Hazera notes this tendency, with regard to the reviews by Caín, in "Cinematic" 45.

41 I owe the idea of *Hamlet* as mannerist as well as the notion of appearances to Sypher. See *Four Stages*, e.g. 92-99, 172-79. Siemens also writes of "the unveiling of the artificial" with regard to *Tres tristes tigres* ("Lewis" 299).

42 See *Oficio* 371 for the origin of this idea as applied to Hitchcock.

43 Feal (*Novel Lives* 41-44) comments on the role of the parentheses, or the "corrections," in *La Habana para un Infante Difunto*.

44 The title is *Pavana para una infanta difunta* in Spanish; hence the sound association with La Habana.

45 When asked if Minnelli interested him, he replied, "*Mucho. Mucho*" (Interview with author). One should also emphasize that Minnelli is not a simple optimist, as films spanning his career, from the early *Undercurrent* to his later *Some Came Running*, *Home from the Hill*, and *The Four Horsemen of the Apocalypse* suggest.

46 Siemens (*Worlds* 160) also notes the relationship of La Estrella to Moby Dick.

47 The point about "imágenes marítimas" is made by Alvarez-Borland in reference to *The Lady from Shanghai* (*Discontinuidad* 125).

48 Menton 69. See esp. Part Two of the study by Menton for information on the political context of *Tres tristes tigres* and the attitudes of its author towards the Castro régime.

49 For a treatment of film as a "realistic" medium, see Siegfried Kracauer, *Theory of Film*.

50 Cabrera Infante expresses a similar idea about "algo diabólico" in "the Fool" and also refers to the knowledge given to Gelsomina by him (*Oficio* 132-33).

51 Alvarez-Borland expresses a similar idea about the connection between the two critical works in *Discontinuidad* 123.

4

Arcadia todas las noches

HE GENRE-ORIENTED CRITICISM of *Un oficio del Siglo 20* is condensed and "clarified" in the essays, or actually in the lectures, of *Arcadia todas las noches* (1978).[1] Here, Cabrera Infante offers evaluations of five directors whose work has encompassed all the film genres mentioned in *Un oficio del Siglo 20*. Alfred Hitchcock worked primarily with the thriller; Howard Hawks with the adventure film and the comedy; John Huston with the drama, the melodrama, and even with the documentary; Vincente Minnelli with the musical and the melodrama; and Orson Welles with the drama.

Cabrera Infante has elaborated on the background of the book. It was originally a series of "charlas" which were planned, he says, not long after "el fiasco de Bahía de Cochinos" and were thus subject to limitations, particularly since their focus was on American movies:

> ...esas charlas me fueron ofrecidas....por una señora que estaba muy consciente del hecho de que yo estaba en Habana sin trabajo...ella me propuso—esta serie de....charlas, y...las charlas dependían de...la disponibilidad de las películas...Yo propuse, más que nada por molestar,...cine americano. Todo el mundo corría a hablar de películas checas, rusas, hacer el conformismo de la mejor manera que ellos supieran.... [yo] no podía hablar de John Ford, porque todas sus grandes películas, incluyendo *The Searchers*, habían sido destruídas por reaccionarias—nada más que habían dejado *Stagecoach* por ser un clásico...había muy pocas películas de Howard Hawks disponibles.... por ejemplo, no estaba *Scarface*.... cosa que no era el caso con Minnelli.... Entonces, yo no podía hacer otra cosa que aceptar—la realidad, ¿no?, aceptar exactamente dónde estábamos. (Interview with author, my ellipsis)

Cabrera Infante has practically disclaimed the book in an interview with Isabel Alvarez-Borland ("Viaje"). He says, in essence, that the opinions in the book are no longer valid:

No creo una palabra de lo que dije en *Arcadia* porque ese escritor no soy yo. Ese *era* yo. Esas conferencias eran meras provocaciones de un rebelde dentro de una causa. Entonces en Cuba el mero hecho de escoger una película americana para criticarla sin que se empleara la torpe jerga marxista, era un alarde de independencia de juicio peligroso... muchas de las supuestas críticas que aparecen en *Arcadia* pueden ser atribuídas a otra persona. No sólo porque esa otra persona escribía prisionera de la ideología sino porque no estoy ya más de acuerdo con su criterio crítico. (66; my ellipsis)

He also tells her that

No son estos ensayos en absoluto lo que me obliga a incorporar elementos cinemáticos en mis libros. Por ejemplo, para nada menciono en *Arcadia* a ese excelente director que es Michael Curtiz... Sin embargo en "Seseribó," en *TTT*, hay un momento que tomé concientemente de otra película de Curtiz, *Young Man with a Horn*.... (66-67; my ellipsis)

Still, the book is valuable as an indication of his thought about film as well as of his method of criticism.

Despite his strong disagreement with *Arcadia todas las noches*, his judgments on Minnelli and Hawks in the book, as will be seen, do not seem far from his present opinion. He still retains as well the general outlines of the ideas regarding "ambigüedad" which he had expressed in the book, as he says to Alvarez-Borland in the same context in which he makes the disclaimer cited above:

...sigo sosteniendo un cierto apego por la teoría de la ambigüedad. Es evidente que son más interesantes los libros y las películas ambiguas que los francamente decididos, unívocos. Esta teoría de la

ambigüedad, por supuesto, tampoco es mía.... Creo sin embargo
que hay otras cualidades más importantes en un libro o en una
película que la ambigüedad, como es la posición poética ante
cualquier fenómeno de la vida o de la literatura, que a menudo
alimenta más los libros que la supuesta realidad. (68; my ellipsis)

Nor does his view of film as concerning "sueño" seem to have changed
much, since he maintained it in an interview with the author of this
study.

Much the same can be said for his general appraisals of the directors
in the book, including, as noted above, Minnelli and Hawks. He gives
an indication of his recent point of view in an interview with Alfred
MacAdam ("The Art of Fiction"), in connection with the topic of "high
and low culture":

And I refuse to make distinctions between high and low culture,
between art and pop art. Movies are for people to enjoy. Films, to
make a distinction, are for snobs and pretentious critics. I don't like
films: you can have Godard, Antonioni, Bergman, Bertolucci, and
all the German *auteurs*. Give me the directors I wrote about in
Arcadia todas las noches, and if you can't, give me Spielberg, DePalma,
Romero, or Scorcese—even Blake Edwards now. (183)

What he seems most interested in denying is the efficacy of
auteurism as a theory of film criticism. He points out the overstated
quality of some of the criticism in *Arcadia todas las noches* as well as the
influence of the *politique des auteurs* on his work at the time ("Viaje" 66-
68):

En *Arcadia* sostuve la teoría cinemática, copiada de Bazin y
Truffaut, de que existen los *autores* cinematográficos, los directores
de cine tan creadores únicos como los escritores. Aprovecho para
repudiar esta teoría ahora. No existen los autores—en ninguna
parte. Solo [sic] existen obras. No hay directores, hay películas. No
hay dramaturgos sino obras de teatro. No hay escritores, sólo
existen libros.

His disclaimer, then, is highly qualified. Even if that disclaimer
were to be accepted without analysis, the book does yield interesting
and consistent insights about his conception of film and about the
transference of film myths into his fiction.

Cabrera Infante elaborates in the talks on his thesis of film as myth. His conception, not much different in tone and thrust from his statements to Guibert about myth (*Siete voces* 410) and his recent remarks in Wellesley on the same subject, revolves particularly around the dovetailed notions of nostalgia and of Arcadia or the Golden Age, with reference to film as evocative of memories of the childhood and adolescence not only of individuals but of the human race more generally. The book, indeed, can be treated as an extended gloss on the idea of film as related to different forms of religion and as therefore sacred, or, in the expression of Manuel Puig, "'holy'" (Katz, *Symposium* 9).

The treatment accorded the directors in the book is a curious one which casts some of them rather in the mold of the "filósofos y artistas de otros tiempos..." (*Arcadia* 179), or, less frequently, places them within the tradition of mythic heroes. The tendency is especially pronounced in the cases of Welles, Huston, and Minnelli. Cabrera Infante employs a technique similar to that used by Sterne in *Tristram Shandy*.[2] He sometimes makes mock heroes out of the directors by providing them with ironic biographies. The method should be familiar to a reader of *Tres tristes tigres*, with its "biographies" of Cuba Venegas and La Estrella.

The apparently flippant method of presentation used in the book conceals some genuine concerns on the part of the critic. He works with the concepts of mannerism, of tragicomedy, of myth and mystery, and of fatalism and stoicism. These concerns flow naturally into his fiction. Many of them, as we will see, derive from the tradition of ancient philosophy and of paganism, to which he alludes when speaking of film.

The essays in the book clearly follow the method of argumentation used by the *auteur* critics. In the lecture on Welles, for example, a clear thread of authorship is traced by Cabrera Infante throughout the work of the director. The images of the mirror and the abyss are examples of recurring trademarks or motifs noted by Cabrera Infante in the films of Welles, whom he even compares directly to Shakespeare (53-58).

Such comparisons as that between Welles and Shakespeare, dear as they are to some auteurists, are of course risky; but Cabrera Infante has firm arguments on which to base his analogy. He sees as an important similarity between the two artists their frequently mannerist approach[3] as well as their "vulgaridad" (35) and that "theatrical bravado" attributed to Welles by Pauline Kael in "Orson Welles: There Ain't No Way" (244). He refers to them in terms which suggest "natural" or "primitive" artists, emphasizing that each "es un autodidacto" (*Arcadia* 35).

In drawing the analogy between Shakespeare and Welles, Cabrera Infante not only erases the value distinction between literature and cinema, thus placing his "influences" on a plane of equivalence, but also attributes more mythic status to Welles. Like that of Shakespeare, the personality of Welles has tended to merge into his work in a particularly noticeable manner, leading to a mirroring of his life by his films and to a type of symbiosis between his life and work. Of course, comparing Welles to Shakespeare gives the director a certain status in cultural history.

For Cabrera Infante, however, Welles has an importance of a different order than that of Shakespeare, since his grasp of film technique has allowed Welles to transcend the purely "verbal" (35-36). Cabrera Infante had expressed a similar idea in his review of *Moby Dick* in *Un oficio del Siglo 20*, in which he spoke of "una grandeza visual que el libro no alcanza..." (143). Note that in both contexts the concept of "illusion" is important, since Welles engages in distortion and exaggeration (see *Arcadia* 36), while the use of special effects, particularly the whale model praised by Cabrera Infante, in the Huston film, contributes greatly to its effectiveness in visual terms (*Oficio* 142).

With the idea of illusion Cabrera Infante is on familiar ground. Myths are in some sense exercises in illusionism, being, as he suggests, exaggerated and super-realistic. Cabrera Infante applies the concept of mythic exaggeration with some aptness to science-fiction movies in which animals acquire mythic or supernatural status through enlargement by camera technique, becoming "dinosaurs" or "mutated ants" (*Arcadia* 30-31). The mannerism of Welles, like that of Cabrera Infante, does not simply rely on exaggeration, or, as Alvarez-Borland says, "afectación" (*Discontinuidad* 124), but rather on the principle of illusion, of the distortion or masking of reality.

Not surprisingly, one of the central images in the work of Cabrera Infante, the mirror, is seen by him to be crucial as well to the films of Welles.[4] Kane, and Welles, acquire the quality of "un Jano bifronte." Welles is reflected in his work, while his work, including of course characters such as Kane, in turn "mirrors" him (*Arcadia* 33). Similarly, Cabrera Infante allows himself to be "reflected" rather explicitly in his work, naming the narrator of *La Habana para un Infante Difunto* "Guillermo" and "Guy" and giving the initials of "'GCI'" to "a character who signs the *Advertencia* and a letter to Silvestre" in *Tres tristes tigres* (Feal, *Novel Lives* 50-51, 48n 43). The duality between Welles and Kane is paralleled and reduplicated by those between Cabrera Infante and the critic G. Caín as well as the screenwriter G. Cain.[5]

The techniques of illusionism and of mannerist obscurantism contribute for Cabrera Infante to the "doble misterio" of the work of Welles as well as that of Shakespeare (*Arcadia* 35). The choice of the term "misterio" seems very deliberate. Welles, in the cinema, like Orpheus in Greek myth, was the founder of a kind of cult. The "cult" founded by the flamboyant director included the use of deep focus and stressed formal experimentation and the open exhibition of technique.[6] The similarities between the work of Welles and that of Cabrera Infante are apparent here, since both rely on the patent exhibition of technical facility in constructing their work.

While Cabrera Infante is certainly not a "didactic" artist,[7] his characterization of the work of Welles and of Shakespeare as expressing, in part, "mensajes exclusivamente para intelectuales" and of mannerist works like *Citizen Kane* and *Hamlet* as vehicles which "contienen un doble misterio: uno popular, inmediato; otro intelectual, más oculto" (*Arcadia* 35) may be quite revealing. Not only does such a characterization appear elsewhere in his critical work, for instance in his remarks on Hitchcock as "un mistagogo" (*Arcadia* 67); but the notion of "un doble misterio" may also be illuminative of his own literary and film work. Thus, *Tres tristes tigres*, while formidable technically, could probably be enjoyed as an entertaining work despite the probability of its vaguely disturbing even superficial readers, who might still sense the underlying seriousness and pathos of its satire.

In connection with the use of illusion by Welles, a humorous tendency from his work, pointed out by Cabrera Infante in *Arcadia todas las noches*, may be mentioned. Cabrera Infante notes the habitual use by Welles of false noses (46-47), which, he says, have resulted in much expense and interesting difficulties.[8] The shifting or chameleon-like appearance of Welles in his films is part and parcel of his mannerist artifice and use of illusion. Welles seems unreal to

Cabrera Infante without his stage or film persona. His dialectic of physical concealment and revelation mirrors that of his films, and his film universe is akin to that of another director studied in *Arcadia todas las noches*, Alfred Hitchcock, because both investigate the truth covered over by surfaces.[9]

In his remarks on the style of Welles, Cabrera Infante praises the marrying of form to context. He says that "Siempre hay en Welles una correspondencia formal con las situaciones dramáticas" (*Arcadia* 40). Such a correspondence is one of the chief tests for the execution of a successful artistic praxis. Cabrera Infante provides a strong defense of the films of Orson Welles against those who would call them "flashy and cheap." The concern with form is important to Cabrera Infante, who wrote a stylistic manual of sorts called *Exorcismos de esti(l)o* (1976).

The appraisal of the Welles style from a perspective of aesthetic congruence is typical of Cabrera Infante, who similarly refers to the equivalence between the film technique and the lifestyle of John Huston by quoting Buffon, an apostle of neoclassical balance (*Arcadia* 148). As his interest in *The Asphalt Jungle* by Huston has shown (see above, 7, 61-62), Cabrera Infante advocates disciplined, economical, though not necessarily sparse, style in film and in literature. His preferences in both areas bear out this thesis: Hemingway, Hawks, Huston, Hitchcock, and Lewis Carróll are all examples of economists of expression. The defense of ambiguity by Cabrera Infante, in which he speaks of "simple razón de economía" (*Arcadia* 27), can now be better understood as a search for something akin to the concept of *poesía pura* espoused by Jorge Guillén: the maximum expression of meaning through the minimum expenditure of word or image.

While Cabrera Infante himself, like Welles, seems to deviate frequently from such a prescription, creating opulent surfaces for his work, the feeling usually remains that these artists work with a sense of the aesthetic necessity of their experiments with form. The short stories and pieces by Cabrera Infante bear out the idea of the economy of style to which he pays tribute in his praises of Hammett and Hemingway,[10] while his longer works seem to veer away from such economy. Nevertheless, even his largest work, *La Habana para un Infante Difunto*, is seamlessly constructed, with little excess in its massive structure.

The concept of economy is also applied by the critic to another important aspect of the figure of Orson Welles, his acting on film and on stage. Here Cabrera Infante deviates from a strictly "auteurist" position and defends an emphasis on the importance of the actor, much as he will do in the essay on Huston, in which he speaks of Humphrey Bogart in mythic terms (139-48). He praises the acting of Welles, often the object of derision in this area by critics, for his capacity to evoke naturalness: "Eso se llama actuación: la técnica de ser un atento oyente de una conversacion sabida de antemano" (*Arcadia* 51).[11] Though Welles struck the attentive viewer as a director relying on artifice, his acting, for Cabrera Infante, has hidden in its best moments its use of artifice through the exercise of skilled craftsmanship and thus achieves a quality of naturalness. He compares Welles to Cary Grant and Humphrey Bogart in this respect and includes him in a list of "los pocos actores verdaderos que ha dado el cine" (49-52). Welles thus fits neatly into both *politiques* espoused by Cabrera Infante in *Arcadia todas las noches*, having been both an *auteur* and an actor.

The view of a director as operating on two levels of meaning, one more accessible and one more "mysterious," is dear to auteurist critics and as such is often abused. Cabrera Infante, while he avails himself of the idea, fits it into his concept of mannerism and implicitly ties it to his ideas in his book *O* (1975) concerning Lewis Carroll, a famous practitioner of hidden message sending.[12] Thus, his analysis of Welles and of Hitchcock as directors with multilevel works seems apt and not merely an auteurist extravagance, all the more so since Cabrera Infante has certainly chosen two worthy subjects for his analysis.

Cabrera Infante extends the idea of double meaning, used in the essay on Welles, by speaking in the piece on Alfred Hitchcock of the concept of "game" as expressed by Johan Huizinga in *Homo Ludens*. The game or play idea is readily applicable to a book like *Tres tristes tigres*, in which word games or plays abound and the characters indulge in games of varying extension and seriousness. Seriousness, in fact, is the quality which interests Cabrera Infante in games such as those played by Hitchcock in his films. The director is ascribed a seriousness akin to that of the Olympian gods, whose games and jests were both political and personal in intent as well as being symbolic for the Greeks of natural or spiritual processes (see, e.g., Graves 1: 13-22).

Cabrera Infante says of Hitchcock that "Hay que tomar en serio a este creador porque sus juegos parecen significar exactamente otra cosa" (*Arcadia* 62-63). He places the director into the category of a mythmaker or "mystagogue"—"un mistagogo" (67)—whose game-playing, including his seemingly frivolous appearances in his own films (63), his flippantly morbid wit, and his mock-serious use of the term "'McGuffin'" to characterize the "'secret'" of his films, hide a serious intent (Hitchcock, *Hitchcock* 98-100). At times, his game-playing expresses absurdity, as in *The Trouble with Harry*, and farce, as in *To Catch a Thief*, which, interestingly, "termina con un gran baile de disfraces que es un festival de pelucas" (65), the wigs recalling a scene in *Tres tristes tigres* (164-68). At other times, Hitchcock becomes more metaphysical in intent, as in *Vertigo*.

The immersion of Hitchcock into "misterio" (*Arcadia* 67) places him, for Cabrera Infante, into a pantheon occupied only by directors such as Welles or Chaplin. "Hitchcock es," as Alvarez-Borland points out, "el director quien más le atrae y fascina" (*Discontinuidad* 126). Cabrera Infante says "que la palabra misterio tiene aquí el sentido trascendente que le da la teología." He associates the idea with "los cuerpos de doctrina paganos y . . . a los misterios de Eleusis, al complejo culto de Démeter y Perséfona" (*Arcadia* 67; my ellipsis). Like Parker Tyler, he places film of this type on a mythic plane:

> Como se sabe, aquellos misterios [los de Eleusis] terminaban en un rito que culminaba en un recinto cerrado y oscuro, en el que se mostraba a los iniciados las visiones del mundo bajo, el descenso al Hades, y retazos de la vida futura por medio de golpes de luz. ¿No les recuerda esto demasiado a esta sala cerrada y oscura? ¿Los golpes de luz no serán 24 en un segundo? (67)

The question posed by Cabrera Infante to his audience, "¿Querrían ustedes ser los iniciados?", will be echoed and extended in the mock-serious Prologue to *Tres tristes tigres*, which in turn, to echo Ardis Nelson, recalls the Prologue in Greek drama, an occasion for the spokesman of the drama to invite the audience to participate in the rite or mystery of the performance (67).

The rites of which Cabrera Infante speaks in the work of Hitchcock, despite their origins in "los cuerpos de doctrina paganos," center, he argues, around Catholicism. He follows, as he says (67), the Rohmer and Chabrol analysis of the director. He quotes Alexandre Astruc as saying in *Cahiers du cinéma*, the French film magazine so influential in the 1950s,[13] that a director like Hitchcock "'es un teólogo'" and that "'La clase de cuestión planteada [en su obra] es siempre, en definitiva, un dilema moral'" (68).

Cabrera Infante has recently clarified his position on Hitchcock, speaking with historical perspective on the *Cahiers* critics and their effect on the director. He has said that his "actitudes" on the director varied from a youthful view to one which was more properly that of a "crítico del cine":

> Hay varias... actitudes... primero, el espectador totalmente inocente—es decir, yo conocí Hitchcock sin saber que era Hitchcock. Esto ocurrió en mi niñez... a fines de los años treinta... yo, antes de salir de mi pueblo en el norte de... Oriente de Cuba, yo había visto ya, pues—*The Man Who Knew Too Much*, *Secret Agent*, and [sic] *Sabotage*... y tan pronto como llegué a La Habana,... los grandes cines tenían un... cartel—un programa—doble—que era *Rebeca* y *La sospecha*... yo estaba viendo Hitchcock sin saberlo. Ésa es una parte.... (Interview with author; my ellipsis)

"La otra parte" of his point of view on the director concerns his historical importance "como técnico del cine." He also spoke at some length on the issue of morality and Hitchcock:

> Yo creo que Hitchcock tiene su mundo particular católico, pero reconocible sólo a partir de que los críticos franceses se lo hicieron conocer. Entonces, él asumió efectivamente esa catolicidad. Los símbolos se hicieron más evidentes, y él se convirtió en un.... director diferente del que era—es decir, diferente de que él se concebía, no diferente del que era; porque en realidad, los franceses lo que hicieron fue señalar algunas.... tendencias que aparecieron una y otra vez en su cine.... (Interview with author; my ellipsis)

He now takes a less definite position on the Catholicism and mythmaking of the director than he did in *Arcadia todas las noches*, stressing especially the technical achievements and importance of the director.

Moral preoccupations, such as those attributed to Hitchcock, are common to the directors discussed by Cabrera Infante in the book, leading one to the conclusion that the critic himself, as has seemed on other occasions in his film reviews, shares a moral spirit or purpose with the directors. Among the directors studied in *Arcadia todas las noches*, it is of Hitchcock that he speaks in the highest philosophical terms, saying that "No necesitaré mucho para reconocer los temas de Hitchcock como trascendentales y a la vez intentar una filosofía hitchcockiana: un estudio de las manifestaciones del espíritu a través de su lenguaje cinematográfico" (68).

The philosophical study of the director by Cabrera Infante finds its highest level in his comments on *Vertigo*, a film which, as noted earlier, is for Cabrera Infante a modern expression of the myth of Orpheus and one of the most important movies in his cinematic mythology. In *Arcadia todas las noches*, he expands on the mythic aspects of *Vertigo*, adding to his Orphic interpretation of it the exegesis by Barthélemy Amengual of the movie as a version of the Tristan and Isolde story (73-83) and the connection, drawn by Cabrera Infante himself, of the film with the myths of Lot and of the Minotaur, the latter being a frequent image in his own work.

Vertigo is a perfect example of the concept of myth in cinema developed by Cabrera Infante. All the myths quoted by him concern death and resurrection (or the failure of such resurrection). The imagery of resurrection, incidentally, is playfully used in *Tres tristes tigres*, with the mock death and resurrection of Cué and the more seriously treated transfiguration of Bustrófedon into the corpus of his linguistic legacy.

In the study of *Vertigo* presented in *Arcadia todas las noches*, Cabrera Infante draws upon the inspiration with which a remark made to Max Jacob once provided him: "Recuerdo no sin estupor lo que le dijo un día un niño al surrealista Max Jacob: 'El cine se hace con los muertos. Se les coge, se les hace caminar y eso es el cine'" (73). Cabrera Infante comments as follows on the relationship of the connection between death and life in the cinema to its fascination as myth: "El horror y la fascinación y el sentimiento ambiguo que se desprenden de esta tesis y antítesis de la atracción me devuelve, una vez más, a ese relato primitivo de lo eterno que se llama, generalmente, mito" (73).

The Orpheus and Lot myths are structurally similar, both concerning a man who loses his wife or lover due to the breaking of an agreement with a god. Like Scottie in *Vertigo*, and like the narrator in *La Habana para un Infante Difunto*, who returns to Violeta to find her only a shadow of herself, Orpheus looks back at Eurydice and loses her forever. The wife of Lot plays a role corresponding to that of Madeleine in the film, since both look back at an image of destruction or evil—in the case of Madeleine, at an apparition, actually a nun, which she thinks to be evil—and die as a result.[14]

The link with the Tristan and Isolde myth impinges chiefly on the "double" motif to be found in that myth. Tristan is, as Cabrera Infante says in his summary of the myth (*Arcadia* 75-76), enamored of one Isolde and betrayed by another. The duplication of women has a near parallel in the Madeleine/Judy pairing in *Vertigo*.

Another myth, that of Pygmalion and his creation of Galatea as a statue which takes on life, is not directly mentioned by Cabrera Infante but certainly has a strong relationship to *Vertigo* as well as to *La Habana para un Infante Difunto* and *Tres tristes tigres*. Like Scottie in *Vertigo*, the narrator of *La Habana para un Infante Difunto* and Códac in *Tres tristes tigres* exhibit a Pygmalion tendency, creating idealized women out of rather inanimate or at least coarse material: the real Violeta del Valle and La Estrella are less ethereal or aesthetically pure than their lovers or admirers would like to believe.[15]

The plethora of mythical allusions in *Vertigo*, as in the work of Cabrera Infante, lends credence to "La declaración," "reclaimed" here by Cabrera Infante and echoing the views of Joseph Campbell in works such as *The Masks of God*, "de que todos los mitos remiten a un solo mito, como todos los hombres regresan siempre a un solo hombre" (*Arcadia* 77). Cabrera Infante extends this statement logically by reference to the Cocteau "film mitológico" called *L'Éternel retour*, itself an allusion to the Nietzschean conception of eternal recurrence.

Here, Cabrera Infante proceeds from what seems to be merely a statement of the permanence of genre, or the unity of form, towards a thesis of cyclic time. Perhaps much of his interest in *Vertigo* can be traced to its evocation of notions such as eternal recurrence or cyclic time.

In *Arcadia todas las noches*, he relates the error of Scottie to that of Orpheus. Both have violated "cyclic" time:

> Dice Mircea Eliade en *El mito del eterno retorno*: "De la misma manera que los griegos, en su mito del eterno retorno, buscan satisfacer su sed metafísica de lo *óntico* y de lo estático [...] asimismo los *primitivos*, al conferir al tiempo una dirección cíclica, anulan su irreversibilidad." Es contra esta dirección cíclica que Orfeo mira atrás en busca de Eurídice: es así que Scottie, el detective de *Vértigo*, reconstruye a Madeleine y vence al pasado: el tiempo no existe, todo no es más que un eterno retorno. Pero al mirar atrás, al tratar de comprobar si es Madeleine-Judy quien le sigue o Madeleine-Eurídice, Scottie la pierde para siempre, porque no ha sabido creer

que el tiempo no es irreversible. (77; original ellipsis and emphasis)

Like Joyce, Cabrera Infante tends towards a unification of language and genre by means of dazzling linguistic transformation and stylistic parody. His fascination with nostalgia and temporal-spatial relations is at least partly motivated by his drive towards a unity of forms. Certainly, such an interest helps to explain his placing literature and film on a plane of equivalence.

Cabrera Infante offers some other interesting observations on the mythic subtexts of *Vertigo* and other Hitchcock films. One of the more intriguing, in view of the apparent predilection of Cabrera Infante himself for certain actresses with blonde, or falsely blonde, hair,[16] such as Monroe, Mae West, and Jean Harlow, is his placing of "el mito de Tristán e Isolda" in "la tradición aria del gusto por los cabellos rubios" and his relating of that tradition to the tastes of Hitchcock (*Arcadia* 80). Another exegetical commentary on the film, to the effect that ancient texts such as the *Symposium* contain antecedents, within the Trojan and Orphic cycles, to the replacing of the real by "'un fantasma'" (80), is not only very illuminating as to the mechanism of the film but also as to the structure of *Vanishing Point*, whose original script contains a scene, excised from the film, with a mysterious "Queen of Spades" who proves to be "'un fantasma'" and who seems to exist in some sort of cyclic time, a reference to her having been made earlier in the script by a character with a related name—Blackie—who could not logically know of her (Cain 136-50, 9). The great importance of *Vertigo* and of the myths and concepts evoked by it for the work of Cabrera Infante is quite apparent.

Cabrera Infante also makes several technical observations in the essay on Hitchcock, speaking of the "astucias técnicas" of the director (81). Much of his admiration for Hitchcock in fact concerns the technique of the famous director:

> La otra parte [of his attitude towards Hitchcock] es—Hitchcock visto como un crítico de cine. Es decir,... visto *por* un crítico de cine—como yo juzgaba las películas de Hitchcock, como yo me aproximaba a ellas; que después, [hay] la actitud... actual, que es—Hitchcock como técnico del cine, y al mismo tiempo, como generador de una mitología que ha alcanzado a gente tan disímil como Brian De Palma ... porque De Palma tiene un concepto del cine que—aparentemente es muy frívolo, pero que... debe mucho a

Hitchcock sin... tener sus preocupaciones que son a veces muy manifiestas—sus preocupaciones teológicas.... también a mí me interesa Hitchcock el técnico. Es decir, Hitchcock, ¿cómo es posible que él supiera tanto cine cuando uno piensa que, por ejemplo, John Ford hizo muchas más películas que Hitchcock, estaba mucho antes que Hitchcock en el cine; sin embargo, John Ford no tiene los conocimientos técnicos que tenía Hitchcock... una capacidad particular o tal vez un interés... en aprender lo más posible para evitar que su concepto de una película desde el guión variara mucho en manos del fotógrafo, etc., etc., el *art director*—toda la serie de gente que están siempre entre el director y la copia final de la película.... (Interview with author; my ellipsis)[17]

In the essay on Hitchcock in *Arcadia todas las noches*, Cabrera Infante follows a fairly straight auteurist line, showing the constancy of certain motifs such as "misterio" and the Catholic concerns in the work of the director. He follows similar procedures in other essays of the book, working in each case with different themes which fit each director.

The Howard Hawks essay shows Cabrera Infante working in part with the idea of ferocity and warmth as two sides of friendship, a theme which flows through the work of Hawks. Hawks, indeed, is identified through his name with the fierce hawk (85) and is injected into a peculiar dialectic with William Faulkner ("Falconer"), who worked with him in Hollywood (108-18).[18] Such imagery of doubles is even more pronounced here than in the other essays and echoes the Cain-Abel motif present elsewhere in the work of Cabrera Infante. The essay is, as Alvarez-Borland notes, quite discursive in its shifting from subject to subject (*Discontinuidad* 126-27).[19] The significance of the interest of Cabrera Infante in Hawks seems clear enough, nevertheless, hinging chiefly, in this book at least, on the focus by the director on male friendship and on the psychological twists of dominance, betrayal, and loyalty which such friendship can acquire.[20]

The concept of friendship between men is given allegorical form in the section of the essay which concerns Hawks and Faulkner. The section exhibits in striking fashion the enthusiasm of Cabrera Infante for language and naming and is a brilliant example of his linguistic dexterity.

He attributes the close working relationship of Faulkner and Hawks to "la legendaria amistad, tres veces milenaria, entre el hombre y un ave rapaz unidos en el arte de la cetrería: ellos son el halcón y el halconero" (109). The fact, noted by Cabrera Infante, that the relationship seems to be reversed—"¿El halcón llama al halconero y éste viene en su ayuda?" (109)[21]—matters little to the allusive structure built by Cabrera Infante. Just as Hawks and Faulkner formed a collaborative and at times almost symbiotic pair, joined by name as well as by profession and interest, so Cabrera Infante typically focuses on pairs of men in his fiction. Most notably, he dwells on the pair of "friends" Cué and Silvestre who alternate between domination and submission; but he also focuses on pairs of men in *La Habana para un Infante Difunto* and, in a stranger manner, on pairings of different types in *Vanishing Point*.

The undercurrents of friendship which flow beneath "el estilo casi impersonal, desnudo de Hawks" (*Arcadia* 100) connect to another important motif of the essay, one which is also present in the section of the book on Hitchcock: the nightmare or dream. The quotation from William Styron (95-96) is a dream sequence; and Cabrera Infante speaks of *The Big Sleep*, a Hawks film, in nightmarish terms:

> . . . recuerdo *Al borde del abismo* . . . no sólo como un film inolvidable, sino como una ocasión en que el cine hizo suyas todas las pesadillas posibles y las transfiguró en una buena pesadilla, esa que termina con el fin del sueño: *Al borde del abismo* muestra como [sic] la paranoia ha informado, en una influencia que complacería a Dalí y a muchos surrealistas viejos, al arte, a la más popular de las formas de arte. (101; my ellipsis)

Dream, while awake or asleep, is a topic of interest for Cabrera Infante, appearing from time to time in his fiction, sometimes in the form of sequences which seem to be nightmares but may only be examples of the fantastic; for instance, the "death" of Cué in *Tres tristes tigres*.

The concept of dream is central to the notion of film held by Cabrera Infante, a point which he recently reiterated (Interview with author). In this respect he is not far from theorists such as Hugo Munsterberg, Béla Balázs, and Parker Tyler. Again in the essay on Hawks is to be seen a mannerist approach to art: beneath the surface of the films lies a mystery, a hidden message to be deciphered by the viewer attuned to the larger mystery of the film.[22]

Some of the movies referred to in the essay are, according to

Cabrera Infante himself, deeply rooted in his memory (88-92). Most especially, he cites the Hawks films *Scarface* and *Tiger Shark* as important to his childhood and as having become nearly part of his unconscious. For example, the theme of betrayal ("la traición") is noted by him as important to *Scarface* (91). Cabrera Infante was deeply impressed by scenes from the movie which concern betrayal: the killing of the gangster played by Boris Karloff, his prior attempt on the life of Camonte, the betrayal by Camonte of his boss, his turning on his friend Guino, the betrayal of faith with his sister by his final surrender (91).

The theme of betrayal is important to Cabrera Infante in more than one respect. It appears in *Tres tristes tigres*[23] in a rather veiled fashion in the sense of loss felt by the "followers" of Bustrófedon after he "betrays" them by dying, in the betrayal of youthful innocence in the career of Cuba Venegas, in the scenes concerning adultery early in the book, and in the betrayal of the memory of La Estrella by publicists after her death. In a more global and abstract sense, the theme appears in *Tres tristes tigres* in the "treason" which language performs on itself, and through translation, on the form and meaning of books—note the final word of one of the closing chapters in the book, "Tradittori" (455). *Tres tristes tigres* has as much of its subject the impossibility of capturing experience in accurate language. On a more personal level, Cabrera Infante feels the revolution, and himself, to have been betrayed by Castro. Thus, the importance of the Cain-Abel myth to his work and life is evident, due to its theme of filial betrayal, as is the concretization of the treason motif in some of the Hawks films.

Examined in the light of the theme of betrayed ideals and trusts, the essay appears less discursive. Marilyn Monroe, a great myth of the cinema, is a poignant example of betrayed hopes and ideals and receives fairly extensive treatment in the essay. A real-life Cuba Venegas, Marilyn, as Ezra Goodman says in *The Fifty Year Decline and Fall of Hollywood* (233), had an unfortunate tendency to use people and then discard them, giving an impression of a character much like the icy one of Venegas. Of course, such a means of living could only lead to a betrayal of self. Cabrera Infante excuses Monroe more than does Goodman, and understandably so, since he sees society as somewhat ogreish. Notwithstanding the difference in treatment from a more objective approach like that of Goodman, the presentation of Monroe in *Arcadia todas las noches* maintains the thesis of ideals betrayed, of innocence corrupted by power. From Cesca, the sister of Camonte, to Marilyn Monroe, is not a great distance, just as the transition from Monroe to figures such as Cuba Venegas and La Estrella is largely one of a filtering through the structure of a narrative which demands certain distortions of the archetype. Monroe is tied closely to other parts of the Cabrera Infante iconography, specifically the Madeleine-Judy "pair" of *Vertigo*, by the linkage between her and two mythic figures: "...Marilyn Monroe, ese mito, vivirá eternamente: la muchacha, Helena de nuevo, la Isolda inmortal está entre nosotros" (*Arcadia* 108).

The mythic approach taken by Cabrera Infante to Hawks leads him to patterns of thought familiar to readers of *Tres tristes tigres* or *Exorcismos de esti(l)o*. One of the striking visual features of *Tres tristes tigres* is its reliance on depiction of word-games through geometric designs, recalling the experiments of Lewis Carroll in works such as *Alice in Wonderland*, for instance, the "'long tale,'" with its design on the page like a mouse's tail (Carroll 39-40). Related to such visualization, which, as in the "dádiva" example (214), often takes on a severely disciplined form, is the fascination, particularly of Bustrófedon, with numerology.[24] Numerology was important to many of the ancients and to medieval thinkers. Of especial interest with regard to the comments of Cabrera Infante on Hawks is the importance of numbers to the Pythagoreans.[25]

Numerical and geometric concerns appear in the essay on Hawks with particular clarity in connection with the films *Land of the Pharaohs* and *Rio Bravo*. Cabrera Infante quotes Herodotus on the grandiose nature of the pyramid of Gizeh, with details of its dimensions, of the number of men who worked on it, and so forth (114-16). In the midst of the reference to the Greek historian, Cabrera Infante injects a quality of "fable" into the film: "Esta parece ser la moraleja de este film espectacular que tiene dentro varias fábulas: la fábula de la reina buena y la reina mala, la fábula del usurpador castigado como por mano divina, la fábula del rey agradecido y el inventor ingenioso" (116).

His commentary on *Land of the Pharaohs*, with its digressions into falconry, thus extending the wordplay with "Hawks" and "Faulkner," is not as pointed with reference to geometry as is the section on *Rio Bravo*. He stresses the "necessity" of the plot elements of the latter film, a qualification which is both Aristotelian and important to mathematicians and logicians. He reduces the film to simple and clear geometric terms. The character relationships "Son términos simples y antagónicos, geométricos, y aquí, como en Pitágoras, un triángulo puede ser base del universo, y una letra, la letra pitagórica, el camino divergente del bien y del mal..." (125-26; my ellipsis).

Cabrera Infante has recently spoken of his interest in Hawks in terms very similar to those of his earlier critical work. He fixes his major interest in Hawks as "la relación que mantenía Hawks entre los personajes y la cámara. Es decir, entre lo visible y el punto de vista..." (Interview with author). He again refers to *Rio Bravo* as a representation of this tendency:

> como, por ejemplo, está muy bien ilustrado al principio de... *Rio Bravo*.... hay una... relación entre los personajes y la cámara que yo no volví... a ver hasta que vi, en Londres, todas las películas, todos los *Westerns*, de Anthony Mann, donde hay también la misma, una muy parecida [sic], tipo de *mise-en-scène*—aunque Anthony Mann es menos... romántico que Hawks—es más...crudo—más—duro.... Está....muy claro en *Rio Bravo*. Hay una relación... absolutamente geométrica entre los personajes y la cámara.... Por ejemplo, en... *Rio Bravo* es la moneda que tiran a... la escupidera. Y luego, con John Wayne. La relación entre....Dean Martin y la moneda es una relación de tensión... la posibilidad de su desmoralización total, y la relación más tarde entre John Wayne [Martin is perhaps intended here] y una gota de sangre.... Esto es,... para mí, precisamente, lo que es Howard Hawks.... (Interview with author; my ellipsis)

Here is seen the number so important to the work of Cabrera Infante, 3, which appears not only in the title of *Tres tristes tigres* but which, in its geometric manifestation as a triangle, is found as an explicit image in his writing, as in his remarks on a set of Hitchcock films under the heading of "*Tres visiones del mundo (o una visión del mundo tres veces)*" (*Arcadia* 64; original emphasis) and as an analogue to the relationships in numerous films significant to the work of Cabrera Infante. The films of Vincente Minnelli, for instance, often concern love triangles; and on a more abstract plane, the spatial relationships between the characters in *Citizen Kane* exhibit the triangular arrangement of figures typical of movies photographed by Gregg Toland.[26] He sees Hawks in more classicist terms than he does Welles,

Hitchcock, and even perhaps John Huston. The work of Hawks appeals to the sensibility of Cabrera Infante due to its purity and clarity of expression as well as for its harmony of form and generic context.

Clarity of form and purity of line are qualities also prominent in the work of John Huston, to whom Cabrera Infante devotes an essay which is interesting because of its essentially negative appraisal of the career of the director. Huston, for Cabrera Infante, is a director whose greatest merit may have been the discovery and mythification of Humphrey Bogart, and with him, the figure of the private detective, as well as of other actors such as Sydney Greenstreet and Elisha J. Cook, Jr. Like Welles, though on a smaller scale, Huston peaked with an early film, *The Maltese Falcon*, and then proceeded, somewhat unlike Welles, to repeat the thematic pattern of his first film, with varying results. The virtues of *The Maltese Falcon* are of a simpler, more classical order than those of *Citizen Kane*; seen today, *The Maltese Falcon* indeed seems classically disciplined, almost austere, in contrast to the lush masterwork by Welles.

The essay on Huston is one of the relative few in which Cabrera Infante deals specifically with film and literature in theoretical terms. He cites a passage from *The Maltese Falcon* by Dashiell Hammett, the basis for the Huston film, and comments on the nature of the prose: "...una verdadera secuencia cinematográfica: algún día habrá que hablar de esta literatura, la de Hemingway y sus epígonos, influida por el cine, que a su vez ha influido al cine..." (*Arcadia* 136-39; my ellipsis). Despite the praise which he reserves for the director of the movie, he cites Bogart as the central figure in the filmic realization of the prose style of Hammett:

> ...¿pero alguien puede pensar en un actor mejor para juntar dramáticamente ese pequeño rompecabezas de miradas torvas, torcidos gestos, diálogos que eluden mencionar su objeto, oraciones sin sujeto...en un actor de cine mejor que Bogart para colocar a Sam Spade en un contexto creíble y dinámico y vital? Yo no lo encuentro, no lo he encontrado nunca. (*Arcadia* 139; my ellipsis)

The discussion of Bogart by Cabrera Infante emphasizes not only his qualities as an actor but also his mythic status. In a vignette in the essay, Cabrera Infante places himself in a fictional situation with three women—the magical number once again—who seem themselves related to images from film and thus, for Cabrera Infante, to myth. The first woman, an intellectual type, wears "un traje-sastre gris o quizá fuera un *chemise* amarillo..." as well as "espejuelos," and asks him a philosophical question. Given the predilection of Cabrera Infante for the work of Stanley Donen, the connection of the woman described with the heroine of *Funny Face* by Donen, an "intellectual" played by an initially mousy Audrey Hepburn, is certainly possible. The second, a black woman, seems a prefiguration of the Queen of Spades in *Vanishing Point*, not only in her blackness but also in her answering of questions with questions of her own; and the third is a blonde—of mythic implication for Cabrera—and, he says, "... [ella] pudo convertirme en un personaje de Mickey Spillane" (140). These women question him about Bogart and his legend. The intertwining of autobiography, or fictionalized autobiography, and criticism recalls *Un oficio del Siglo 20*;[27] and Bogart and his legend are made even more mythic by the apparently fictional intervention of the three iconographic women.

The Bogart myth, for Cabrera Infante, was brought to fruition by the films of Huston and in turn fed the cinema of that director:

> ...la mitad del cine hecho por Huston sería otra cosa (y dudo que fuera otra cosa *mejor*) si no hubiera contado con la presencia de Humphrey Bogart in *El halcón maltés, A través del Pacífico, El tesoro de* [la] *Sierra Madre, Huracán de pasiones, La burla del diablo* y, última pero no la última, *La reina africana....* (*Arcadia* 141; original emphasis)

Cabrera Infante briefly reviews the actor's career and proceeds to summarize some sketches of him by critics such as Robert Lachenay and André Bazin.

In the midst of the biographical material on Bogart appears the argument, now familiar to us, for "la importancia del actor en el cine" (142-43). Cabrera Infante supports the thesis of Néstor Almendros, who sees a significant difference in two films by the same director but with two lead actors of sufficient power: "Un film de Clark Gable o de Frank Sinatra, razona Almendros, es radicalmente distinto a uno de Henry Fonda o de Gene Kelly, aunque sean dirigidos por el mismo director, producidos por la misma compañía, escritos por los mismos guionistas" (142). Thus, says Cabrera Infante, "Es evidente que la personalidad del actor opera un cambio en la película en que actúa" (142). The thesis contradicts the perceived overemphasis on the directorial role in cinematic creativity and certainly fits with the ecumenical tastes of Cabrera Infante with respect to actors, many of whom he tends to mythify to a degree at least equivalent to his praise for certain directors.

The section on Bogart is continued with some commentary which forms the poetic center of the essay on Huston and is one of the more interesting attempts by the critic to place film into a mythic ambience. Cabrera Infante briefly establishes, by analyzing some of the roles played by Bogart in Huston films, that Bogart is the motive force in the tragic upshot of these movies—*Key Largo* (*Huracán de pasiones*), *The Treasure of the Sierra Madre*, and, apparently, *The Maltese Falcon*. As such, Bogart is, for the critic, the leader or "el motor de estas expediciones" in ambition and "avaricia," "el agente que convoca la catástrofe..." (144).

The role of Bogart in the cinema of Huston recalls for Cabrera Infante the part played by the Greek Jason in the expedition of the Argonauts, a group of men who were in the majority, like the "argonauts" of *The Treasure of the Sierra Madre*, decidedly unsentimental about their reasons for trying to retrieve their prize, the Golden Fleece, as well as about their methods for doing so (145). Cabrera Infante has hit upon a most interesting mythic parallel to the films of Huston mentioned in this connection, despite the fact, noted by Borges, "'...que, en los libros antiguos, las buscas eran siempre afortunadas: los argonautas conquistaban el Vellocino y Galahad, el Santo Grial'" (qtd. in *Arcadia* 145); while Huston films typically end, Cabrera Infante suggests, in "fracaso" (145). Nevertheless, the parallel between *The Treasure of the Sierra Madre*, with its search, noted by Cabrera Infante, for gold on a mountain with hostile "guardians," and the voyage of the Argonauts is quite clearly established in the essay, as are the similarities between the quest of the Argonauts and those of the searchers in *Key Largo*—led by Rocco (Edward G. Robinson) and looking for the return of Prohibition—[28] and in *The Maltese Falcon*.

Again Cabrera Infante concentrates on the motif of the voyage or search, which, as noted above, is central to his fiction and to his film work. The motif also plays a central role in the work of Huston, whose "estoicismo" is respected by Cabrera Infante even though he criticizes the aesthetic failures of the director. The critic offers a clear summary of "las tendencias adheridas a la filosofía de Huston" (146-47):

Reconocidas, se sabe que son la ambigüedad (dada siempre por
Humphrey Bogart y desaparecida con él) y la negativa a la derrota
(tomada por otros actores: Sterling Hayden, Audie Murphy,
Trevor Howard) y el anacronismo (ofrecido por Walter Huston y
Edward G. Robinson y Katharine Hepburn, y, rara sorpresa, Clark
Gable).

He concludes "que en la obra de Huston las fuerzas anacrónicas
impulsan el espíritu de pelea" (147).

The notion of "anacronismo" is of interest to readers of Cabrera
Infante. His novels are characterized by their emphasis on the past of
La Habana and, by implication, on the author and his memories as in
a sense anachronic, out of step with the Cuba from which he has
exiled himself. Like Welles, Huston exhibits a certain predilection, if
not a exactly a romanticism, for anachronistic figures. The
predilection of Huston is noted by Cabrera Infante, who qualifies his
statements by adding that the work of Huston has moved away, "ha
terminado con el tema de los anacrónicos" with films like *The Roots of
Heaven, The Asphalt Jungle,* and *The Misfits* (149). Cabrera Infante
continues to connect the content of, in particular, *The Asphalt Jungle*
with Greek myths; but the connections have become more tenuous:
"Al final, cuando el matón Dix Hanney regresa al lar paterno, los
caballos parecen reconocerlo como al hijo perdido, como Argos a
Ulises regresado. ¿O se trata, simplemente, de la curiosidad animal
ante la muerte?" (149). The film, part of the "'mitología privada'" of
Cabrera Infante (*Siete voces* 410), is a good example of the "estoicismo"
which is so conspicuously lacking from the comportment of the
characters of his novels, even though the tone of those books, and of
Vanishing Point, carries such a thrust. The opposition of Cabrera
Infante to "la literatura didáctica" (Alvarez-Borland, *Discontinuidad* 125)
appears here when he dismisses the "psicologismo fácil que aparece en
los comienzos" of *The Asphalt Jungle* (*Arcadia* 149-50). Instead, he
applauds the establishment by Huston in the film of "el realismo, el
método documental" (150), qualities which place the film on the level
"de tragedia griega"—not the romantic tragedy of *Little Caesar,* but a
more Sophoclean, purified, unsentimental tragedy—and which
"Sirven para una concepción poética del personaje central, no muy
lejano de los parias sureños de Tennesse [sic] Williams y William
Faulkner" (149-50).

The theme of stoicism is given extensive treatment here by

Cabrera Infante. His attraction to the topic may be related to his interest in Petronius, a writer who is said to have died a Stoic death by suicide. Cabrera Infante does not appear to share, or at least to exhibit, the deep "cinismo" of Huston (157); rather, his often flippant humor would seem to be an attempt not to indulge in the sort of pessimism towards which Huston has gravitated and which perhaps has a similar attraction for Cabrera Infante. One of the more cynical films of Huston, according to Cabrera Infante, is *The Misfits*, in which, incidentally, there are three chief protagonists.

The film interests Cabrera Infante because of its "síntesis epicúrea" and "verdadero cinismo" (157). The qualities cultivated by Hemingway, those of resignation in a heroic mode before the inevitable fact of death, attract Cabrera Infante as an admirable philosophy. Of particular poignance for him, as for the characters in his novels, is the sense, conveyed by the film, that a way of life has been lost or transformed into something mechanical. Like Kowalski in *Vanishing Point*, the "misfits" do not belong in their time. They, as Cabrera Infante suggests of Rocco in *Key Largo*, are throwbacks or "anachronisms" "que cazan caballos salvajes, matan águilas y actúan en rodeos pero utilizan el avión, el auto, los camiones, es decir, la técnica moderna, aunque su edad efectiva ha quedado paralizada en otros días, otro lugar" (157). Significantly, too, these characters, like those of *The Roots of Heaven*, are sympathetic to animals, carrying to its logical conclusion the distrust of the cynic for humans. For Cabrera Infante, as a lover of animals, a man who could devote extensive passages of *O* to his cat, and a great memorialist of a past culture in *La Habana*, the cinema of John Huston, though perhaps the work of "un epígono" (155), should have a strong emotional attractiveness.

Of a different sort is the attraction which the cinema of Vincente Minnelli exercises on Cabrera Infante. He is strongly drawn to the overt "optimism" of Minnelli (see *Arcadia* 155), perhaps as an antidote to the note of stoicism which colors his own work, and does not, contrary to the suggestion by Alvarez-Borland (*Discontinuidad* 127), deprecate the work of this director because of its "feminine" qualities. The "urbanidad" of Minnelli, who in this respect as in others, Cabrera Infante suggests, "es la exacta contrapartida de Howard Hawks" (161), is naturally attractive to Cabrera Infante due to his own concentration on the city. Much of the action of *Tres tristes tigres* occurs in cabarets, bars, and parties, all of which are important to the work of Minnelli; and the tone of the book is set by an emcee who introduces the reader or the "audience" to a show. In *Arcadia todas las noches*, Cabrera Infante sees Minnelli as a "superbo *entertainer*" (161), and his probable influence on *Tres tristes tigres* especially should not be ignored. Cabrera Infante speaks of him in terms which he usually reserves for artists such as Welles, Hitchcock, and Lewis Carroll:

> Es además, después de Orson Welles y después de Alfred Hitchcock, el primer *showman* del cine: el hombre capaz de tomar una escoba, vestirla con una bufanda y hacerla pasear frente a la cámara y, con un pase elegante de la mano ilusionista, divertirnos, entretenernos, hacernos olvidar las penas de vivir todos los días y tenernos, así ilusionados, una hora y media y dos horas y hasta dos horas y media, haciendo verdadera la exacta frase de Lebovici: "El cine es un sueño...que nos hace soñar." (162; original ellipsis)

Minnelli is not just the apostle of American optimism for Cabrera Infante. He devotes some space to a seemingly atypical Minnelli film, *Undercurrent*, "un melodrama romántico" which treats in a rather frightening and very somber fashion the theme of "la doble personalidad" which can be very easily found, as Ardis Nelson notes in "El doble, el recuerdo y la muerte," in the work of Cabrera Infante himself (*Arcadia* 163). The film is fitted into the Minnelli canon by Cabrera Infante with reference to its camera style and its use of a party as a motivating plot force.[29]

The party, Cabrera Infante suggests, is a leitmotif for the work of Minnelli, and is used in a most individual fashion. The echo of such parties is perhaps to be found in a gathering such as the one in *Tres tristes tigres* in Códac's house (122-26). The Minnelli party is typically, Cabrera Infante says, "obsesivo, recurrente" not only in its repetition in the films but in its nature, "frenético y ruidoso" (*Arcadia* 164). A notable example, in a lighter vein than the one in *Undercurrent*, is to be found in *Bells Are Ringing*, a film with a party in which the heroine (Judy Holliday) begins to understand her unsuitability for the social world inhabited by her boyfriend, played by Dean Martin.

In a reverie of Silvestre in *Tres tristes tigres* (305-06), a technique is used which is similar to that employed by Minnelli in *An American in Paris* as well as by Donen and Gene Kelly in *On the Town*. In the Minnelli movie, Lisa (Leslie Caron) is pictured to the hero, played by Gene Kelly, by her lover, Henri Borel, in a series of narrated vignettes, each showing a different character trait. In *On the Town*, Ivy

Smith is pictured in a similar fashion by the three sailors played by
Kelly, Frank Sinatra and Jules Munshin, who, however, have no prior
knowledge of her character. The reverie by Silvestre contains internal
commentary which could serve as a good summary of the techniques
used in the two musicals: *"(esta espalda porque la veo ahí o, en el decir de la
gente, la tengo ahí como si la estuviera viendo)..."* (305; original emphasis).

Minnelli is the Renaissance artist of the group of directors studied
in *Arcadia todas las noches*. Indeed, he could be thought of as a movie
equivalent of the author of the famous *Arcadia*, Sir Philip Sidney, both
in his flamboyance and in his creation of musical worlds of myth.[30] The
world of Minnelli balances for Cabrera Infante the baroque system of
Welles, with its negative coloration (see *Arcadia* 165-66). The director,
as noted above, is also described in *Arcadia todas las noches* as:

> ...la exacta contrapartida de Howard Hawks. Donde Hawks exhibe
> una virilidad casi cruel, Minnelli deja ver una sensibilidad
> femenina;[31] donde Hawks se ve tenaz, aguileño, como un halcón,
> Minnelli parece un pingüino inteligente, un canario que baila, una
> amable cacatúa que canta bonito; donde Hawks es casi un fascista,
> un violento, un duro, Minnelli es un demócrata completo, un
> hombre de sociedad, un *citadino* generoso que sabe que urbanidad
> viene de urbe, que las buenas maneras se inventaron en la ciudad.[32]
> (161)

Much of what appeals to Cabrera Infante in the Hollywood cinema,
its exuberance, urbanity, and optimism, is found summarized in the
films of Minnelli. Such qualities are certainly present in the work of
Cabrera Infante, with its almost inexhaustible humor and its
characters who, despite their frequent cynicism, refuse to be defeated
by adverse circumstances, as in the attempts by Cué and Silvestre to
get two women to laugh (*Tres tristes tigres* 370-91).

The Americanism of Minnelli is apparent in the chief focus,
identified by Cabrera Infante as "ese problema [que] se llama familia"
(*Arcadia* 176). He points out the presence of the motif of "la parábola
del hijo pródigo" in several Minnelli films (176). The emphasis by
Cabrera Infante on a "parábola" is familiar enough, and the
concentration by Minnelli on familial "problems" or maladjustments,
such as the "adolescente-problema" of *Tea and Sympathy* or the
humorously rebellious adolescents and children in *Meet Me in St. Louis*,
is close to the atmosphere of *La Habana para un Infante Difunto*, with its

often chaotic family relationships and rebellious "adolescente-problema," the narrator, who is a cousin of "el... famoso adolescente-problema del cine moderno, el que James Dean convirtió, doble, en meta y mito, en *Rebelde sin causa* (176; my ellipsis; see also Feal, *Novel Lives* 62-93).

An excellent example of the "family problem" theme is to be found in *Home from the Hill*, in which "el hijo pródigo" is also a prominent motif. Cabrera Infante speaks as well of the Cain and Abel complex in this connection (*Arcadia* 175-76). In this movie, the conflicts between Theron, the Abel figure (played by George Hamilton) and Rafe, the Cain character (played by George Peppard) are resolved after Theron leaves town upon avenging the murder of his father Wade (Robert Mitchum). The terms are interestingly reversed, however, since Rafe, a " 'bastard' " of Wade and thus "marked" as an outcast, does no killing and returns to his mother after Theron leaves.[33]

The essay on Minnelli is generally less concentrated and philosophical than some of the other sections of the book. Much of it is devoted to the kind of "mock tribute" which, as Ardis Nelson says, is so well practiced by Cabrera Infante (*Cabrera Infante* xi). The latter part of the lecture, however, does focus seriously on the general thrust of the book in terms of the treatment of cinema as "la única fuente moderna de mitos, exceptuando a la publicidad y a Adolfo Hitler" and as "no sólo una fábrica de sueños (y de pesadillas) sino una fuente constante de la vida otra, de la creación poética" (*Arcadia* 179). Cabrera Infante gives the highest marks to musicals for their capacity to express the "magic" of film:

> Creo también que nada dentro del cine como la comedia musical para expresar este sortilegio creador, para animar la belleza de la vida y poner en juego al alma y al cuerpo como las fiestas dionisiacas ponían en juego el cuerpo y el alma del antiguo: la comedia musical es un cine pagano en el sentido que Nietzsche le dio a esa expresión. (181)

For Cabrera Infante, Minnelli is the master of the musical, a creator "que en media docena de comedias musicales ha demostrado ser un mago para hacer baile, canción, diversiones prácticamente de la nada..." (182). The magic of Minnelli is summarized by Cabrera Infante as his evocation of "Arcadia," a concept which was understood by "los antiguos" in the following manner:

La Arcadia fue para los antiguos algo más y algo menos que el Paraíso. Era tierra prometida, pero estaba habitada por dioses y animales prodigiosos y toda la perfección acumulada por el hombre: la belleza y la ilusión y la poesía de la vida. Era también la tierra del dios Pan, perdida para siempre. (182)

He says that "en estas ocasiones paganas, las comedias musicales, la recobramos en la oscuridad del cine" (182).[34]

Brigadoon, Cabrera Infante suggests (182-84), is an expression of the Arcadia myth, which can be placed within literary tradition as the *topos* of *locus amoenus*. The hero of the film, played by Gene Kelly, loses his faith in the modern world and can then discover, and rediscover, Arcadia in the form of the "paraíso intemporal" Brigadoon. The movie centers on the process of his finding, losing, and rediscovering love in this paradise and thus rejecting the modern world in favor of a mythic, eternal past.

The impulse towards such extreme nostalgia is common in the work of Cabrera Infante, in the overall ambience of his novels as well as, more specifically, in the flashbacks of *Vanishing Point*, in which Kowalski remembers the "Arcadia" of his idyll with Vera. Cabrera Infante, however, states that "Yo... rechazo esta filosofía naturalista y simple y romántica de Vincente Minnelli: me quedo con el siglo, con nuestro mundo, con ustedes" (183; my ellipsis). His work confirms this statement, for in spite of his focus on such impulses towards a *locus amoenus*, he, like Orson Welles, does not believe in the possibility or, in terms familiar to John Huston, in the morality of such narcissistic escape. He says that, despite his emotional attraction for such Arcadias, he will not evade the present:

Escojo este momento que significa muchas cosas desagradables, casi siniestras. Pero no puedo olvidar que junto a estas calamidades que hacen de las pesadillas cosas diurnas, nuestro tiempo, el mundo actual, hace también posible a Brigadoon, a la Arcadia, no cada cien años, sino todas las noches. (183-84)

The cinema fulfills for Cabrera Infante a need for poeticism and peace. His interests and concerns with regard to film, investigated in the foregoing chapters of this study, will be seen to play an important role in his creative work for the cinema. The concentration on myths in *Arcadia todas las noches* will appear in still more intensive form in his screenplay, *Vanishing Point*.

NOTES

¹ Alvarez-Borland, *Discontinuidad* 123. She makes a point very similar to mine concerning the connection between the two works.

² The technique is noted by Ardis Nelson as pertinent to Cabrera Infante (*Cabrera Infante* xi).

³ The connection is also noted by Alvarez-Borland, *Discontinuidad* 125.

⁴ Ferguson discusses the use of mirrors in *Tres tristes tigres*, in a limited context, and also refers to the importance of "the looking glass house" and "funhouses" in the work (142-43). Her reference to the analogy between Alice "In the looking glass house" and the four major characters of *Tres tristes tigres* is not only apt but suggested to me another link between Welles and Cabrera Infante:

> In a mirror world everything will be the opposite. Alice has to walk backwards to get anywhere . . . In the looking glass house, Alice has to run as fast as she can just to stay in place. Cué, Silvestre, Codak [sic], and Eribó aren't getting anywhere either, although they are living a fast paced life. Cué and Silvestre speed through Havana, only to turn around and return the way they came. Their journeys differ very little from night to night. They are staying in place. (142; my ellipsis)

Like Alice, Michael O'Hara (Welles) in *The Lady from Shanghai* is trapped in a funhouse in which he does a good bit of running. Like the characters in the Cabrera Infante book, O'Hara is trapped in a maze, symbolized by the circular motifs which recur in the movie as well as by the funhouse and by Chinatown itself; and like those characters, he ends up more or less where he started. The film makes this explicit not only for him but for the other characters (those played by Hayworth, Sloane, and Anders) in terms of their "natures" by means of an "'old Chinese proverb'": "Those who follow their nature keep their original nature."

⁵ The expression "'Jano Bifronte'" is also used by Cabrera Infante with reference to Caín in *Oficio* 25.

⁶ For remarks on the influence of Welles, see Bazin, *What Is Cinema?* 28.

⁷ Alvarez-Borland points this out in *Discontinuidad* 125.

⁸ Bazin also discusses the disguises used by Welles (*Orson Welles* 40-41).

⁹ See *Oficio* 370-71, 383, for discussions of this idea.

¹⁰ For his remarks on these two writers, see *Arcadia* 132-45, 151-56.

¹¹ Cabrera Infante was probably influenced here by the Lachenay article on Bogart which he cites later. See Lachenay 37: "Lorsque, dans un film, Bogart téléphone, tout se passe comme s'il y avait quelqu'un à l'autre bout du fil." Truffaut used "Robert Lachenay" as his pseudonym; I am indebted to Hillier (300) for this information, as well as the location of the Bogart article.

¹² See *O* 97-110, for a discussion of Carroll.

¹³ For an overview of the influence of the magazine, see Peter Graham,

The New Wave: Critical Landmarks Selected by Peter Graham, Cinema World 5 (Garden City, NY: Doubleday, 1968).

¹⁴ Alvarez-Borland also refers to the "analogía" of these myths to the film as being established by Cabrera Infante (*Discontinuidad* 126).

¹⁵ See Weinberg (*Lubitsch* 56) for interesting comments on von Sternberg as a Pygmalion to the Galatea of Marlene Dietrich.

¹⁶ He comments to Magnarelli on the "false" nature of the blondes in *La Habana para un Infante Difunto:* " 'El libro no trata de blancas sino de falsas rubias, de esas mujeres para quienes el oxígeno era vital' " (29).

¹⁷ See *Oficio* 371 for comments on the innovative role of Hitchcock in film history.

¹⁸ This dialectic is based on a play on word meanings and their translations. As Cabrera Infante explains, "Faulkner no es más que una forma ortográfica, alterada dos veces, sajona, del nombre de un oficio común en la Inglaterra medieval: Faulkner, Falkner, Falconer: Halconero" (*Arcadia* 109). Hawks, whose name is etymologically related to "Faulk" (falcon, hawk), is thus, as Cabrera Infante points out (109), related by name to Faulkner.

¹⁹ Much of the reason for the thinness of the essay may rest upon these points revealed by Cabrera Infante about the climate of the "charlas":

...había muy pocas películas de Howard Hawks disponibles... por ejemplo, no estaba *Scarface.* Había... *Tiger Shark*...había *Ceiling Zero*...yo podía hablar muy poco de esas películas [the films of Hawks]...porque yo no podía verlas, y otra cosa peor era que no podía exhibirlas.... Por eso Howard Hawks aparece tan...malo. (Interview with author; my ellipsis)

²⁰ Cabrera Infante now belittles the importance of "la camaradería" in the work of Hawks:

...la temática de la camaradería... no pertenece a Hawks; como muchas cosas de Hawks, viene de John Ford.... para mí, precisamente, lo que es Howard Hawks... más que la camaradería... hay una.... especial relación entre... la cámara y sus personajes que es muy particular del cine americano.... (Interview with author; my ellipsis)

²¹ Alvarez-Borland also comments on this section in "Ensayos" 165.

²² This approach could also be understood as a Gnostic one, bringing one's critical perspective close to that of William Siemens.

²³ For a discussion of "betrayal" in this novel, see Nelson, "Betrayal in *Tres tristes tigres* and Petronius's *Satyricon.*"

²⁴ See Siemens, *Language and Creativity,* esp. 146-53; and *Worlds* 154-57. See also Pereda 57-75 for a study of the importance of numbers in *Tres tristes tigres.*

²⁵ Siemens comments on Pythagoras and Cué in *Worlds* 154-55.

²⁶ Bazin, "Aesthetic" 39-45, alludes to the photography of Toland when writing about the work of William Wyler and of Welles:

Over the surface of the screen, the director and the director of photography have managed to organise a dramatic chessboard from which no detail is excluded. The most obvious, if not the most original, examples of this are to found in *The Little Foxes*, where the *mise-en-scène* has the precision of a blueprint (with Welles, the baroque overtones make analysis more complicated).

For formulating the idea of a triangular spatial arrangement by Toland, I am indebted to Dr. Ron Stottlemyer.

27 See, e.g., Jiménez 47-51, for remarks on this aspect of *Un oficio del Siglo 20*.

28 Cabrera Infante speaks of the search of Rocco and his men in terms of "anacronismo":

Los gangsters de *Huracán de pasiones* también son navegantes anacrónicos: Rocco obliga a su lugarteniente a repetirle una y otra vez que la Ley Seca volverá, que el apogeo del contrabando vendrá de nuevo, que las grandes pandillas estarán de moda como en los años veinte. Es Bogart, con su heroísmo desesperado, su desengaño moral...y su reserva espiritual, quien hace fracasar a estos argonautas del mal. (*Arcadia* 146; my ellipsis)

29 I owe the concept of "motivation" in film plots to Bordwell and Thompson (54-55).

30 This is the *Arcadia* most well-known to English-speaking readers. As Eliana Rivero pointed out to me, however, other works in the same vein preceded it, including the *Arcadia* (1504) by Sannazaro, imitating the *Ameto* (1341) of Boccaccio; and *La Diana* (1559) of Jorge de Montemayor. *La Diana*, she notes, "influenced Sir Philip Sidney to write his *Arcadia*, published in 1590."

31 As an aside to the remarks of Cabrera Infante, one could compare his distinction between the two directors to the contrast in the Minnelli film *Home from the Hill* between the exaggeratedly virile Robert Mitchum character and his son (played by George Hamilton), who, as Thomas Elsaesser notes, "wants to assume adult responsibilities while at the same time he rejects the standards of adulthood implied in his father's aggressive masculinity" (301; see the discussion of the film, 300-03, which helped to clarify for me the familial conflicts in the movie).

32 *The Four Horsemen of the Apocalypse*, a 1962 film by Minnelli, is an interesting case study for his conception of manners and democracy. Good manners and urbanity, he demonstrates, can be qualities associated with Nazis and their sympathizers, while brusqueness, in this context, is frequently associated with the democratic spirit. Significantly, however, the film is set largely in Paris, the center of European urbanity which was violated so tragically by the Germans.

33 See the stimulating discussion of this film in Elsaesser 301-02. *The Four Horsemen of the Apocalypse*, which is not discussed in the collection, probably because of its late release date, is also a good example of the theme of family conflict and of the prodigal son who redeems himself, ironically, through a type of fratricide (instead of a brother, it is a cousin who suffers death because of his actions).

34 Cabrera Infante still holds a high estimate of Minnelli and evaluates him in terms very similar to those used by him in *Arcadia todas las noches*, despite his qualified disclaimer of the book (see above, 81-83). When asked in November 1985 if he was still interested in Minnelli, he confirmed his earlier great partiality for the director. He then spoke in terms which suggest his continuing interest in the director

> ...en la medida en que se pueden ver sus películas—no es fácil verlas ahora. Pero yo creo que Minnelli tenía una habilidad para recrear ciertas situaciones sociales que nadie tenía en Hollywood como él. (Interview with author)

5

Vanishing Point

ANISHING POINT, the most commercially impor-
tant filmscript written by Cabrera Infante, is,
like *Arcadia todas las noches*, set in mythic terms.
The script also bears the mark of the interest of
Cabrera Infante in film genres such as the
Western and the detective film. As in *Arcadia
todas las noches*, Cabrera Infante concentrates
heavily in *Vanishing Point* on myths as a source of
inspiration and reference. In *Arcadia todas las noches*, he had dealt with
film in terms of a return of the Golden Age (Arcadia) and as a
revitalization of the mythic experience for modern man. He treated
film myths as modern versions or retellings of older myths. For
example, the story of *Vertigo*, with its attempt by the hero Scottie to
recapture his lost love, is cast by Cabrera Infante as a retelling of the
myths of Orpheus, of Lot, and of Tristan and Isolde. Other mythical
figures of antiquity which appear in *Arcadia todas las noches* include
Jason, Pan (the god of Arcadia), Odysseus and Penelope, Adam and
Eve, and Achilles. Cabrera Infante also works with the myths created
by film itself, concentrating especially on actresses such as Jean
Harlow, Marilyn Monroe, and Greta Garbo, who have become
mythified through the cinema. In *Vanishing Point*, he weaves his
allusion to myths both ancient and modern into the fabric of a
creative structure which is strongly grounded in Hollywood genre.

The mythic allusions in *Vanishing Point* form a subtext of the
screenplay. Odysseus and Theseus, as well as the Minotaur, are
predominant in it. The approach reminds one of *Ulysses*, in which a
complex mythic structure is used by Joyce as a narrative and thematic
basis for a modern story.[1] The references to film myths in the script
are not as extensive as in *Arcadia todas las noches* but are important

nevertheless. Humphrey Bogart, Mae West, Lee Marvin, and the Keystone Kops are all mentioned.

While the screenplay bases itself rather strongly on myths, the movie derived from it takes a different tack, concentrating on the adventures of the hero in a context appealing to youthful audiences of the early 1970s. Cabrera Infante refers to this difference between the script and the finished film when he comments on the movie as "una película de acción" [que] "ha ganado hasta ahora 28 o 30 millones de dólares" but which differs in important respects from his original script (Interview with author). He does speak in rather positive terms of the film in an interview with Alfred MacAdam, pointing out its contribution to the American mythic lexicon: "'Thanks to John Alonzo, a cinematographer of genius, my screenplay is now a piece of Americana, a cult film, and a very successful movie'" (182). The film is useful as a reference point for understanding the script but does show considerable change from the original treatment by Cabrera Infante. It remains the only film based on one of his scripts which has achieved much fame. Some of his scripts, as we have seen, have been unproduced, while the one for *Wonderwall*, produced "'en el año 1967,'" was unsuccessfully realized ("Cabrera Infante habla" 67; see above, Cinematic 10). Another called *The Salzburg Connection* bore, he says, little or no relation to the movie of the same title (Interview with author; "Art" 182).

Cabrera Infante has spoken with Jorge Nieto about the background of the screenplay for *Vanishing Point*. He says that

> *Vanishing Point*, es en realidad la extensión de una idea, una idea concebida por un fotógrafo inglés que vivió en los Estados Unidos durante mucho tiempo en los años cincuenta y sesenta y escribió un breve argumento de dos páginas, y eso fue lo que yo extendí hasta convertirlo en el guión de la película. A mí me contrataron para hacer un guión con esta idea y entonces procedí como si estuviera alquilado para hacer una película, ni más ni menos que como si estuviera haciendo cualquier otra actividad más o menos mercenaria. (66)

He has, as he says, expanded on this "'idea,'" making of it a screenplay which is recognizably in line with his concept of film as expressed in works such as *Arcadia todas las noches*.[2]

The tendency of Cabrera Infante to cast film in terms of myths is nowhere more evident than in this script. *Arcadia todas las noches* had shown a trend towards creating or restating mythical narratives in which to fit film figures, such as the essay on "*Bogart y los argonautas*" (139-48; original emphasis). The trend is not so apparent in his more properly fictional works *Tres tristes tigres* and *La Habana para un Infante Difunto*, since the mythologized film allusions are woven into much larger narratives. In *Vanishing Point*, however, the device used in *Arcadia todas las noches* becomes central to the narrative, with two myths based on mutually related motifs forming important subtexts.

The screenplay is also in line with the generic preferences of Cabrera Infante with respect to film, and this fact partially explains the importance of myths in the text. *Vanishing Point*, as written by Cabrera Infante, is essentially a revamping of the Western genre.[3] Kowalski, the protagonist, is a lone Western hero and is referred to as such by Super Soul, the disc jockey in the film, who calls him "'the SUPER-DRIVER OF THE GOLDEN WEST....'" (Cain 52).

Kowalski rushes westward in his car, a vehicle which is here the modern equivalent of the horse for the Western hero. He craves an escape from civilization and the disillusionment with which it has left him. In the film, for instance, one of the flashbacks shows an argument which Kowalski, once a policeman, had with his partner about being "on the take" and taking advantage of a female prisoner. Kowalski is an idealist, a frustrated figure who yearns for purity and tries to find it in a reckless escape to the frontier.

The importance of myths for *Vanishing Point* can be understood more clearly with reference to the kinship of the script to Western film. The Western, as Jenni Calder notes (xi-xiii), has served as a great source of myth for Americans and, for outsiders, about America. The West, or the image of the West presented in movies and fiction, represents the heroic age of the United States.

It is hardly surprising that the classical myths used in the script are also derived from the "heroic age" of Greece (Burn 47-48). Odysseus, Theseus, and the Minotaur were all, to follow the interpretation of Burn, figures attributed to that period in Greek history. The human heroes mentioned here, Odysseus and Theseus, were both adventurers and essentially loners. They both fought for survival and occasionally for high ideals, using their wits and stamina like Kowalski or like Shane, Wyatt Earp, and other figures from the corpus of Western myths.

The generic and mythic aspects of the script follow parallel lines of development and treatment. Just as the script is an updating of the Western genre, so too the myths of the classical tradition are revised and commented upon by their inclusion in the text of *Vanishing Point*.

The more immediately apparent of the two myths is that of Odysseus. Kowalski is cued for the reader as an Odysseus figure. He goes on a seemingly impossible journey in a car, using magical aid in the form of the monologues of the blind, mock-Homeric disc jockey Super Spic, called "Super Soul" in the movie.[4] The car originates from "Argo's Car Delivery Agency" (7), reminding one both of Odysseus' dog and of Jason and the Argonauts. Later in the script, Vera professes her affection for his "tremendous scar," a mark which he, rather like Odysseus, is reluctant to show or to have touched (82-84). The myth is not carried through to its full conclusion, but the parallels are evident; and surely a joke on the Kowalski figure is meant by the obvious gap between his general stolidity and befuddlement (despite his clever driving) and the legendary craftiness of Odysseus.[5] More extensively and successfully treated in the screenplay than the story of Odysseus is the myth of Theseus and the Minotaur.[6] The introduction to the script places the hero in a "labyrinthine tragedy" (iii). Death Valley eventually becomes the incarnation of the labyrinth, from which Kowalski-Theseus seemingly escapes by following an old Prospector along an "invisible road" (100). The Minotaur can be discerned in the film as the fear and guilt about the past which Kowalski feels he must "kill" by escaping his present through risk and velocity.

Super Spic plays the part of Ariadne for Kowalski, acting as "his guide through the maze of patrol cars, police forces, barricades" on a "thread of a voice" except when Kowalski apparently loses patience and cuts his radio, getting lost in Death Valley and using the Old Prospector as a surrogate Ariadne (3, 100-07). Later, in the film version, an apparently brainwashed or traitorous Super Soul becomes a false Ariadne, leading Kowalski into a trap which results in his death.

Super Spic even makes a hidden allusion to the Minotaur story. He says, "'*I* listen for my footsteps, *you* listen for *your* footsteps....'" (44; original emphasis). The allusion may or may not be conscious but is strikingly reminiscent of the Jorge Luis Borges story "La casa de Asterión," in which an anguished, intellectualized Minotaur awaits the coming of his slayer, listening with mixed reactions to his approaching footsteps.

Kowalski is also repeatedly connected with centaurs, as in the reference by Super Spic to him as "'our Love Driver, the last American hero, the electric centaur, the demi-god, the SUPER-DRIVER OF THE GOLDEN WEST...'" (52). This and other references seem to be deliberate attempts to connect him with the members of the mythical race.

In one sense, the analogy is clear: Kowalski and his car, like the man-horse body of the centaur, form a unit. The implications of the comparison are more complex, however, and enrich the mythic structure which has already been established for Kowalski.

Kowalski has already been linked obliquely with Theseus, the slayer of the Minotaur. The hero of the movie thus acquires a dual patina of idealism, because of his link with the hero who struggled against the evil Minos and his man-bull, and of a primitive savagery. After all, the exploits of Theseus were set in the "heroic" or more primitive age of Greece[7] and were hardly the acts of a genteel man. Borges develops this point in his story, showing the Minotaur as existentially trapped, and frightened as well as relieved by the approach of the merciless Theseus.

Concentrating, then, on the savage side of the character of Theseus, a link can be drawn by etymological means to the centaur figure from Greek myth and thereby to the hardly gentle figure of Kowalski. Robert Graves offers the interesting observation on the actual Centaurs that "Both Lapiths and Centaurs claimed descent from Ixion, an oak-hero, and had a horse cult in common... They were primitive mountain tribes in Northern Greece...." He continues by saying that "*Centaur* and *Lapith* may be Italic words: *centuria*, 'war-band of one hundred', and *lapicidae*, 'flint-chippers'. (The usual classical etymology is, respectively, from *centauroi*, 'those who spear bulls', and *lapizein*, 'to swagger'.)"[8] The importance of the centaur allusions now becomes more apparent, since, like Theseus, they had a reputation as slayers of bulls.

The centaur analogy has another significance which is somewhat lacking to the Theseus myth. Graves comments (1: 361-62) on the "erotic orgies" of the Centaur tribes. In the screenplay as well as the film, Kowalski is depicted repeatedly as making love. Super Spic calls him "'our Love Driver.'" Whether or not Cabrera Infante had delved into the legends surrounding the Centaurs, his choice of the analogy certainly seems apt for the character.

The use of the Centaur as an analogy for Kowalski also relates to the generic nature of the script. A connection is made from Kowalski and his car through the mythic image of the cowboy on his horse to the unifying concept of the Centaur. Kowalski is identified with his car to the same extent that the cowboy or Western hero was with his horse.[9] The identification is summarized and made concrete in the image of the Centaur. Incidentally, the name of the hero is suggestive of the Westerner; *Kowalski* is the modern *cow*boy who finds that his time has run out, as Super Spic reminds him (73-74).

Through the harangues of Super Spic, Cabrera Infante relates the Minotaur reference to an allusion to Orpheus, a figure even more important to his previous work than the Minotaur.[10] When Kowalski is about to enter Death Valley, the disc jockey implores him not to do so because of the labyrinthine quality of the desert:

> ...Now you're gonna need some more luck... because—Kowalski baby—*the desert is like a maze*. The maze to end all mazes! You can beat the police, I kid you not, as Captain Queeg [of *The Caine Mutiny*] would say... You can even beat the clock. But you can't beat the desert, for out there, there's no time left. All is space down there. (73-74; original emphasis; my ellipsis)[11]

The reference to time and space recalls the musings of Silvestre in *Tres tristes tigres*, and the specific reference to "beating the clock" harks back to the comments of Cabrera Infante in *Arcadia todas las noches* about the failure of Scottie in *Vertigo* "porque no ha sabido creer que el tiempo no es irreversible" (77). Super Spic has less faith, or less *hubris*, than Kowalski because he does not believe that one "'can beat'" space as well as time.

Perhaps the point made by Ardis Nelson about "la trascendencia espiritual" attained by Kowalski at the end of the film is applicable here ("El doble" 512), since Kowalski, by refusing to look back, seems to conquer, to reverse, or to deny time, as the alternative endings of the movie demonstrate. Although the alternate endings do not appear in the script, their interpolation into the narrative structure lends credence—intended or not—to the connection with Orpheus.[12]

The issue of time which is raised by the movie is expressed, as Nelson suggests, through its use of flashbacks and other devices ("El doble" 512 and throughout). One of the most important sets of flashbacks shows the relationship of the hero with Vera, who committed suicide or was accidentally drowned in the ocean, recalling the narrowly escaped fate of Judy/Madeleine at the bay in *Vertigo*.

Vera seems connected, on the strength of several textual hints, to Venus or Aphrodite, although the analogy is not exact. She is thought to be "a beautiful hermaphrodite" (76-77), and questions Kowalski's judgment by wondering "'How could you possibly have taken me for a man?'" (80).[13]

Earlier in the script, but chronologically later in the plot because of the flashback technique, is a love encounter in the Galaxie—aptly named in the mock-astral context—between Kowalski and a blonde who calls herself the "'Mae West of the West'" (22-25). He later throws her out of the car, where she stands "almost as if she were re-enacting the famous virgin's stance in 'September Morn.'..." On page 80, Vera tells the hero that he was playing "'at the time'" with "'plastic Mae Wests.'" Here one sees a case of temporal distortion, or of an apparently deliberate confusion of the temporal scheme of the script, since the remark by Vera about "'Mae Wests'" is textually supported only by a later incident in the plot. The allusion to the "virgin" is significant, too, in terms of Aphrodite, who, says Graves, "went to Paphos, where she renewed her virginity in the sea...." (1: 68). This reference leads again to the flashback with Vera, in which she disappears into the ocean, usually a metaphor of death or rebirth.

Mae West, as a modern parody of the Venus fertility figure,[14] is one of the contributions by the cinema to modern myths, within the terms used by Cabrera Infante. In addition to West, Humphrey Bogart is referred to, with Super Spic "imitating" his "voice": "... (imitating Bogart's voice) [:] 'Play it again, Sham!'" (68). And Lee Marvin, while not exactly as high in the movie pantheon as West and Bogart, is given a berth here when Kowalski ejects a girl from his car after some lovemaking: "'Like the man said'—(parodying Lee Marvin) 'I haven't got the time, lady!'" (25). The Marvin parody, an allusion to *The Killers* (1964), is quite appropriate within the context of *Vanishing Point*, since the reference raises the problem of time: "As with other films of this period, time pulses throughout [*The Killers*]; the fear of death and destruction are [sic] central."[15]

One of the significant points about the film myths used here is that they are employed in the dialogue of the characters themselves,

thus demonstrating that the characters of the script have a consciousness of film history. These characters, then, are akin to such
figures as Cué, Silvestre, and Códac, from *Tres tristes tigres*, and the
narrator of *La Habana para un Infante Difunto* in their relationship to film
culture. Notice, too, that their references to actors are frequently to
stars who became known largely through detective films. The detective film and the Western may be seen as closely linked.[16] Thus, the
generic provenance of this script is strengthened by the allusions to
actors such as Bogart and Marvin, as well as by other indications, like
the "wanted poster" which is displayed at the office of the "'NEVADA
STATE HIGHWAY PATROL...'": "'poster...DEAD OR ALIVE!'" (44-45;
original spaced periods).

By means of allusion to films, two genres are interlocked as
subtexts to the screenplay. Similarly, a technique of interlocking or
overlapping allusions is employed in the filmscript. The method was
used with the Venus and Mae West references noted above and is
utilized even further with the hermaphrodite motif. Kowalski picks
up two "women" who turn out to be homosexuals in drag (112 and
following pages). Later, he meets the Queen of Spades, who appears
rather asexual because of her being "shaved all over" (144).

The system of repeated allusion, familiar to readers of *Ulysses* or of
Tres tristes tigres, is used with regard to other motifs in the filmscript,
such as that of the Minotaur. One of the more representative examples of such allusion, which works also as an effect of linguistic
montage, refers to a character as a possible "bull-dike," thus
combining in one image the motifs of the Minotaur and of the
hermaphrodite, with all its sexual connotation (47). Kowalski is to
hear his name pronounced by the Old Prospector as "'Cow-alski'"
(98) and is found to have been born under the sign of Taurus (143),
identifying him perhaps with the Minotaur and indicating a fluidity of
role for him which is consonant with the theme of the double or
"*second self*" which is applied by Ardis Nelson to the work of Cabrera
Infante ("El doble" 510; original emphasis).

The figure of the Hitch-hiker is the most ambiguous in the script.
She possesses mythic status almost equal to that of Kowalski and
exemplifies the use of ambiguity by Cabrera Infante to create an
artistic figure of myth. She is introduced as an image of death,
recalling an Egyptian goddess: "She has a remote, ancient aura about
her, like a Nubian priestess stranded in the 20th Century" (138). Her

dress connects her, by its black color, with the Queen of Spades and reminds one of the animated playing card characters in *Alice in Wonderland*:

> She is very tall, dressed all in black—black bell bottom pajamas, an enormous black bag hanging from one shoulder, and a big flopping wide-brimmed black felt hat over her head. On the ground there is a much travelled, battered brown suitcase.... (Cain 136)

"Marihuana" is her incense; like a Delphic priestess, she makes predictions (139-49). The Borges story "La casa de Asterión" is perhaps recalled by her asking Kowalski for his "'sign'" and by her telling him "'...I was waiting for you. I've been waiting for you a long, long time. How I waited for you!'" (141-43).

The use of incense by the Hitch-hiker, as well as her wearing black or dark clothes, reinforce her oracular status. She speaks in rather less enigmatic terms than those used by well-known oracles such as the one at Delphoi,[17] saying clearly to Kowalski, "'Please don't go to San Francisco'" and revealing herself as "'the Queen of Spades'" or the spirit of death (149). The coming of the Hitch-hiker is itself foreshadowed or predicted at the beginning of the script by Blackie, a relevantly named man at the Car Agency, who exclaims, while playing solitaire, "'The Queen of Spades! A hopped-up bitch'" (9).[18]

Her prediction of the death of the hero is borne out, as he dies by crashing into the portentously named "bulldozers" to the tune of a *"Bull-fighting trumpet call-momento-de-la-verdad theme"* (157-58; original emphasis). The film as it stands is much less allegorical or referential than the script, which maintains its mythic quality throughout by means of a network of allusions.

Cabrera Infante has stated that little of the script remains in the film *Vanishing Point*:

> Entonces—con *Vanishing Point* ocurrió que el guión, para mí no está [en] la película, es decir, está como la clásica imagen del guante dado vuelta...está todo el material,...pero es otro guante...Eso ocurrió con....*Vanishing Point* en términos de expresión del guión. (Interview with author; my ellipsis)

The script was in fact reshaped to a large degree, and many of its mythic overtones ignored, to fit it into the scheme of a film for mass distribution. Cabrera Infante has also pointed out the differences in thesis between the script and the film

> Entonces, para mí, la película, era esencialmente, se trataba de un hombre con problemas en un automóvil. La película ha resultado ser un hombre en un automóvil con problemas—que es muy diferente proposición.... (Interview with author)

Even in the finished movie, however, the imprint of his concerns can still be seen, as well as some of his virtuosity with language. Despite its changes in emphasis, the movie preserves its generic links, the mythic relationship between Super Soul and Kowalski, and some of the punning, comic monologue of Super Soul, and even attempts to mythicize Kowalski in a direction different from that of the script by linking him to pop icons such as bikers and flower children, thus placing him squarely, as Cabrera Infante has noted, in an ambience of American myth ("Art" 182). The preservation of at least some of the original intent of Cabrera Infante may well account for much of the popularity of the film.

Film, myths, and generic allusion receive limited but intensive treatment in *Vanishing Point*. The filmscript is of course on a smaller scale than was the linguistic *tour de force* of Cabrera Infante, *Tres tristes tigres*, to which we will turn our attention next, and which drew extensively from sources in film, continuing and extending many of the concerns of Cabrera Infante in his books of criticism.

NOTES

[1] The notion of the mythological structure of *Ulysses* is derived from Stuart Gilbert, *James Joyce's* Ulysses: *A Study*. For Cabrera Infante, Joyce, and myth, I am indebted to Kadir, "Stalking" 15-22.

[2] The original conception of Cabrera Infante, as developed from this "'idea,'" is discernible in the first draft of the screenplay, used here for reference purposes. His screenplay evidently underwent some changes, such as the change in the name of the disc jockey (see below, n 4); but, from the statements made by Cabrera Infante to the author of this study and to other interviewers such as Alfred MacAdam, the points of difference between the script and the finished film, such as the musical notations in the screenplay which did not appear in the movie (a fact pointed out to me by Cabrera Infante), have apparently been maintained, in general, throughout the drafts made by Cabrera Infante.

[3] Cabrera Infante confirms this idea and also connects the hero of the film with Ulysses (see *Siete voces* 412).

⁴ Cabrera Infante, speaking with Jorge Nieto, elaborates on the history of the disc jockey character:

... "Supersoul" estaba en principio en la idea original. Se llamaba Superspade. Estaba más o menos basado en un personaje de la vida real, uno que se llamaba el Superspade, que después creo que murió o se suicidó, pero no era un "discjockey" como en la película. Entonces, en la primitiva idea, venía este "discjockey," que era negro. Lo único que yo hice fue transformarlo en un discjockey ciego, además de negro, porque me pareció que había una suerte de ironía en el hecho de que un ciego condujera a un chofer a alta velocidad, y que gracias a un ciego el chofer pudiera liberarse de una serie de obstáculos y triunfar en una persecución verdaderamente encarnizada, y así fue como surgió el personaje que para mí en la película está bastante bien, porque el actor que lo hace es bastante eficaz. (68-69)

Apparently the change from "'Super Spic'" to "'Supersoul'" was made in a later draft than the one that I consulted.

⁵ Braun (60) imputes the stolidity of Kowalski to the unfortunately "impassive... performance" of Barry Newman [my ellipsis] and compares his acting unfavorably with that of Marlon Brando, whose mythic echo he sees in the name Kowalski (from the hero of *A Streetcar Named Desire*).

⁶ See the chapter devoted to the Minotaur in Cabrera Infante, *Exorcismos* 67-84.

⁷ For the origin of my use of the term "heroic" as well as for a useful discussion of that period, see Burn, Chapter 2.

⁸ Graves, 1: 361-62 n 1 (my ellipsis). The idea of etymological connection to the centaurs of history is Graves'.

⁹ Notice the similarity to the placing of Cué and Silvestre in a car on the Malecón and their use of Western dialogue.

¹⁰ See the references in n 1, 6, above. The Orpheus allusion can be extended through film, since Kowalski, like the hero of the Cocteau film *Orphée* (1949), receives radio messages from a "partner" with possibly supernatural qualities. Braun (60) refers to the "strange echoes of saintly guidance in some of the characters most notably, of course, Super Soul...." Ardis L. Nelson deals with the double motif in Cabrera Infante, specifically in *Vanishing Point* and *La Habana para un Infante Difunto*, in "El doble" 509-21. My notion of the double in the work of Cabrera Infante is indebted to her study, which also points out the links between *Tres tristes tigres* and *Vanishing Point*. She deals with the film but not with the script.

¹¹ This passage echoes the 1964 film *The Killers*, in which similar references are made to cheating time.

¹² Cabrera Infante may be speaking of the alternate endings when he refers to the participation of the famous producer "'el viejo Darryl Zanuck'" in the script as he "'ideó una breve escena para el principio de la película que está muy dentro del espíritu del film'" (Cabrera Infante, *Siete voces* 411). One of

the endings actually occurs at the beginning of the film.

13 Graves, 1: 18 d, speaks thus of the origin of Hermaphroditus: "Flattered by Hermes's frank confession of his love for her, Aphrodite presently spent a night with him, the fruit of which was Hermaphroditus, a double-sexed being . . . ."

14 The parodic element in Mae West was suggested to me by Tyler, *Hollywood* 94-99; and by Haskell 19-20, 115-17.

15 Kaminsky 76. I owe to Kaminsky the attribution of the Lee Marvin quotation to *The Killers.*

16 See the treatment of *Rio Bravo* as a recasting of the detective film in Western terms in Cabrera Infante, *Oficio* 355-59. My linking of the detective film and the Western is also indebted to Warshow 127-54, for his comparisons between gangster and Western films; and to Clarens, *Crime Movies* 13.

17 For a sketch of the methods of such oracles, see Burn 171-73.

18 The incident with Blackie is interestingly parallel to the film *Manhattan Melodrama*, in which Blackie Gallagher (Gable), awaiting execution for murder, is given a pair of dice by a sympathetic guard so that he may entertain himself during his last twelve hours of life. Notice once again the motifs of time and death.

6

Tres tristes tigres

RES TRISTES TIGRES, the most widely known work by Cabrera Infante, has strong ties to film. The influence of film on the work has been studied and noted by several critics, including Ardis Nelson and William Siemens. Parallels between *Tres tristes tigres* and film are easily enough established, since the book abounds with allusions to movies and shows a cinematic influence in its style. Less apparent but quite revealing of the particular flavor and content of the work of Cabrera Infante are the reasons for the existence of such parallels as well as the functioning of film allusion within the fictional structure. The themes of myth, memory, eternal return, and the urban settings common to many of the movies favored by Cabrera Infante as critic are here placed into a fictional context, and developed with even greater resonance than in criticism such as *Arcadia todas las noches*.

The thematic continuity between the criticism of Cabrera Infante and his fictional output clearly exists and has already been sketched by Isabel Alvarez-Borland. A lack of such continuity would be surprising, since the critical pieces by Cabrera Infante deal with many films in which he is personally interested and which could therefore be expected to exert some influence on his fiction. He has himself noted the dependence of his fiction on films, and his tastes and opinions as expressed in his criticism should be present as well in his fictional works.

The actual degree and depth of the continuity have yet to be investigated, but Cabrera Infante has offered his views on the connection between his criticism and his fictional work. The following

124

exchange is taken from an interview with Cabrera Infante by Jorge Nieto:

> JORGE NIETO: Esta experiencia de la crítica cinematográfica, ¿no deja una marca sobre el escritor de *T.T.T.*?
>
> GUILLERMO CABRERA INFANTE: De una cierta manera sí. En *T.T.T.* está además el autor como espectador, mientras que en *Un oficio del Siglo XX* está el autor como crítico.... En *T.T.T.* siempre se hace referencia aun a las películas como vistas, es decir, como recuerdos o como vivencias, pero siempre de una manera pasiva, mientras que en las críticas de cine yo trato de intervenir en la producción de la película, no en la producción inmediata, sino en la producción mediata. Claro que es una pretensión demasiado grande, porque era imposible que alguien desde Cuba pudiera influir en Hollywood, o pudiera influir en las producciones francesas, pero, tal como se presenta la crítica, es siempre como buscando un modelo ideal, es decir, buscando hacia la película ideal, es por lo tanto un espectador activo el que está escribiendo las críticas. Y en *T.T.T.* ocurre lo contrario, es un espectador pasivo, un espectador que acepta las películas como parte de su propia vida, pero como parte del pasado, es decir, algo que no se puede reconstruir, algo que está ahí sedimentado como una vivencia, pero sin ninguna posibilidad de reforma, sin ninguna posibilidad de actuar sobre ese material, como ocurría en las críticas de cine. ("Cabrera Infante habla" 73-74; my ellipsis)

Cabrera Infante is here speaking basically of the difference between a critical and a biographical or existential point of view with regard to movies, but he does support the notion of a continuity of experience with film which goes from his critical perspective into the point of view which is present in his fictional work. One would not expect the films which serve as referential material in *Tres tristes tigres* to vary significantly from those reviewed in the columns. It is rather the prescriptive emphasis noted by the author in his criticism which will be exchanged for an experiential concern on the part of the characters, for a tendency to think, speak, and act in terms of films already absorbed.[1]

Probably the most important aspect of the cinematic presence in the lives of the characters of *Tres tristes tigres* is the ability of that presence to transport them into another reality, to represent for them a world outside their own existence, which may seem drab in comparison. The key to the fascination with film evinced by the characters of the book, as by Cabrera Infante and his literary persona, Caín, is not so much of a political or social nature, representing a window on another presumably more attractive, exotic, and economically inviting culture, as Giordano suggests (164-69, 175), but rather of a psychological or spiritual order.

For example, the interest of Silvestre in film is, as Cabrera Infante has said, tied to the experiences of his childhood, just as are some of the film preferences of Cabrera Infante himself (Interview with author). Film allusions are generally treated by Silvestre and Cué, the chief manipulators and parodists of the allusions, on two levels: one intellectualized and flippant, and the other poetic, irrational, and filled with dream elements or memories. Silvestre typically attaches metaphysical or extrinsic significance to movies. Cué takes the impressions made on him by the medium to a less serious conclusion, as Siemens suggests (*Language and Creativity* 34). Silvestre sounds at times like the Caín of *Un oficio del Siglo 20* or the Cabrera Infante of *Arcadia todas las noches*, making statements on the nature of film as an art, such as his musing about "una velocidad uniforme y constante a un punto dado, que es el secreto del cine..." (*Tres tristes tigres* 294).

Lydia Hazera has also pointed out the technical continuity extant between *Un oficio del Siglo 20* and *Tres tristes tigres* in terms of the response by the characters in the latter book to film and language. She refers to the interest of Caín in the capacity of the camera to "achieve" effects of which language is incapable, as demonstrated in his review of *North by Northwest*, and notes "...the critic's obsession with reproducing in writing as graphically as possible what he is seeing on the screen, and his awareness of the limitations and capabilities of language to render the visually-perceived" ("Cinematic" 44-45; my ellipsis). She connects the perspective of Caín to that of Cabrera Infante as author of *Tres tristes tigres*: "This concern with language as a graphic means of representation pervades the novel *Three Trapped Tigers* and links it to his experience as a critic..." ("Cinematic" 45; my ellipsis).

Hazera comments aptly on the roles of the characters in *Tres tristes tigres* as elements of a film composition, likening the structure of the book to that of a sound film. Referring to some of Silvestre's narration in "Bachata," she says that:

This passage exemplifies the fusion in written form of the fundamental elements of film: sight, sound, and movement. This fusion also characterizes the overall composition of the work[,] encompassing four narrative voices whose discourse is dominated by acoustic and visual images. Eribó, the musician, perceives his world in terms of rhythm and movement; Silvestre, in movement, sight, and sound (film); Cué, theater actor, in conversation, sound [and, one might add, in costuming and appearance]; and Códac, the photographer, in surface description of characters and actions.... ("Cinematic" 46; my ellipsis)

William Siemens states, concerning Silvestre, that he "has been preoccupied with the visual in the form of the cinema, but at the point of writing has already become a professional writer for whom words are supreme" (*Language and Creativity* 59). While Silvestre does attach great importance to words, his sensibility is deeply imbued with film. Hazera asserts that "Silvestre...is an embodiment of Cabrera Infante's alter ego, G. Caín the critic, who speaks the language of film" ("Cinematic" 46; my ellipsis). More precisely, Silvestre is a development of Caín, since, as Cabrera Infante pointed out to Jorge Nieto (see above), Silvestre thinks of film as assimilated "more or less passively" to his experience and does not "mediate" film or approach it in an actively critical fashion. As Siemens also notes (*Language and Creativity* 59-61), Códac, named for the Kodak camera, is visually fascinated with film, matching the interest of Silvestre in the medium. Códac, however, does not tend to become involved in metaphysical speculation to the degree of Silvestre.[2]

Silvestre and Códac share a tendency to exercise their visual sensitivities through dreams, an activity which is for some film theorists, such as Hugo Munsterberg, the core of cinema. Dreams and memory are two of the most important mechanisms examined and employed in the book and link it directly to the concept of film expounded in *Arcadia todas las noches*. As we already saw when considering *Un oficio del Siglo 20*, the dream state, in which the unconscious can function freely, is, according to Joseph Campbell, the arena of myths, of the working out of conflicts or struggles between the "hero" and the demons of the unknown (*Hero* 4-10).[3] Silvestre and Códac narrate two dreams which recall in their imagery and thematic content some of the film iconography important to Cabrera Infante and which evidence his statement that the aspect of film that most

influenced him when he began to write fiction "Fue fundamental-
mente la habilidad que tiene el cine para crear situaciones totalmente
oníricas, la capacidad de fabricar sueños que tiene el cine, y al mismo
tiempo, la capacidad que tiene de fabricar mitos..." (Interview with
author).

The dream of Códac (160-62), which contains strange sea imagery,
is rather Wellesian in its grotesqueness and exaggeration of visual
qualities in a baroque fashion. Certainly a parallel to *The Lady from
Shanghai* can be seen in the dream, with its strange emphasis on
distorted and nightmarish fish imagery.[4]

Códac, whose narrative sequences are distinguished by their
especial use of cinematic cutting, often relying on the use of "y" as a
joint between cuts, becomes a kind of subjective camera, supplanting
in fact the instrument by which he exercises his professional skill and
after which he is nicknamed. Like Silvestre, he is not an "objective"
reproducer of reality in the fashion claimed by neorealist filmmakers.
His dreams as well as his interjection into his narration of
conversations, for example, his repeated use of "'decía'" as a kind of
ironic commentary during the party at his apartment (125), are, like
the dreams and speculations of Silvestre, in direct contradiction to an
objectivist style of presentation. Códac and Silvestre represent rather
the oneiric and irrationalist qualities of the cinema which are stressed
by Cabrera Infante.

The passage of "Ella cantaba boleros," which contains the dream of
Códac (160-61), opens with his recollection of the dream and is thus
colored by his visual organization of its elements. The narrative
elements of the dream are reminiscent not only of *The Lady from
Shanghai* but also of *The Old Man and the Sea*, a film whose original
inspiration, the novel by Hemingway, is the subject of a disagreement
between Cué and Silvestre (34).[5]

The dream is a jangling piece of surrealist narrative redolent of
Lautréamont but containing devices which are interestingly akin to
the "'intellectual montage'" of Sergei Eisenstein (see Bordwell and
Thompson 179-83). Like the images in an Eisenstein film such as
Potemkin, the imagery in the dream suggests other associations in the
mind of the "viewer" and seems transformed through its juxtaposition with other images. Thus, the "'pez fosforecente'" [sic] is
connected first to "'Cuba,'" a linkage which brings to mind not only
Cuba Venegas but also the fact that the "old man" of *The Old Man and*

the Sea fishes in Cuban waters. The image then undergoes several transformations which drastically affect it as a percept:

> ...venía un pez fosforecente [sic] que era largo y se parecía a Cuba y después se achicaba y era Irenita y se volvía prieto, negruzco, negro y era Magalena y cuando lo cogí, que picó, comenzó a crecer y a crecer y se hizo tan grande como el bote.... (160; my ellipsis)

The pace of the transformations in the dream passage is so rapid and the visual quality so strong that one is reminded of the process of animation, in which such effects are easily achieved through drawings and by very rapid and abrupt cutting. One image quickly supersedes another, hardly leaving time for the previous one to register perceptually. The tonal quality of the colors and the lighting in the dream also recall the dream sequence in *Vertigo*, during which Scottie mentally views his past experience with Madeleine in an old mission in severe perceptual distortion. At the end of the dream, Códac suffers a claustrophobic attack, a near-suffocation which also recalls the vertigo of Scottie; but instead of the bleak awakening experienced by Scottie, Códac awakens comically to another transformation. His "'pez fosforecente'" is actually La Estrella, in bed with him. Her nickname is, appropriately, "'la Ballena Negra'" (64).

Later in the sequence, Códac begins to refer to film technique itself, initiating a kind of "metacinematic" narrative, similar in literary terms to the self-conscious film style of Jean-Luc Godard, in which the spectator is made aware of his watching a film by, for example, seeing the lead numbers on the reel during the movie itself or by observing the characters discussing the technical aspects of the film in which they are appearing. The torso of La Estrella is divided into "'rollos,'" suggesting film reels besides pointing to layers of fat (161).[6] The implied analogy is later made more explicit when the same word is used in connection with photographic technique: "'leyendo esas indicaciones que vienen en cada rollo Kodak....'" Here one sees an interesting use of montage technique, in which La Estrella, the "'rollo,'" is linked to Códac through the origin of his nickname. The narrative then becomes mockingly "technical" in quality: "'leyendo esa cómoda simpleza que divide la vida en Al Sol, Exterior Nublado, Sombra, Playa o Nieve (nieve, mierda, en Cuba) y finalmente Interior Luminoso...'" (163; my ellipsis). When Silvestre enters with news of the death of Bustrófedon, cinematic references, both technical and contextual, begin to appear.

Silvestre begins to recount his experiences with Ingrid Bérgamo. The scene contains not only evidence of cutting technique but also overt analogies to the actress Ingrid Bergman and to actors, such as the comparison which Silvestre draws between himself and George Sanders: "'yo tratando de calmarla, más razonable que George Sanders...'" (165). Silvestre also alludes to technical aspects of cinematography: "'momento en que el viejo Hitch[cock] cortaría para insertar inter-cut de fuegos artificiales...'" (166).[7] The scene also recalls the striking montage technique used in the dream of Códac: "'la cama es un mueble como otro cualquiera, que puede ser un asiento...'" (166).

The mock surrealism of the Bérgamo sequence and its use of the bizarre transformation of Ingrid into a bald woman perhaps suggest once again the strange transformation sequence in *Vertigo*, when the red-headed Judy becomes the blonde Madeleine. While the overall technique seems similar, the tone of the two sequences is quite different, one comically grotesque and one hauntingly beautiful.

The sequences with Silvestre are more typically characterized by speculations about dream, memory, and time and space than are the sequences dealing with the other characters. The elements which are found in the musings and reveries of Silvestre are important to film theory. In particular, the problems of dream and memory have been prominent in the remarks of Cabrera Infante concerning film. Like *La Habana para un Infante Difunto*, *Tres tristes tigres* represents in large part a search for the past through memory.[8] The external referents of politics and current events are perceived by the characters as secondary to the internal processes of memory and dream. Andrew Sarris has stated penetratingly, in "Rerunning Puig and Cabrera Infante," that "Cabrera Infante has chosen to treat recent history as an hallucination..." (46), much as Scottie in *Vertigo* refuses to acknowledge the death of Madeleine and tries to force Judy into the role which she apparently only acted out for money. Silvestre, like Scottie, tries to, or is caused to, escape into his memories instead of giving his full attention to the occurrences around him.

The preoccupation of Silvestre with the process of memory is shown in his interior monologue (305-06). This monologue is closely related in tone to the central memory scene in *Vertigo*. His concern with memory is also apparent in his interpretation of Cué's dream (313-14), which is even more closely related to the *Vertigo* love scene which is set by the bay outside San Francisco.

In the love scene from *Vertigo* by the bay, Scottie and Madeleine realize their passion for each other. The love of Scottie for Madeleine will be linked to his memory of her faked suicide attempt, which also occurred by the bay, and his "rescue" of her. The waves of the bay form a visual metaphor for the flow of time, or the eternal return, and his mnemonic obsession with Madeleine.

We may remind ourselves that in Proust's *A la récherche du temps perdu, la petite madeleine* (tea biscuit) was the trigger of *"la mémoire involontaire."*[9] Silvestre, preoccupied with the process of memory, reflects on his reverie about the girl, speaking of it in terms strikingly similar to those of Proust (see the remarks by Cabrera Infante, quoted below):

> Esta imagen me asalta ahora con violencia, casi sin provocación y pienso que mejor que la memoria involuntaria para atrapar el tiempo perdido, es la memoria violenta, incoercible, que no necesita ni madelenitas en el te [sic] ni fragancias del pasado ni un tropezón idéntico a sí mismo, sino que viene abrupta, alevosa y nocturna y nos fractura la ventana del presente con un recuerdo ladrón. No deja de ser singular que este recuerdo dé vértigo: esa sensación de caída inminente, ese viaje brusco, inseguro, esa aproximación de dos planos por la posible caída violenta.... (306)

When asked about his use of allusions to *Vertigo* in the passage containing the reverie, allusions such as "madelenitas," which recalls the name Madeleine as well as the image of the Proust novel, Cabrera Infante affirmed his conscious use of the film here:

> Pensé... no solamente conscientemente sino que siempre me ha sorprendido que Hitchcock.... llamara a este personaje Madeleine, porque ella representa el recuerdo. Yo no sé si eso fue consciente en Hitchcock, pero claro era muy consciente en mí, porque yo conocía los dos antecedentes, es decir la película y la novela de Proust. (Interview with author; my ellipsis)

Silvestre even speaks of the sea in terms which suggest *Vertigo* and which tend to cast the maritime imagery of the book into terms relating to memory, death, and resurrection. He says that:

El mar nos rodea, el mar nos envuelve y finalmente el mar nos lava los bordes y nos aplana y nos gasta como a los guijarros de la costa y nos sobrevive, indiferente, como el resto del cosmos, cuando somos arena, polvo de Quevedo. (307)

The reverie of Silvestre concerns a girl he had once loved. He remembers her with some difficulty, but the image which emerges is not unlike that of Madeleine in *Vertigo*:

Traté de recordar varias mujeres y no pude pensar en ninguna y cuando me iba a dar por vencido, pensé no en una mujer sino en una muchacha. Recordé su pelo rubio, su frente alta y sus ojos claros, casi amarillos, y su boca gruesa y larga y su barbilla partida y sus piernas largas y sus pies en zandalias [sic] y su andar y recordé estarla esperando en un parque mientras recordaba su risa que era una sonrisa de dientes perfectos. (304-05)

Silvestre becomes irritated when Cué accuses him of "inventing" the girl, rather like Scottie reinventing Madeleine after her "death": "— Que no estuviste enamorado, nunca, que esa mujer no existe, que la acabas de inventar. Debo enfurecerme, pero yo ni siquiera puedo ponerme bravo donde todo el mundo echa espuma por la boca" (305).

At the end of the reverie, Silvestre contributes his Proustian comments on its mnemonic significance. For Silvestre, as for Swann in the Proust novel, memory occurs outside of time.[10] Time and memory are antithetical or at least non-analogical processes.

Cabrera Infante and Hitchcock, like Proust, attempt in such passages to capture the "timeless moment," "during which a forgotten incident floats up from oblivion in its pristine form and seems thereby to become free of time" (Bluestone 56). The "timeless moment" in all three cases refers to the mental state experienced in *"la mémoire involontaire,"* which comes to Silvestre "violently" as it does to Scottie.

Scottie, like Swann, uses devices to remember Madeleine. The devices used in the film are the objects of clothing and the hairstyle which he imposes on Judy in "reconstructing" Madeleine. The recall of Madeleine by Scottie is truly violent and involuntary on other occasions, to the point of obsession. He undergoes trauma as a result of her "death," he has an obsessive dream, and he wanders haunted by disturbing memories. Even more violent is the memory of the fall of his partner, a memory which appears to cause his vertigo.

The interest of Cabrera Infante in vertigo is clearly shown by his frequent use of the term in different forms ("vértigo," "vertiginoso") and is here expressly linked to his concern with memory, time, and space. Silvestre links the concepts when commenting on his reverie:

> No deja de ser singular que este recuerdo dé vértigo: esa sensación de caída inminente, ese viaje brusco, inseguro, esa aproximación de dos planos por la posible caída violenta (los planos reales por una caída física, vertical y el plano de la realidad y el del recuerdo por la horizontal caída imaginaria) permite saber que el tiempo, como el espacio, tiene también su ley de gravedad. Quiero casar a Proust con Isaac Newton. (306)

Silvestre, proceeding somewhat in the manner of Hitchcock, who uses spatial or cinematic technique to convey the mental state of Scottie,[11] would like to "marry" Proust, whose literary efforts must be based on time, with Newton, who worked with spatial laws. Silvestre, then, is attempting a marriage of literary expression to cinematic discourse, carrying to a technical plane his habit of using cinematic allusion in his speech and writing. In passing, the commentary by Silvestre, with its reference to "caída violenta" and the "aproximación de dos planos," is a pointed allusion to *Vertigo*, with the fear of Scottie of falling from heights being vividly demonstrated in the film by a technique involving a combination of a dolly shot and the use of a zoom lens, so that "two planes," the floor and the location of Scottie on the stairs during the shot, seem to converge in a sickening fashion.[12]

The dream, then, and its companion, memory, are important to *Tres tristes tigres* and are closely intertwined with the attraction of film for Cabrera Infante. The concern with cinema as "una manifestación irracional" and the opposition expressed by Cabrera Infante to the approach of John Huston, who "ha reducido el cine a la razón" (*Arcadia* 128), find creative embodiment in *Tres tristes tigres*. Perhaps the labored and overly logical narrative of "Historia de un bastón" could be seen as the end result of such a rationalization of film, or literary, language.

Just as an ideological continuity exists between the criticism of Cabrera Infante and his fiction, as demonstrated by the creative incarnation of his ideas on the irrationality of film, so thematic or allusive and stylistic continuities and patterns are not difficult to find.[13] The predilections of Cabrera Infante as a film critic are echoed by the characters of *Tres tristes tigres*. Thus, Silvestre and Cué refer to films such as *The Treasure of the Sierra Madre* and *A Double Life* (307-08). Furthermore, echoes of the films of directors such as Hitchcock, Minnelli, and Hawks appear in the book.[14]

A very important tendency in the Hitchcock films, his ritualized mythmaking with the "juego," as Cabrera Infante says in *Arcadia todas las noches* (62-63, 65), is equally crucial to *Tres tristes tigres*. The remarks applied to Hitchcock by Cabrera Infante in *Arcadia todas las noches* concerning his gamesmanship could easily fit Cué, Silvestre, and their mentor Bustrófedon.[15]

Like Hitchcock, the "tigres" are gamesmen. The friends in the book are virtuosi in the verbal field as is Hitchcock in the visual area. The games are often humorous in both cases but conceal more serious preoccupations.

Since *Tres tristes tigres*, as Cabrera Infante has said in a class lecture at Wellesley College, is formally a detective story, built around the notion of *"cherchez la femme,"* the gamesmanship between Cué and Silvestre can be illuminated by seeing their banter as revolving around the motif of the woman who is at the center of the plot of the book.[16] The analogy between the book and Hitchcock films such as *Vertigo* and *Rear Window* also becomes even more apparent, since such films focus either on the search for a loved one or on the woman as the motive for or the object of a crime.

Underlying the banter between Cué and Silvestre is a competitiveness, both intellectual and amorous, which culminates in the declaration by Silvestre that he will marry Laura, the woman who is the "criminal" in the life of Cué because she has seduced him away from his provincial innocence.[17] Laura Díaz, the romantic actress, has attracted, and, to use the term of Silvestre, "corrupted" Cué. Silvestre, on the other hand, sees her simplicity, revealed in her humble origins.

In the dichotomy of attractions experienced by "'el dúo,'" as Eribó terms the complementary pair of Cué and Silvestre (107), one can see a close parallel to the structure of *Vertigo*. Scottie is lured away from his existence with the stolid Midge by the fatal attractiveness of Madeleine, who is impersonated by the rather simple "actress" Judy. Scottie later discovers that Judy is a fairly naive girl from Kansas who has inexplicably found within herself the capacity to impersonate a complexly ethereal creature like Madeleine, or, more precisely, to create the personality of Madeleine.

Thus, like Scottie, Cué has been "corrupted" by the charm of an image, an ideal of cultural mystique represented by Laura Díaz. Silvestre, whose provincial simplicity has already given way to literary sophistication, tends to seek the simpler qualities of Laura, seeing her "real" self. Unlike Scottie and Cué, Silvestre has been able to some extent to "reverse time" by looking at the former self of Laura. Perhaps, because, as Nelson notes, "A Silvestre le gusta recordar" ("*Tres tristes tigres*" 19), he has been capable of avoiding the predicament of Cué, for whom "Su único recuerdo es doloroso: cuando ve la puerta del apartamiento de Livia, asocia ese objeto espacial con un acontecimiento en el pasado: la pérdida de Laura" (20). Cué, like Scottie, "no ha sabido creer que el tiempo no es irreversible" (*Arcadia* 77). Since, as Nelson points out (7), "Laura Díaz, ya casada con Silvestre," later sees a psychiatrist in "un *flashforward*," the future of the couple is not altogether rosy. Perhaps Silvestre falls after all into the trap which ensnares Scottie and Cué, losing himself in the search for the ideal woman.

Tres tristes tigres as a whole contains much of the investigation effected by Hitchcock and Welles into "el misterio" which is hidden behind the exterior of everyday life or behind the surface of a figure like Charles Foster Kane in *Citizen Kane* (*Arcadia* 35, 67). Cuba Venegas, La Estrella, Cué, and Laura are all subjected to scrutiny which recalls almost any Welles film in its biographical emphasis on stripping away layers of pretense and social veneer.

In the process of the discovery of social truth, the mannerist aesthetic ascribed to Welles by Cabrera Infante is seen in action. The mannerist painter or poet who concerns himself with the importance of appearance and its deceptive shadowing of inner conflict would understand the tendency of the narrative of *Tres tristes tigres* to look behind surfaces. The "gothic" nature of the characters, so like the atmosphere of a Welles film, is epitomized by Cué, who, like the alien villain of the Roger Corman film *Not of This Earth*, but rather comically wears dark glasses to conceal his disconcerting eyes. He is seen as conflictive in nature by Silvestre, who remarks of him that "'En cada actor hay escondido [sic] una actriz'" (308). Several other characters in the book undergo such revelation of their personalities, or, as in the case of La Estrella, concealment or frustration of their true natures. The air of betrayal and falsity which pervades the work of Welles is also prevalent in *Tres tristes tigres*.

The narrative organization used by Cabrera Infante in *Tres tristes tigres* is reminiscent of that of *Citizen Kane*.[18] In this film, several characters narrate the life of Kane from their differing and somewhat overlapping perspectives. The life of the magnate is thus, as Bordwell and Thompson show, subject to "reconstruction" by the viewer (60-68). Similarly, Nelson suggests, "No hay narrador omnisciente en *Tres tristes tigres*," and "Casi toda la narrativa del libro está en el pretérito: *flashbacks* de sucesos recordados" ("*Tres tristes tigres*" 7).

The book not only employs flashbacks but uses them at times in a manner which indicates to the reader the artificiality of the device. Similarly, the characters in the films of Jean-Luc Godard may suddenly address the audience, reminding them that they are watching a film and that the character is aware of his true nature.[19]

Thus, in Godard films such as *Masculin/Féminin*, the viewer is shown the ends of film reels, with the numbers for the projectionist; the film starts and stops and seems to run off the sprocket; and the characters even address the audience directly. A major effect of such practices is to lessen the distance between viewer and film, making the spectator, at least in theory, a participant in the process. Conversely, however, the fictional illusion is vitiated and the film is placed in danger of being turned into an academic exercise. This is not quite true of *Tres tristes tigres*; but its characters do maintain a certain consciousness of their playing a role. Hence stem to a significant degree their frequent comparisons of themselves to actors. Códac appears to show a self-consciousness pertinent to a character from a Godard movie when, in one of the sections entitled "Ella cantaba boleros," he opens his narrative with the apostrophe "'¿Qué quieren?'" (120), apparently addressing the reader as if speaking to an audience.

The question by Códac not only opens a sequence but, since it is asked in a novelistic present, functions as a temporal frame for the rest of the passage. The next words of the sequence, "'Me sentí Barnum y seguí los torcidos consejos de Alex Bayer,'" in the preterit (120), are perceived as initiating a flashback analogous to those in *Citizen Kane*. In this film, the flashbacks begin, like the sequence in *Tres tristes tigres*, with a line of dialogue addressed to an offstage or invisible listener (the reporter). The time in which the *Kane* flashbacks are framed is the present, although their content deals with the past.

In connection with the technique of piecemeal narrative used by

Cabrera Infante in *Tres tristes tigres,* another analogy to *Citizen Kane* can be discerned. William Siemens, without referring to the Welles film, observes that

> ... Cabrera Infante appears to feel that their [the "literary characters'"] presence, thoughts, feelings and actions are of no interest without the verbalized interpretations of them by several narrators, each of whom presents to the reader his private view of the situation in which they are living. Often, in fact, the reader gains knowledge about a character or situation only by piecing together fragments from several narrators, none of whom can be trusted to be completely reliable. (*Language and Creativity* 42; my ellipsis)

A similar feeling is instilled in the viewer of *Citizen Kane* by the narrative technique of Welles. Each narrator, some of whom, such as Kane's servant and Jed Leland, the former friend to the magnate, seem unreliable for personal or financial reasons, presents his versions of parts of the Kane story. The viewer gleans many facts about the history of the publisher by comparing the stories, but the uneasy feeling remains of Kane as a shadowy figure who only comes alive through the perspectives of the narrators. The unease is enhanced by the dreamlike nature of the camera and sound techniques used by Welles. Perhaps Kane, as in a lighter vein Bustrófedon, was of more interest for his effect on others than as a flesh and blood person.

Despite its links to such relatively gloomy films as *Citizen Kane* and *Vertigo, Tres tristes tigres,* with its use of mannerism and gamesmanship, must not be seen in deadly serious terms. Cabrera Infante has warned against losing the thread of comedy which pervades his work and to which purpose the punning and association of ideas tend. Speaking of the associations based on the conceit of La Estrella as "'La Ballena Negra,'" for instance, he comments that

> Eso. ... viene del intento de. ... intensificación de la relación, es decir, una intensificación de la metáfora o una intensificación, en este caso, de la analogía .... el resultado puede ser barroco, pero ... la intención primera es fundamentalmente cómica. (Interview with author; my ellipsis)

The particular comic quality in the fiction of Cabrera Infante does not lie exclusively, however, in its brilliant use of punning and associations. Although "puros juegos," as Cabrera Infante calls instances of the humor in *Tres tristes tigres* such as the jokes about the translations by Rine Leal (Interview with author),[20] are prevalent in the book and lend to it a very lighthearted quality, the kind of pathos found in the films of Chaplin or Billy Wilder is certainly not absent.

The case of La Estrella is, as we have already mentioned (see above, 56), illustrative of the pathetic side of comedy as it is practiced by Cabrera Infante. Códac mourns the decline of La Estrella from the idealized creature who sings *boleros*, themselves, as Cabrera Infante pointed out in lecturing to a class at Wellesley, sad songs, to the singer who dies of overeating and is cheapened into a pornographic image. Certainly a deeply ironic comedy lends its hue to her life, but the fact remains that, as with Chaplin in the Tramp films, the work attempts to elicit compassion for the misunderstood figure of the singer.

As already noted, the comedy of Billy Wilder is significant in *Tres tristes tigres*. The chief representative of the comedy of Wilder which finds an echo in the book is *Some Like It Hot*. The Cary Grant imitation, itself an allusion to a master of film comedy, by Silvestre in his seduction of Ingrid Bérgamo (164-68), recalls the method used by the Tony Curtis character in his pursuit of the girl played by Marilyn Monroe. The very pairing of the figures of Grant and Ingrid Bergman, represented by Bérgamo, to whom Silvestre says "'que le dimos ese apodo porque así es como ella pronuncia el nombre de Ingrid Bergman'" (165), ironically echoes the often comic encounter of Grant and Bergman in *Notorious*.

In more generalized terms, the problems of identity and the donning of various masks by the characters of *Tres tristes tigres* are analogous to the difficulties experienced by the characters in Wilder films such as *Some Like It Hot*. The veiled reference by Silvestre to Cué as having within him an "'actriz'" is easily understandable in terms of *Some Like It Hot*, in which the Jack Lemmon character in particular suffers a sexual identity problem due to his assumption of a female role.

Another aspect of *Some Like It Hot* is of some importance to *Tres tristes tigres* and leads to considerations of the debt owed by the book to two cinema genres: the detective film and the musical. *Some Like It Hot* is a parody of the old-fashioned gangster film. The gangster film plot and the "suspense" of *Some Like It Hot* are used to comic effect, just as the "detective structure" of *Tres tristes tigres*[21] is the occasion for much comedy and witty interchange between the characters.

The parody of gangster films is only one aspect of *Some Like It Hot*, however, and the importance of music and musical settings to its plot should not be ignored. The Curtis and Lemmon characters are rather cheap cabaret musicians, one a saxophonist and the other a horn player. Thus, the film combines three elements important to *Tres tristes tigres*: comedy, a detective plot, and a musical environment. In connection with the musical environment, the chain of association between the fact that one of the heroes of *Some Like It Hot* plays a sax and the reference by Códac to "'un saxofonista que parece el hijo del padre de Van Heflin con la madre de Jerry [sic] Mulligan'" should be noted (130). Also relevant is the declaration by Cabrera Infante to Isabel Alvarez-Borland that "'en «Seseribó,» en *TTT*, hay un momento que tomé concientemente de ... *Young Man with a Horn*, biografía ficticia de un gran jazzman, Bix Beiderbecke'" ("Viaje" 67; my ellipsis).[22]

With respect to the importance for *Tres tristes tigres* of detective and gangster movies and fiction, Cabrera Infante has noted his specific indebtedness to the work of Raymond Chandler. In an interview with me, he said that the scene of the visit by Cué to the house of an important personage, when he is shot, actually with blanks, and as he says, "'caí para delante, sin ver ya, mi cabeza golpeando, duro, el brocal de un pozo que había en el suelo y caía dentro'" (60), is taken from a Philip Marlowe novel in which the hero is beaten and falls unconscious into a dark hole. The novel may be *Farewell, My Lovely*. For the purposes of the present study, it is important to note that the technique of first person narration used here, with its cynical reactions to decadence and somewhat moralizing tone, traits also seen in the narrative by Códac and Eribó, is quite reminiscent of the style used by Philip Marlowe.

Silvestre, in fact, identifies himself specifically with Marlowe during an evening car excursion with Cué. As in a detective movie, the action of the book is set in the city, mostly at night, with a car serving as a center of operations for its characters. Silvestre reacts to the streets of La Habana much as Marlowe does to those of Bay City, the mythical evocation of Santa Monica by Chandler (320-21).

The association with Marlowe is triggered by a visual experience, lending more credence to the observation of Siemens (*Language and Creativity* 63-64) and Nelson ("*Tres tristes tigres*" 12-13) concerning the appeal of the visual art of cinema for Silvestre. He sees "los canales, las radas y el mar paralelo" as if in a tracking shot, noting that they "pasaban lentamente" (320). The phenomena of the outside world are deliberately subjected to a process of visual selection as if seen through a camera lens.[23]

A connection is made with Philip Marlowe partly because of the technique used in a particular film with Marlowe as its hero, and partly because of the typically Chandleresque setting in which Silvestre finds himself. The camera technique used in *The Lady in the Lake* was an attempt to control the perspective of the film in order to produce a "subjective camera" effect. The face of Robert Montgomery, who directed the movie and played Marlowe, was shown only once in the mirror.[24] He is therefore, like, in varying degrees, the characters of *Tres tristes tigres*, the perpetual observer. The movie unreels from his perspective, just as much of *Tres tristes tigres* unfolds from the point of view of the movie watcher Silvestre.

Cué, as Nelson suggests (14-15), does not share the obsession of Silvestre with movies, saying to Silvestre that "—Por mi madre que estás completamente loco—" (320). Nevertheless, he does identify with Silvestre in a rather strange fashion by remarking that "'¿Es mi culpa si Bay City me dice más que Combray [an important location in *A la recherche du temps perdu* by Proust]? Sí, supongo que sí. ¿A ti también? Tú lo llamarías el Síndrome de Chandler'" (326).[25] His point concerns the equivalence of "popular" and "high" cultures, a concept which Cabrera Infante supports by saying that: "Para mí, el valor, por ejemplo, de una novela de Corín Tellado no es inferior como tema...a el *Quijote*.... Para mí, es lo mismo" (Interview with author; my ellipsis). Cué, who, as Nelson points out, does not like to remember his past (20), is perhaps also speaking of the precedence of fantasy over the type of memory indulged in by Silvestre.

The fact that Silvestre identifies himself with Philip Marlowe also points to the participation of many of the male characters in the book in generic Hollywood versions of the hero. Marlowe is one of the most romantic of screen heroes and draws not only on the detective tradition but also on the image of the Westerner who must uphold civilized morality in a wild or corrupt environment (Warshow 137). Silvestre, Cué, and Códac are repeatedly cast in terms of Hollywood protagonists. Silvestre and Arsenio are both linked to Marlowe. Códac is less specifically associated with film heroes but seems placed in the typical position of the hero of a screwball comedy, since he endures comic mishaps in his pursuit of La Estrella. Eribó, as Cabrera Infante has stated, is connected at least indirectly to the figure of Bix Beiderbecke as treated in *Young Man with a Horn*.

If the men in *Tres tristes tigres* are identified with film figures or types, the women almost without exception fall into the categories of American film types as proposed by Wolfenstein and Leites in *Movies: A Psychological Study*. In their scheme, the image of women presented on the screen ranges from the "bad girl" through the "good" girl and the "good-bad" girls. The division, while obviously simplified, is quite useful in studying the imagery presented to the average moviegoer, especially in the 1930s and 1940s.

Vivian Smith-Corona is an ingenue type, a kind of Audrey Hepburn figure whose virginity becomes the subject of drunken banter between Cué and Silvestre at the expense of Eribó, who seems enamored of her. Wolfenstein and Leites state that the good-bad girl in American movies is a figure whose virtue is called into question to give her erotic interest, but who typically is found not to have consummated her relationships with the men in her life other than, perhaps, the hero of the movie (see 27-47). The tension of the film, often but not always comic, therefore lies in the uncertainty of the hero and perhaps of the audience about the virtue of the heroine, as, for instance, in *Gilda*, cited by Wolfenstein and Leites (27-29). In *Tres tristes tigres*, the mystery about the good-bad girl is given a humorous slant because of the barroom debate over Vivian and because of her droll last name. She eventually admits to having made love to Tony, but her motives were those of a "good" girl. She was, she says, interested more in pleasing Tony than in indulging in sensuality.

The step from Vivian to Laura Díaz is only a matter of a little maturity. Laura is somewhat more ambiguous than Vivian and is definitely sensual but can hardly be termed a "bad" girl or a "vamp." She merely seems to have "been around" and exhibits the kind of "fun girl" or "masculine-feminine girl" assertiveness noted by Wolfenstein and Leites in roles such as those usually played in the 1940s by Lauren Bacall or Rosalind Russell (76-85).

Laura clearly exhibits the approach of the "masculine-feminine girl," who, as Wolfenstein and Leites say, "admits without

euphemisms that she is interested in sex" but "does not carry the
unrelieved aura of it" (76). She participates with Livia, her double, in a
very straightforward game with Cué which involves sexual teasing
(149). Perhaps more appropriate to the case of Laura than the analogy
of Bacall or Russell is the heritage of Jean Harlow, who was
notoriously open about sex and quite fun-loving. An implied analogy
is even made between Harlow and Laura when Cué uses *Red Dust* as
an example to warn, or threaten, Silvestre from marrying Laura
(443). The warning implies that Laura will dominate Silvestre because
of her sensuality. Laura is the most complex female figure in the book
but is still remarkably close to film types, amalgamating the
"masculine-feminine girl" with the "good-bad girl" and the Bette
Davis type of neurotic heroine.

Cuba Venegas also fits well within the framework of film types.
Like the Kim Stanley protagonist in *The Goddess*, she is the "bad girl"
who corrupts men and has lost whatever innocence she once had in
the provinces. The picture presented in the book of various women is
not merely a one-dimensional catalogue of sexual objects[26] but a
hierarchy of figures which match American film typology, with Cuba
complementing the figure of Vivian in the formation of a triangle
whose hypotenuse is Laura Díaz, a girl with mixed traits. In other
words, Laura is a meld of the tendencies represented by Cuba, the
actress gone bad, a figure seen in Hollywood films such as *The Goddess*
and *All about Eve*, and Vivian, the good-bad ingenue who has populated
the Hollywood movie at least since *It Happened One Night*.

La Estrella appears to violate the pattern of American film
typology present in the book, but that is part of the essence of her
character. She violates patterns physically, occupationally, and
socially. As an obese mulatto woman who refuses to sing with
accompaniment and has embarrassing habits in public, she is an
anomalous, mythic figure. Certainly she is closer to a Fellini figure
than to a type from a mainstream American movie. She actually
stands outside the cast of female characters in the book because a
true romantic involvement with such a grotesque being is never
really entertained even by Códac.

If the female characters are susceptible to identification with film
types, the male characters of *Tres tristes tigres* consciously link
themselves to film stars and situations. As Rivero notes, "...los
personajes masculinos principales...se realizan en discursos que los

proyectan como poseedores de una vasta cultura 'pop'...son conocedores de literatura, música, cinematografía y arte..." (284-85; my ellipsis). The stars with whom they identify often represent projections of their self-images. Silvestre, who suffers from a virulent romanticism, connects himself explicitly and implicitly with loners such as Marlowe and Scottie in *Vertigo*. Cué, the glossy show business personality, thinks in terms of a figure like Fred Astaire. Eribó, who despite being a bongo player has worked as a graphic artist, refers to Kirk Douglas, as Van Gogh, in *Lust for Life* (95), thus identifying himself with a visual artist.

The process of identification with film characters on the part of the men in the book certainly contains elements of campiness and parody. The names of the actors and the film characters are frequently distorted and their dialogues parodied, as in the aforementioned reference by Eribó to Kirk Douglas:

—José Pérez es mi nombre, pero mis amigos me dicen Vincent. No pareció entender, sino que se extrañó.... Le expliqué que era una broma, que era la parodia de una parodia, que era un diálogo de Vincent van Douglas en Sed de Vivir. Me dijo que no la había visto y me preguntó si era buena y le contesté que la pintura sí pero la película no, que Kirk Fangó pintaba mientras lloraba y al revés y que Anthony Gauquinn era un bouncer del Saloon de Rechazados.... (95)

Another example of such humorous identification with film characters is the remark by Cué, who almost does a pratfall in one scene, that "«Soy la respuesta cubana a Fred Astaire»" (53).

Nevertheless, the fact of identification with movie characters is a solid one and is not altogether romantic in the usual sense of the word. Much of the answer lies in the assertion by Cabrera Infante that he once saw Hitchcock films as "el espectador totalmente inocente. Es decir, yo conocí Hitchcock sin saber que era Hitchcock. Esto ocurrió en mi niñez...a fines de los años treinta" (Interview with author). Extending such a youth's-eye view of movies to a character such as Silvestre, one could say that film actors were, and to some extent are, partial role models for conduct, cultural ideals, and marks against which to measure oneself.

The tendency of the characters in the book may be towards a participation in the culture of the United States which bears out the

view of Jean Franco that Cuba had "'... in 1959—the bastard culture of
an island dependent on North Americans'" (272; quoted in Rivero 291
n 21). A good formulation of the trend in the book, as in the works of
Cabrera Infante generally, would be to say that the characters,
constantly bombarded by American tourism, consumer products, and
access to mass media,[27] share as Cubans, and more specifically as
Havana dwellers, in the idealized picture of American life in which
Americans themselves want to believe and which, as Michael Wood
says, "is not life...It is *the movies*" (*America* 8; my ellipsis; original
emphasis). Movies are a *lingua franca* for these characters, much like the
language of art or literature, but on a more intimately assimilated
level.[28]

In writing *Tres tristes tigres*, Cabrera Infante operated on the
assumption of a readership which shared a common movie culture[29]
but, to borrow a phrase which Michael Wood uses in a different
context, "The classics here being the public's classics, rather than the
critics': Fred Astaire rather than Flaherty; Lubitsch rather than von
Stroheim" (*America* 11). His direction of the book to this median
audience is revealed in a change which he performed on the pratfall
scene with Cué which was mentioned above. The line about Astaire
originally read "«Soy la respuesta cubana a Gene Kelly»," but Cabrera
Infante thought that Astaire would be more well-known to the
Cuban public and therefore changed the reference (Interview with
author).

The characters of the book would in general have no trouble in
determining such a reference, as they operate at some remove from
the supposed readership of the book. These characters do not see film
as esoteric or campy; it is rather the reader who may feel himself
distanced from the cultural landscape in which many of the characters
operate. The effect is either strangely humorous or faintly absurd,
allowing the reader to experience the book as an entertainment much
as a reader of Dickens or Fielding was able to do. Comic distance is
maintained for the reader, who cannot quite take seriously all the
banter about films but who can nevertheless identify (at least
partially) with the cultural basis of that banter. Similarly, a reader of
Pickwick Papers at the time of its publication probably did not take very
seriously the adventures and mishaps of the characters, seeing in
them an element of sophisticated caricature which nonetheless stayed
grounded in a common culture.

The book should also be placed in a proper context relative to Cuba. It was largely written when Cabrera Infante was falling from favor with the government. The book underwent, as Seymour Menton explains, two versions which differed significantly. The first, "1964 version," "was entitled 'Vista del amanecer en el trópico' and portrayed Havana night life as the symbol of the decadent Batista regime of the late 1950's" (67). According to Menton, Cabrera Infante called it "'a politically opportune book'" and "has since morally repudiated" it. The second "version was inspired by the Cuban government's confiscation of the twenty-five-minute film *P.M.* made by Cabrera Infante's brother Sabá" (67).

The Cuban public of whom Cabrera Infante would have been thinking when he wrote the second version was the public raised on American movies and perhaps identifying with Hollywood figures. Cabrera Infante shared the background of his readers, whom he thought of as restricted to people experienced with the Havana of the period due to the difficulty of understanding the references (Cabrera Infante, qtd. in Pereda 104).[30] As is now clear, the book has an appeal which transcends such local barriers. Nevertheless, the films spoken of in the book would generally have been available to the moviegoer of the period with more facility, perhaps, than now.

Cabrera Infante has spoken about the relationship of the book to *P.M.* He says that he searched for a form into which to put his ideas and came upon his first book, a procedure similar to that followed by Manuel Puig (see Puig, Interview with Christ 53-55):

> ...oí que había muerto Fredy, una gran cantante de boleros que era del pueblo pero no popular. Entonces supe que podía realizar algo que me preocupaba desde que prohibieron el documental, que ocupaba mis ocios y mis noches como una obsesión casi clínica: hacer *P.M.* por otros medios—y los únicos medios que me eran asequibles eran los medios literarios. Así surgió *TTT*, del cine y de la música popular, pero aunque hay muchos que han querido llevar si no el libro por lo menos sus fragmentos al cine y hasta hay una película chilena [*Tres tristes tigres*, directed by Raúl Ruiz (1968) (Chanan, 99)] que para atenuar su mediocridad ha robado el título a mi libro, no creo que *TTT* tenga que convertirse en cine. ¿Para qué? Ya lo fue antes de ser libro y se titula *P.M.* (Cabrera Infante, "Viaje" 63)

The cultural background and context of *Tres tristes tigres* is deeply involved in films and film references,[31] many of which not surprisingly follow and extend the salient points in the criticism of Cabrera Infante. He has said that "Hay muchas películas conscientes en ese libro, y otras inconscientes" (Interview with author). Recurring elements in his criticism are notably present in *Tres tristes tigres*: references to *Moby Dick*, *King Kong*, *Lust for Life*, and the motif of Cain and Abel, with *East of Eden* as one of its chief embodiments. The list of elements presented here is certainly not exhaustive but is significant because of the insistence with which the motifs recur as well as because of their thematic resonance within the book.

All the films just cited function as repeated motifs in *Tres tristes tigres* and concern misunderstood or outcast characters. Like the characters in the book, the movie figures are in essence isolated from the world and struggle against it with results which vary from disaster to forced surrender. The movie characters are also, with the possible exception of Cal in *East of Eden*, grotesques either in physical or emotional terms. One should not carry the parallel with *Tres tristes tigres* too far, but *Moby Dick*, for instance, is a good negative image of La Estrella.[32] The connection is well supported in the text, with Vítor Perla telling Códac, "'Ten cuidado que es la prima de Moby Dick, La Ballena Negra'" (64), and Códac even referring directly to the movie version when he relates her to the whale: "'...y entonces levantó la cabeza o no levantó la cabeza, la ladeó solamente y levantó una de las rayas finas que tenía pintadas sobre los ojos y me miró y juro por John Huston que así miró Mobydita a Gregory Ahab. ¿La habría arponeado?'" (123; my ellipsis). The motive here is largely comic, serving as a good example of the process of "intensificación de la relación" by which the author says he achieves humorous effects (Interview with author).

In other instances, film influence or parallel is not so explicit but is rather on the level of stylistic analogy. The partying in the book, with its marathon dance quality, seems to parallel the frenzied parties in Minnelli films. Cabrera Infante does not deny the existence of a parallel here (Interview with author); and the analogy is difficult to reject, since both Minnelli and Cabrera Infante portray such parties as microcosms of frenetic modern emptiness.

The purely technical influence of film on the book, or the parallels in technical terms between film elements and parts of the book, has been treated in some depth by Ardis Nelson in *"Tres tristes tigres* y el cine." While her comments cover many of the possible analogies to film technique which are to be found in the book, Cabrera Infante has revealed two particular points in the work which, he feels, are not conceivable "sin el cine." While he says that he does not "necessarily" think in terms of film technique when writing, he does feel that its influence on him has been important in terms of narrative (Interview with author).[33]

One of the sections in the book of which he speaks occurs during the pursuit of Vivian by Eribó. The point specifically referred to precedes a visit "'al Focsa'" in order to, as Cué says, "'Dar una vuelta por la piscina'" (100). Cabrera Infante comments, concerning the scene, that

> ...en el misma [sic] fragmento de *Tres tristes tigres* en que se introduce concretamente a Cuba Venegas, hay dos o tres elementos de narración que no existirían sin el cine. Por ejemplo, digamos, ciertos cortes...hay un momento en que...Eribó....dice que no iba a ir como estaba vestido a acercarse a una piscina....y hay un corte y en la próximafrase él está en la piscina mirando cómo se bañan las niñas...eso es un corte típicamente cinematográfico. (Interview with author; my ellipsis)

The other scene to which Cabrera Infante alludes in this connection takes place when Cué and Silvestre are about to enter a club. Here, Cabrera Infante also admits to a "conscious" use of film technique:

> ...Conscientemente, hay un momento en que Silvestre, en el capítulo de "Bachata," se acerca a una fuente....y esa fuente es una especie de ninfa de bronce desnuda...la aproximación que él hace es típicamente cinematográfica...porque él mismo lo quiere, él mismo lo dice, él está produciendo eso que es privativo del cine, que se llama un *dolly* o un *travelling*,...es ese momento en que la cámara, moviéndose lentamente, se acerca a un determinado objeto o a un determinado actor. Estos son momentos conscientes de utilizar las técnicas del cine como técnicas de narración.... (Interview with author; my ellipsis)

In remarking that Silvestre "mismo" refers to his approach as "cinematográfica," Cabrera Infante appears to be speaking of the comment by Silvestre that, when replying to Cué, "Lo que no le dije fue que llevaba un ojo cerrado mientras le daba vuelta" (412). Just as he closes an eye during the scene echoing *The Lady in the Lake*, gaining thereby a cinematic viewpoint on el Malecón,[34] so here he indicates his use of a film technique in viewing the statue (411-12).

Cabrera Infante has thus pointed out some instances of technical use of cinematic elements in his work, and, as Nelson has shown, numerous other examples are to be found. Direct and extensive thematic borrowings are less prevalent, the approach used by Cabrera Infante, as Sarris has noted ("Rerunning" 46), being rather more scattered. Nevertheless, Cabrera Infante has noted that, as already mentioned, he based the scenes with Eribó in the bar and playing the bongos on *Young Man with a Horn*. He has stated in two interviews (an interview with me and one with Alvarez-Borland) that the scenes which he used had either not appeared in the original film (perhaps the result of distorted recall) or, since he has most recently seen the film on television, may have been cut for commercials.

An important area of borrowing from movies is found with regard to cinematic genres. The major genres treated in *Un oficio del Siglo 20* exercise considerable influence on *Tres tristes tigres*. The musical has already received some attention in the present study, as has the detective film; but the horror film or thriller, the comedy, and the Western are also quite important.

The imagery of fear and of nightmare associated with the thriller recurs in the book in several circumstances, some less comic than others. The nightmare of Códac about La Estrella is rather comic because of its context, while the scene in which Silvestre looks at the aquarium (336-38), an episode which recalls *The Lady from Shanghai*, is not so humorous. Generally, the fear imagery is associated with animals and especially with marine ones.[35] Animals, after all, are the prototypes of the threatening gods of myth (see Kirk 50-52) and are the essential figures of much nightmare and fears of darkness.[36] Cabrera Infante in fact ascribes the strong mythic appeal of the Paul Muni *Scarface* to the fact that the figure of Camonte seems animalistic:

> *Scarface* tiene, en realidad, yo creo que...por la presencia de Paul Muni...esa calidad mitológica, por una concepción del *gangster* como algo más primitivo que un hombre primitivo, como algo...que pertenece al mundo de los monos, más que...al mundo del ser humano. (Interview with author; my ellipsis)

The scene in which Silvestre watches the aquarium is chilling despite its faint campiness because of its self-conscious mention of film names and situations. The chill comes from the flashback experienced by Silvestre in which he connects his childhood to his present visual sensations through a chain of associations leading from a ray, a type of fish, to Dracula (a relationship of physical resemblance), through Dracula to a crucifix, and through a crucifix to the truly frightening image (particularly for a child) of "mi tío que en un acceso de furia blasfema rompió su cadena-detente..." (336-37). The sense of fear is dissipated, however, by means of the comic ending to the story about his uncle, who was so frightened by *Dracula* that he began a frantic search for the crucifix:

> ...cuando vino del cine de ver El Vampiro andaba como el Mad Doctor por el patio con un farol en la mano, Diógenes cristiano y jorobado y nocturno, buscando el crucifijo por todo el orbe hortense y no se fue a dormir hasta que lo encontró.... (337)

The film imagery presented in the aquarium scene not only operates on the level of memory and presents a childlike view of fear but also relates to the fear felt by Silvestre towards Cué, whose masculinity seems, like that of the monsters in the films, to devour women. The fact that Silvestre relives or recalls his childhood perspective on the movies *Dracula*, *The Mark of Dracula*, *King Kong*, *Cat People*, and *The Leopard Man*, all of which concern rape or domination, is not only quite realistic since most people have stored memories of frightening movies from their childhood, but also represents in fictional form the process by which Cabrera Infante admits to having been heavily influenced by the films of Val Lewton, the important producer of horror movies:

> Val Lewton es, en realidad, un generador de imágenes en el cine que yo no vine a conocer hasta que ya yo era mayor, aunque yo absorbí todas estas películas...y sobre todo el *Leopard Man*, que está casi narrada totalmente en *Tres tristes tigres*.... y lo mismo que esa, digamos, colección de imágenes influyó mucho a Manuel Puig,...tuvo una gran influencia también en mí...en determinado momento, en los años cuarenta, era un niño capaz de sentir miedo ante esas películas, pero al mismo tiempo buscarlas como una suerte de droga. Eso le ocurrió a Puig, eso pasa conmigo. (Interview with author; my ellipsis)

The remarks of Cabrera Infante in *Un oficio del Siglo 20* on the importance of nostalgia in the perspective of film critics acquire added depth from the filmic reveries of Silvestre.

The other movie recalled here by Silvestre, *The Thing*, is of a somewhat different order. The film can be seen as an allegory on McCarthyism and the irrational xenophobia of the America of the 1950s.[37] Certainly the Cuba of Batista was, like the contemporary society of the United States, no stranger to xenophobia and political abuse and paranoia. In such a context, the remarks of Silvestre on the movie, revealing a perspective more adult than his childish viewpoint on the other thrillers, become easily comprehensible:

> ...cuando llegué al cine Actualidades el 21 de julio de 1944 había ocho o diez personas sentadas separadas, pero poco a poco, sin darnos cuenta, nos fuimos juntando en un grupo y a la mitad de la película [*The Leopard Man*] éramos un ovillo de ojos botados y manos crispadas y nervios destrozados, unidos allí en las delicias del pavor falsificado del cine, igual que cuando vi en el Radiocine el 3 de enero de 1947 La Cosa de Otro Mundo, que pasó lo mismo, pero era un terror diferente que sentí, que sentíamos, que sintió el grupo apelotonado en medio de la tertulia, un terror que ahora sé que es menos atávico, un terror actual, casi político... vieron, vimos, vi, que era redondo, que parecía un plato, que era, sí eso: *una nave del espacio exterior.* ¡Ellos! (338; original emphasis; my ellipsis)[38]

The imagery used in the second part of the reverie, with expressions such as "apelotonado,"[39] contrasts in its suggestion of political terror with the picture of physical fear presented by visions such as "manos crispadas," which leave an impression of a group of ordinary people seeing a horror movie.

Where the horror film helps to show the dark underside of the life of Silvestre, including his rivalry with Cué, the comedy film often serves to depict them at their best in terms of comradeship. The major importance of comedy films here revolves around the dialogue between the two friends, who have developed a sort of detached, bantering rivalry. Thus, the two directly imitate the non-sequitur dialogue of Abbott and Costello when trying to amuse the two prostitutes whom they have picked up.[40] The reference to the comedy team is explicit, setting the stage for a meandering dialogue very reminiscent of their films (387-90).

Cabrera Infante has stated to Rita Guibert that he was "doing nothing else" in *Tres tristes tigres* but following the philosophy of the Marx Brothers (see above, 31). The generally flippant attitude of the main characters of the book, as Levine notes (561), certainly fits into the class of humor used by the Marxes. While the use of puns can certainly be of literary inspiration, the particular brand of give and take between Silvestre and Cué is frequently quite reminiscent of that between Groucho and Chico. The emcee who introduces the book, speaking a Cuban-English jargon, exhibits a flippancy towards his audience which is rather like that of Groucho in his "public speaking" scenes, such as those from *Cocoanuts* and *Horse Feathers*.

The humorous dialogue between Cué and Silvestre is often cast into purely cinematic terms. Nowhere is this tendency more apparent than in their parody of the Western film genre when they are running low on money (373-74). The dialogue in the car appears in parodied Western English, with explicit references later on (379-80) to Cué as imitating Gary Cooper and to Silvestre as mimicking "Katy Jurado, en *High Noon*." Beba and Magalena, the prostitutes, are left out of the joke by dialogue such as the following:

—Sheriff Silver Starr, we're running outa gas.
Afectaba un acento tejano. Ahora era un marshal del oeste. O cheriff adjoint.
—Gas? You mean no gasoline?
—Horses all right. Trouble in July. I mean the silver, Starr. Long o'women but a little this side of short on moola or mazuma. Remember? A nasty by-product of work. We need some fidutia, pronto! (373)

Not only the use of Western accents but the activity of roaming through the streets seem not too far removed from the Western activity of wandering through towns on horseback.

The Western does have its importance for *Tres tristes tigres*, although this importance seems less extended than that of the other genres of film. If less extended, however, the influence of the Western on the book is no less intense than that of the horror film. In particular, the "duelo" in a "café"[41] which Silvestre witnessed as a youth on the way to a Ken Maynard serial takes on an intensified reality when applied to the context in which the incident is recounted. Silvestre narrates the story of a gunfight between a man named

Cholo and a rival, two men who "Habían sido amigos y ahora eran enemigos y entre ellos había ese odio que hay solamente entre rivales que fueron una vez camaradas" (436). One of the men is killed in front of Silvestre, a real scene which seems pallid to him when compared to the movie he sees a little later (436-37).

The analogy is not difficult to draw. Cué and Silvestre, having been friends, are now possible enemies and are certainly rivals in love. The relationship between Silvestre and Laura, like that between "El crótalo misterioso, malvado, y la muchacha bella y pálida y virtuosa,"[42] seems more "real [ ]" than the "duel" between him and Cué (437). One of the more significant points about the parallel here is that neither relationship is valued in very real terms: one is placed in the realm of "sueño y . . . recuerdo" (437; my ellipsis),[43] while the other is a movie relationship despite being placed under the rubric of the real. Silvestre betrays here a romanticism rather typical of his nature and apparently totally foreign to the more hardened Cué.

Silvestre, as Nelson says, tends to associate movies with personalized or private experience more than do the other characters. Movies, nevertheless, are a benchmark against which practically every character in the book measures his experience. Códac, Eribó and the others tend to evaluate other characters and situations in terms of movies; for example, Códac listens to "'un saxofonista que parece el hijo del padre de Van Heflin con la madre de Jerry [sic] Mulligan y me pongo a oírlos tocar *Tonite at Noon'*" (130). The saxophonist must be compared to an actor as well as to a real saxophonist in order to seem real to Códac. The combination of Heflin and Mulligan actually lends ontological substance to the sax player. Códac sees him through his memory of the appearance of the actor and the famous jazzman. As with Silvestre, movies, or movies and show business, usurp for Códac, as well as for the other characters in the novel, the facts of, as Cabrera Infante says, "real life" (Interview with author).

The implications of such a reversal or substitution of ontological values are twofold. The more negative implication is that the protagonists of the novel, somewhat like Toto in *La traición de Rita Hayworth*, have begun to shut out the reality of La Habana, to interpret and revalue it in terms of the projected "reality" of another culture. Thus, as Phyllis Mitchell says, the characters are living in a mythical reality (25-28).[44] The second and related point is in some sense more positive or at least more neutral. Movies have become a true mythology for these characters and are in fact not so much an escape as a kind of creed and basis for culture. If movies are, then, in a sense an "escape" for these inhabitants of La Habana, they are no less healthy an escape, from their point of view, than the creeds of religion have been for many people.

The book does not hereby fall into vague spiritualism or a naïve apology for the movies. The notion of the substitution of movies for religion is in fact ironized by the remark of Cué that "«El cine es el opio de los espectadores»," an opinion which he offers with reference to "Gregory LaCavia," a parody of the name of the influential director Gregory La Cava (322). Nevertheless, an error of perception would be committed by seeing the novel as some sort of indictment of the effect exercised by mass culture on people with empty lives, or, more penetratingly, by admitting the palliative effect of the "opio" of movies but deploring their content. Cabrera Infante does neither, rather suggesting that movies are a viable and permanent part of world culture and that this is to be encouraged instead of denied.

Movies have in fact become a force for cultural unification, allowing the characters in *Tres tristes tigres*, for example, to speak a kind of *lingua franca*, full of its own meanings and implications, which cuts across social and national distinctions. As has been shown, Cabrera Infante will have none of the distinctions so often made between "pop" and "high" culture. One of the successes of *Tres tristes tigres* is, according to him, its equal valuation of all forms of culture:

> ....lo que *Tres tristes tigres* hace, a mi modo de ver, es llamar la atención acerca de[l] traspaso de elementos de una cultura popular a *high culture* sin llamar la atención de que se trata de un *high culture* en ningún sentido.... Entonces... eso es lo que... tenía *Tres tristes tigres*, para mí, personalmente, de importante.... (Interview with author; my ellipsis)

The easy admittance of the values of all cultural forms into the lives of the characters of the novel results from this attitude on the part of its author, and the problems and maladjustments of the characters cannot be imputed to some victimization by a monolithic mass culture. Movies, then, are not viewed in especially "camp" terms in *Tres tristes tigres*. Neither are they seen with undue reverence. They are simply a major part of the daily experience and the background of the people in the novel.

A variation on the approach to film which is seen in *Tres tristes tigres* will appear in *La Habana para un Infante Difunto*. Here, as Cabrera Infante has suggested in an interview with me, the narrator will directly attack and rebel against the institution of movies, much as Don Juan blasphemed against the Catholic Church. The treatment of film in the most voluminous work of Cabrera Infante, then, is our next subject of inquiry.

NOTES

[1] This tendency, with reference to "la mitología del cine," is noted by Guillermo and Hernández (27-28).

[2] In another article ("Mirrors"), Siemens connects Códac with "Korda... Cabrera Infante's photographer friend" (303 n 7; my ellipsis). Merrim calls Caín "the model for *TTT*'s Bustrófedon" (see *Logos* 75-76). The book by Merrim, as well as Scheybeler's study, includes some observations similar to mine. Since I came upon these works after my own book was in the final stages, I have not cited them extensively.

[3] Kirk dismisses such theories as having no empirical grounding (see esp. 69-79). Nevertheless, the fact that Cabrera Infante makes such a connection between film, dreams, and myths is the important point here.

[4] The link between this film and the work of Cabrera Infante through the similarity of sea imagery was suggested to me by Alvarez-Borland in *Discontinuidad* 125.

[5] Siemens also notes the fact that "the dream is a personal reworking of *The Old Man and the Sea*" and provides some analysis of the transformations in the sequence. His analysis is not, however, cinematic (*Language and Creativity* 77-78). Notice also the pun on the title, "'El Viejo y el Mal'" ('mar-mal'), which appears on p. 411 of the novel.

[6] I owe the suggestion about "fat" to Eliana Rivero.

[7] The reference is to the love scene between Cary Grant and Grace Kelly in *To Catch a Thief*. Siemens, *Worlds* 149, comments on this scene but does not connect it specifically to *To Catch a Thief*. The scene also recalls *Notorious*, which has Grant and Bergman but no fireworks effects.

[8] "'—*Tres tristes tigres* se propuso, antes que nada, explorar una nostalgia, al tiempo que celebraba una ciudad perdida: La Habana'" (Cabrera Infante, Interview with Montaner 166). Referring further to La Habana, he says, in terms which are relevant to both books, that:

> ...yo padezco tremendas nostalgias de La Habana, pero no de la Habana real, la que está ahí, sino de una Habana histórica que se perdió en el pasado. Quizás sea esta tierra mítica la única que necesito. Pero siempre puedo reconstruirla en la memoria, y también en esa forma de memoria que es la literatura. (168)

I am indebted to Eliana Rivero for these citations, and for other suggestions concerning this chapter and the sources used in it.

9 Nelson ("*Tres tristes tigres* 18-19) also notes the use of *"la mémoire involontaire"* in the passage and cites part of the quotation which appears directly below in this study.

10 See the comments of Amengual on time and *Vertigo* (esp. 45-46). He speaks of "une victoire sur le temps" (46).

11 For the origin of my ideas on space, time, and film and literature, see Bluestone 56-64.

12 The nature of this technique in *Vertigo* was explained to me in a course at the University of Arizona by Dr. Ron Stottlemyer. A "dolly shot" involves movement of the camera: "Dolly Shot (n.). Shot taken while the camera is in motion on a truck or dolly" (Lindgren 306). Cabrera Infante provides a good explanation of this type of shot: "...es ese momento en que la cámara, moviéndose lentamente, se acerca a un determinado objeto o a un determinado actor" (Interview with author; see below, 147, for another mention of the dolly shot). The use of the "zoom" technique is defined by Reisz and Millar as "To magnify a chosen area of the image by means of a zoom lens (variable focal length) so appearing to move the camera closer to the subject" (402). Thus, for the example from *Vertigo* referred to here, Hitchcock has told François Truffaut that, to achieve the desired effect,

> The viewpoint must be fixed, you see, while the perspective is changed as it stretches lengthwise. I thought about the problem for fifteen years [after a failure to achieve the similar effect in *Rebecca*]. By the time we got to *Vertigo*, we solved it by using the dolly and zoom simultaneously. (Hitchcock 187)

See also Monaco, *How* 63 (cited in Prawer 208) for a discussion of the technique used here.

13 I am indebted to Eliana Rivero for the concepts and the phrasing of this sentence.

14 Examples of films by these directors appearing in the book are: *Lust for Life* by Minnelli (95); *Spellbound* (443) and *Vertigo* (305-06) (while the film is not mentioned, the reference to it seems quite deliberate) by Hitchcock; *Tiger Shark* (351-52) and *The Thing* (338) by Hawks (see Brosnan and Willis 140-47 for Hawks and the direction of *The Thing*).

15 See Ferguson, esp. chapter 4 (126-53) for a study of gamesmanship in *Tres tristes tigres*.

16 Cabrera Infante also says, in accord with his remarks in the lecture, that "'... TTT fue una intención fallida de hacer novela policial por otros medios: los cuerpos del delito, un asesinato temprano, las pistas falsas y, sobre todo, su *cherchez la femme* ...'" (Cabrera Infante, "Viaje" 55).

17 Nelson, in "*Tres tristes tigres* y el cine," suggested to me the connection between Silvestre and Laura and their link with Cué. She concurs with me on other points such as the use of Proust and of time and space. The remarks of Cabrera Infante quoted here were made on 21 November 1985 in his class at Wellesley College.

[18] In this connection, the following remarks by Malcuzynski are supportive:

> TTT is primarily a series of *formal* manipulations by which the object of the artistic representation becomes the creative process of organizing the structure of the text.... The "Prólogo" sets the scene for the whole novel [much as does the newsreel at the beginning of *Citizen Kane*] on at least two different levels of the text. (35; my ellipsis)

Referring to the "characterization" of Bustrófedon, Malcuzynski says:

> The novel's sections called "Rompecabeza" and "La muerte de Trotsky referida por varios escritores cubanos, años después-o-antes" ...are *structuralizations* of his polyvalent nature: Bustrófedon's characterization comes to be an analogy of the structuring processes of the novel. (38; my ellipsis)

[19] Eliana Rivero suggests the interesting similarity between the awareness of the Godard characters of themselves as playing parts and the experience undergone in "some oneiric occurrences," in which it is possible to "see" oneself as being in a dream.

[20] Cabrera Infante has also said of *Tres tristes tigres* that "'Preferiría yo que todos consideren al libro solamente una broma que dura cerca de 500 páginas'" (*Siete voces* 424).

[21] The reference to "detective structure" is derived from the remarks of Cabrera Infante in his class at Wellesley College.

[22] Cabrera Infante also mentioned the link with Beiderbecke in an interview with me at Wellesley.

[23] Nelson, in "*Tres tristes tigres*," comes to conclusions identical to mine concerning the camera analogy and points out the link to *The Lady in the Lake*.

[24] Not having seen the film, I owe this information to my father and am indebted to Dr. Ron Stottlemyer for applying the concept of "subjective camera" to the movie.

[25] Here is made an obscure connection to *Un oficio del Siglo 20*, in which Caín is said to suffer from what Carlos Clarens once referred to as "'*el* síndrome de [Norma] Talmadge'" (31; original emphasis).

[26] Rivero argues that, in this novel, "no existe una sola figura femenina que no se halla, directa o indirectamente, perfilada en relación a su interés o conducta sexual, sea como actor o como espectador-*voyeur*" (284). The female characters in the book are indeed evaluated in sexual terms and can be seen, in general, as foils for the men. Rivero makes this point in saying that "...los [personajes] femeninos...no son figuras de acción y ni siquiera—en la mayoría de los casos—de habla propia determinante" (282; my ellipsis). This state of affairs does not differ greatly from that found in the traditional Hollywood film, which "is a rich field for the mining of female stereotypes" (Haskell 30). In *Tres tristes tigres* as in the Hollywood cinema, certain female characters, while fitting into a scheme of types or of stereotyped objects, nevertheless exhibit individual qualities which suffice to make them

memorable on their own terms (e.g., La Estrella in *Tres tristes tigres*, Brigid O'Shaughnessy [Mary Astor] in *The Maltese Falcon*, Elsie [Rita Hayworth] in *The Lady from Shanghai*).

[27] Bonnie Frederick states that

> The domination by the United States was a domination by means of commercialism. Practically no manufactured items were Cuban in origin, breeding a dependence on the United States and at the same time stifling Cuban economic growth. (27)

Giordano makes a similar point concerning the "devaluation" of Cuban culture relative to that of the United States (see, e.g., 165).

[28] I am indebted for the idea of *lingua franca* to Mitchell, who also applies the notion to Puig (25-26). Rodríguez Monegal ("New" 47) uses the same phrase.

[29] He also apparently assumed a readership who shared a common pop music culture. On almost every page, a line or word is taken from a *bolero* or song. This could escape a reader unfamiliar with the song lyrics. (I owe these last two points to Eliana Rivero.)

[30] Cabrera Infante also refers, in the *"Advertencia"* to *Tres tristes tigres*, to the difficulty of understanding the book due to the culturally specific nature of its language: *"El libro está en cubano.... predomina como un acento el habla de los habaneros y en particular la jerga nocturna, que, como en todas las grandes ciudades, tiende a ser un idioma secreto"* (9; original emphasis; my ellipsis). Guillermo and Hernández also refer to the restrictive effect of the allusions (46).

[31] In fact, as Eliana Rivero pointed out to me, Cabrera Infante calls *Tres tristes tigres* "'el escape como espectáculo'" (Interview with Montaner 170).

[32] Siemens notes this fact in *Worlds* 160.

[33] In answer to a question by this interviewer as to whether he thought specifically of film technique when writing, he replied, "No. No necesaria-mente."

[34] Nelson, in *"Tres tristes tigres* y el cine," reaches a conclusion similar to mine concerning the use of film technique by Silvestre on el Malecón.

[35] Frye points out the demonic imagery associated with animals, frequently marine ones, and the sea, in *Great Code* 151-52. For dragon and Leviathan imagery, relevant here, see esp. *Great Code* 186-93.

[36] The Hammer film *Five Million Years to Earth* offers an interesting treatment of these notions in the context of insect inhabitants of Mars who could have, as the fiction of the movie suggests, been the origin of our fear of horned demons.

[37] This idea is derived in part from the comments of Thomson with regard to *Invasion of the Body Snatchers* (225-26). See also the review of *Invasion of the Body Snatchers* by Ernesto G. Laura, in which he says "... that allegory is the key to *Invasion of the Body Snatchers* ..." and notes "the facile McCarthyism" in the book which served as the source for the movie (72; my ellipsis; see also 71). Merrim also notes the connection by Cabrera Infante of horror films

with politics but refers especially to *I Walked with a Zombie* and *Invasion of the Body Snatchers*, without mention of McCarthyism: "Hence Silvestre portrays Cué the *poseur* as a pod from 'The Body Snatchers' [sic] and the political *desaparecidos* as zombies, while images of vampires, underwater creatures, martians [sic] and panther women proliferate ("Through" 301; original emphasis. See also 306, 308.).

[38] The exclamation "¡Ellos!" comically recalls the screams of the little girl in the science-fiction film *Them!* (1954) after giant ants have killed her parents. Note the additional link to demonic animal imagery.

[39] This word as used in Cuba, Eliana Rivero has told me, does not necessarily have the connotation of "before a firing squad." Nevertheless, such an interpretation does exist in Spanish.

[40] Merrim interprets the episode somewhat differently (see *Logos* 79-80): "...Cué and Silvestre contrive to speak a language unknown to the women, thereby purposely alienating them."

[41] Nelson, in *"Tres tristes tigres* y el cine" (2-3), refers to the "duelo," drawing a conclusion which agrees with mine about the greater reality of film for Silvestre. She does not connect the incident to the Silvestre-Cué rivalry. I use her terminology of "café."

[42] Perhaps some reference to such a relationship (parodic, of course) between the Mae West and Joseph Calleia characters in *My Little Chickadee* is intended.

[43] See 420-21 of *Tres tristes tigres* for the dream with which Silvestre associates Laura on p. 434.

[44] Frederick says that "The island and its people have lost their identity, taking on instead a borrowed one from a foreign culture" (30). Julio Rodríguez-Luis negatively evaluates *Tres tristes tigres* because of its failure in escaping from the cultural domination of the United States, in which, he claims, it actually participates:

> Si *TTT* falla en su empeño es, a mi ver, porque su estupenda adaptación literaria de la cámara cinematográfica y de la grabadora—del cine sonoro—no consigue trascender, apropriándoselo, ni el modelo literario original, el *Ulysses*, ni tampoco el cine, la fascinación con el cual en cuanto ventana al mundo del capitalismo avanzado, impide que se lo adapte eficazmente al propósito de construir una novela que trastorne nuestra noción del género. Burlándose del subdesarrollo, *TTT* lo subraya: lo que leemos es una versión insular o provinciana de la alta cultura, mas ininteligible fuera del medio original. (98)

Giordano makes a similar point about shutting out La Habana (see esp. 164-69).

7

La Habana para un Infante Difunto

F MAJOR IMPORTANCE in considering the role played by film in *La Habana para un Infante Difunto* is the concept of parody. While the narrator preserves some of the genuine interest felt by earlier characters and personae of Cabrera Infante towards movies, his prevailing attitude becomes one of cynicism and disenchantment. Despite his analogies between women 'in La Habana and actresses, and his frequent references to films which evidently interest him greatly, movies receive a treatment which is often ironic or ambivalent. This treatment fits well with the rather negative tone of the book, in which parody serves as an important mechanism for the establishment of irony.

The narrator cannot, or will not, live uncritically in the film fantasies which had so absorbed Silvestre in *Tres tristes tigres*. Despite the large degree to which the narrator indulges in film culture, he does not seem, like Silvestre, to elevate the reality of film stars and figures so that their power overshadows the characters in the book. To an extent, the narrator uses movies to escape from or to obscure reality, as does Silvestre, who, "In choosing to act out his feelings in terms of the cinema," "effectively removes himself from the situation" (Frederick 25).

Both Silvestre and the narrator of *La Habana para un Infante Difunto* use movies to shunt reality to one side. Silvestre is more thoroughgoing in this activity than is the narrator. Since Silvestre does not like the reality around him, which includes disagreements and jealousies with Cué over Laura, he prefers to live in his movie reveries. The narrator, on the other hand, uses movies more as comparison points or familiar markers to orient him in an often confusing but very full and present reality, the city of La Habana, which strikes the reader of the novel as abundantly alive and often very satisfying to the narrator.

The strong presence of the urban environment for the narrator of *La Habana para un Infante Difunto* is to be seen in his presentation of women. He frequently compares the girls or women he has known at different stages in his life to actresses.[1] The women known by the hero are, however, not pale versions of movie figures, since they often have their own memorable qualities which are added to the mythifying of the actresses to whom they are compared. His analogies to actresses are wide-ranging, covering varied types of stars. The effect of the technique is to universalize the women of La Habana for the narrator, placing them into the movie culture which has a special meaning for him.

An instance of movie analogy which demonstrates the special qualities possessed by some of the women of La Habana for the protagonist is that of Zenaida, one of his neighbors as a youth. He establishes an analogy between her and Valli, "la actriz italiana" (*La Habana* 74) who appeared memorably in *The Third Man*. The comparison, however, is set in terms which heighten the reality of Zenaida in the memory of the narrator, for whom Valli becomes more a convenient point of reference for a girl who was fully realized as an image for him before seeing Valli in the movies and even meeting her later:

> De una muchacha indiferente [Zenaida] devino en días una mujer de rara belleza: blanca, con el pelo castaño rojizo y los ojos violeta...y precedió en sus rasgos a la popularización de la imagen de una estrella de cine europea captada por Hollywood y su máquina de mentiras maravillosas y rebautizada con su medio nombre italiano, Valli. Esta estrella en su declinar—de su fama de actriz, no como mujer: nunca la vi más bella que cuando la conocí— fue a caer en México. (72; my ellipsis)

The actresses sometimes receive ironic treatment through their comparison with the women and girls known to the narrator, thus becoming the subjects of parody. While this tendency was not absent from *Tres tristes tigres*, as in the remark by Cué that "«Soy la respuesta cubana a Fred Astaire»" (53), it is more pronounced in *La Habana para un Infante Difunto.* The actresses used as examples by the narrator seem to lose some of their sheen when linked to the often earthy women of the city.

The unequal juxtaposition of women in La Habana and movie stars is found to varying degrees in the book. For instance, the narrator repeatedly evaluates women known to him in terms of Hedy Lamarr. Examples of girls or women compared to Lamarr are Elvira (152-53) and Magaly (490-91). Magaly is mythified by her connection with the actress:

> ...y ahora ella devolvía mis besos con más técnica que pasión, lo que no me impidió gozar sus labios latinos, bien besados, y admirar de vez en cuando su perfecto perfil: toda la belleza que la hacía una copia cubana de Hedy Lamarr...Ella, con su pelo partido al medio, para ser la más exacta versión de la Venus vienesa, hasta se había agenciado un millonario que la compraría en cuerpo y cara—porque alma nunca tuvo. (491; my ellipsis)

The actress is seen as an essence of beauty which is incarnated in Magaly.[2] The narrator says that he could only evaluate the "exotic" appearance of Elvira in the movie terms familiar to him:

> Hoy diría que [Elvira] era bella, entonces me pareció exótica. Exótica en Cuba debía ser una sueca o alemana, pero mi vocabulario estaba sacado del cine y así Hedy Lamarr, embadurnada de maquillaje oscuro, era exótica en su imperecedera aparición como Tondelayo, la nativa de Malaya. [Notice the implied equivalence of Tondelayo with Elvira not only because of their link to Lamarr but because of their tropical provenance.] (152)

Elvira, however, had her own qualities which distinguished her from Lamarr:

> Pero Elvira (ése era su nombre: nunca supe su apellido: en Zulueta 408, como en el partido comunista entonces y luego en Hollywood, todo el mundo se llamaba por su nombre) era a su manera exótica pero no se parecía a Hedy Lamarr, mi amor gigante y en dos dimensiones. (152-53)

The only equivalent for Elvira who occurs to the narrator, apparently completely in retrospect, is María Félix:

> ...Elvira imitaba a María Félix o tal vez la prefiguraba [note the

similarity to the remarks about Elvira and Lamarr quoted above]
porque María Félix no era conocida en Cuba en esa época: quizá
fuera que María Félix encarnaba el epítome de la belleza de los
tiempos en América Latina. Pero María Félix fue celebrada como
María Bonita mientras Elvira no era considerada bonita por los
hombres del edificio y no creo que tampoco fuera bella con un
criterio cubano. (153)

Since María Félix was, he says, not famous in Cuba at the time of his
contact with Elvira, the narrator was apparently at a loss to evaluate
this woman who did not seem beautiful to him at the time, perhaps as
much because of her failure to fit his cinematic version of beauty as
because of her not meeting the "criterio cubano" for beauty.

An example of mythification of women through their connection
with actresses which has a particular significance within the system
of film allusions established by Cabrera Infante in his other work
concerns a girl named Chelo (*La Habana* 136-39). Unlike the analogy
between Hedy Lamarr and Magaly, the connection between Chelo
and Cesca, the sister of Tony Camonte in *Scarface*, was made by the
narrator only with hindsight:

(Años después me puse a analizar por qué me enamoré de Chelo y
descubrí que tenía su origen en su parecido con Ann Dvorak, la
impronunciable, casi caquéctica hermana de Paul Muni en
Caracortada, que fue uno de mis amores de sombras en mis años
infantiles.). (138)

The similarity between the characters is extended by the alliteration
of their names, since the 'C' in Cesca is pronounced 'ch' in Italian.[3]
The Cesca figure is dealt with at some length in *Arcadia todas las noches*,
during the discussion of *Scarface* found there (70-76).

An instance of a comparison between a woman of La Habana and
a movie star which is meant to indicate a negative valuation of the
pair is found with the character Dulce, taken repeatedly by the
narrator to a "posada" or house of assignation (463-83). The allusion
to the makeup worn by Dulce not only demythifies her but also
refers to the carnality of "early Dietrich" (in *The Blue Angel*) and the
artificial attempts at femininity by the "late Crawford" (for instance,
of *Whatever Happened to Baby Jane?*): "La besé bien duro olvidando su boca
pintada a lo Joan Crawford tardía o Marlene Dietrich temprana—..."
(466).

The tendency of the narrator to place women on a pedestal, making of them sexual objects by reference to movie stars, does not necessarily mean that they are seen by him in terms completely restricted to the characteristics of those actresses. A good example of the exhibition of individual qualities, or at least of qualities distinct from those of a film actress, by one of the women in the life of the narrator is found in the character of Carmina. Despite her resemblance to Hedy Lamarr, she maintains her own outlines for the narrator, much as did Zenaida:

> ...ella tenía el pelo negro, partido al medio y los ojos claros y aunque se veía que imitaba a Hedy Lamarr, mi fetiche femenino favorito, era también muy suya, su imagen más propia que apropiada. Estaban además sus labios indelebles que reían mucho, dejando ver una dentadura blanca, perfecta, saludable, que era su mayor atractivo. (253)

As seen from the above examples, the narrator does not uniformly evince a reverent or uncritical attitude towards movie stars or, by extension, towards movies. While he uses films as reference points or cultural markers, and while his interest in them is substantial, he has stepped over into a mode of discourse concerning movies and life which allows him, unlike Silvestre in *Tres tristes tigres*, to desecrate or mock the "temple" of film.

Cabrera Infante has spoken at some length of the contrast between *La Habana para un Infante Difunto* and *Tres tristes tigres* with regard to the "sacred" status of movies. He has elaborated on the importance of film myths in the two books and on the differing approaches apparent in each case:

> ...la presencia de....mitos encarnados—es decir, mitos de veras creados por el cine—porque es exactamente igual que como se crearon los mitos en la Grecia Antigua—a partir de un determinado ser humano, que.... se convierte en un héroe, ese héroe se convierte en un dios, y ese dios genera su propio mito. Y esto es lo que está siendo utilizado mucho en *Tres tristes tigres*, al revés ... por ejemplo, de *La Habana para un Infante Difunto*, donde hay una presencia mayor del cine como lugar adonde se va como sitio de reunión social, y esto apenas aparece en.... *Tres tristes tigres*. (Interview with author; my ellipsis)

The local movie house, in its function as a "sitio de reunión social," is also the site of many pursuits of women by the narrator. He engages in burlesquing the myths of film. Such actions, despite their reversal of any reverent tone towards film, are signals to the reader familiar with the film criticism of Cabrera Infante, who has spoken of the cinema in religious terms, characterizing the local movie house as the site where such religious feeling may be experienced: "...digo que si hay una ocasión mágica, si hay un momento en que el juego se hace religión, ese milagro ocurre todas las noches y se llama cine, *le cinéma, the movies*" (*Arcadia* 181). The narrator of *La Habana para un Infante Difunto* refers to a movie house as "este alto templo de la religión del cine" (99); but the reference is tinged with a certain irony because the theater has a "Vestal Virgin" attending its rites who nevertheless has connections for the narrator with less than virtuous situations:

> La primera vez que visité este alto templo de la religión del cine (con estrellas luminosas en el cielorraso) oficiaba felizmente, vestal vestida, Ingrid Bergman, que había sido mi amor perverso desde que vi su espalda marcada mórbida en *El hombre y la bestia*, amada simiescamente por Mr. Hyde,[4] contra quien concebí unos celos solamente desplazados por la envidia que sentí por Humphrey Bogart en *Casablanca*. (99)

The attitude of the narrator towards movies is revealed as somewhat different from that of most of the characters in *Tres tristes tigres* by his use of theaters as places for seduction. Cabrera Infante has pointed out the similarity of the narrator to Don Juan, in this instance a Don Juan who desecrates the "temple" of the movies:

> En parte....[el cine] es un lugar sagrado ...En *La Habana para un Infante Difunto* es mi intento de re-escribir desde un punto de vista habanero el mito de Don Juan.... Creo que...es muy visible en el libro. Pero—Don Juan era también originalmente el Burlador de Sevilla. Es decir, Don Juan se burlaba de la iglesia, se burlaba de los muertos. Y, en realidad, el personaje....sin nombre de *La Habana para un Infante Difunto* se burla un poco del templo del cine, que es—un teatro. (Interview with author; my ellipsis)[5]

A good instance of such blasphemy occurs near the end of the book, during its final seduction scene:

> Le toqué un brazo para llamar su atención pero no atendía. Lo único que le interesaba era el maldito espectáculo—y así me encontré blasfemando al maldecir el cine en un cine. Me quedé paralizado por el terror religioso. (700)

Later in the scene, he says, after disturbing the other patrons in the theater, that: "Mandaban a callar de todas partes del cine, en un comportamiento extraordinario, como si estuviéramos en una iglesia y todos los congregados fueran feligreses feroces—¡yo era el pagano en el templo!" (701-02).

The motif of the narrator as a defiler of the movies is cemented by the epigraph of the book, a quotation from *King Kong* which reads:

> CARL DENHAM (after taking a good
> look at the natives):
> "Blondes seem to be pretty
> scarce around here".
> *King Kong* (9)[6]

The reference to the lack of blondes not only establishes an analogy between primitive Africa, the setting of the first part of *King Kong,* and La Habana, a city in which the narrator is certain to be at least somewhat frustrated in his search for true blondes, but also has mythic resonance. Cabrera Infante has spoken of "la tradición aria del gusto por los cabellos rubios" as containing "el mito de Tristán e Isolda" (*Arcadia* 80). Hollywood has become notorious for propagating the latter-day versions of the blonde mystique, as many of the figures in its corpus of film myths, such as Harlow, Lombard, and Monroe, demonstrate.

In such a context, a reference such as the epigraph quoted above, applied to the book and by extension to La Habana itself, could constitute a comment on the lack of Hollywood myths and consequently of the force exerted on the narrator by the "religion" of movies. The narrator lends some credence to such a view about the "scarcity of blondes" when he says that "Es verdad que había en Cuba un culto a la mulata, sobre todo en su aspecto sexual, pero ésta era una actitud masculina" (51). Such an interpretation accords well with the indication by Cabrera Infante that the narrator is a Don Juan who blasphemes against movies, since Don Juan, for all his blaspheming, was yet fascinated with the object of his sacrilege. So too the narrator, in the midst of his desecrations, seeks the blondes who form such an important part of the Hollywood pantheon.

The Don Juanism of the narrator is not only indulged in through the actual pursuit of women but in the practice of voyeurism. A chapter of the book is entitled "La visión del mirón miope" (394-415), and contains the exploits of the narrator as he practices "la violación visual del voyeur" (401).

The fact that the narrator is an adept at "el arte de mirar" (398) is hardly surprising, since he is also a devotee of the film. The inference is easily drawn: film viewing is suggested to be a voyeuristic activity, another function of the donjuanesque desire for power over women which overt voyeurism also satisfies. The narrator is not alone in his voyeurism, since, as he says, "En La Habana, donde el voyeurismo era una suerte de pasión nativa, como el canibalismo entre los caribes, no había una palabra local para describir esta ocupación que a veces se hacía arte popular" (400). He does, however, exhibit an aestheticized preoccupation with the habit which lends it an obsessive quality: "Curiosamente esto era lo más excitante de la caza visual: aguardar a que se produjera un desnudo, no importaba si parcial o total, ofrecido a la vista, era más excitante que la presencia del cuerpo desnudo" (401).

In his role as voyeur, the narrator notes his similarity to the James Stewart character, "inválido con un ojo único de largo alcance, en *La ventana indiscreta* [*Rear Window*]..." (407). He differs from the Stewart character, he says, in that

> Descubrí varias escenas caseras (ninguna tan interesante como las que se revelaron a James Stewart...pero tampoco tenía yo una Queen Kelly, Grace under pressure, que viniera a darme un blondo beso lento para distraerme de los diversos espectáculos vistos por las ventanas, y así me pasaba las noches libres ejerciendo mi solitaria afición voyeurista) que podían ser patéticas o dramáticas pero que a esa distancia, sin el auxilio del sonido, resultaban terriblemente aburridas. (407; my ellipsis)

Here he reveals a very significant difference between himself and the hero of *Rear Window*. The narrator evaluates the "escenas caseras" seen by him only in aesthetic terms, showing no doubts as the morality of his enterprise. The protagonists of *Rear Window*, in contrast, voice their doubts about watching the lives of other people; and, for the heroes of the movie as for the audience, the activity is only morally justified because a crime has been committed and is solved thanks to the prying of the Stewart character.[7] No such justification is offered or, apparently, even contemplated by the amoral narrator of *La Habana para un Infante Difunto*.

The narrator has less respect for the privacy of others than for the "temple" of film. He exhibits an aesthetically determined approach similar to that of the Seducer, the Don Juan figure of *Either/Or* by Kierkegaard. The narrator says that he has no interest in the "escenas caseras" because, like silent movies in the opinion of Caín in *Un oficio del Siglo 20* (242-43),

> ...a esa distancia, sin el auxilio del sonido, resultaban terrible-mente aburridas. Aun de haberlas podido oír con oído telescópico, sé que habrían sido diálogos como éstos: "¿Trajiste el pan?" "No, mi amor. Se me olvidó, perdona." "¡Comemierda! ¿Cuántas veces voy a decirte que debes apuntar los mandados?" "Ya lo sé, mi vida, pero es que con tantas cosas en la cabeza"—que serían otra tanta basura en mi cabeza: neorrealismos, mientras yo buscaba lo extraordinario en la vida cotidiana. (*La Habana* 407-08)[8]

His search for "lo extraordinario" fits him quite well for a role like that of the Seducer, who says, disparaging grown women as being dull, that:

> ...I constantly seek my prey [note the vampiric overtones] among young girls, not among young women. A woman is less natural, more coquettish; an affair with her is not beautiful, not interesting; it is piquant, and the piquant is always the last stage—I had never expected to be able again to taste the first fruits of infatuation. I am submerged in love, I have been given what swimmers call a ducking; no wonder that I am a little dazed. So much the better, so much the more I promise myself from this affair. (*Either/Or* 320)

Both the Seducer and the narrator of the book by Cabrera Infante try to fill up their essential hollowness by pursuing women, visually as well as physically.

As Cabrera Infante has pointed out when speaking to William L. Siemens, *La Habana para un Infante Difunto* does not glorify the exploits of its narrator but rather shows his constant disillusionment as a result of his erotic pursuits:

> This book is really the chronicle of Don Juan's failure, and this
> is one thing that the militant feminists who have criticised it have
> missed. This is true even when he is "successful."...
>
> The accusation of *machismo* or sexism is only possible in the
> present day, and my narrator doesn't live in the present day; he
> acts and lives and speaks as a man of his time and place. It must be
> recognized that the narrator lives in a different epoch from ours,
> one in which there is no equality between women and men, least
> of all in the Cuba of those days. ("Caín" 10-11; my ellipsis)

The women who are the subjects of his interest often disappoint him
by being less than ideal either as love or as carnal objects (a dilemma
shared by the men in *Tres tristes tigres*). While he compares several of
the women in the book to actresses who attained mythic stature, for
instance, the "imitation" of Hedy Lamarr by Carmina (253), the
comparisons are largely physical and become ironic by the obvious
and inevitable failings of the women to become such goddesses. The
overall effect contributes to a tarnishing of the mythology of
Hollywood.

Hollywood myths, despite the critical attitude with which they are
sometimes treated in the book, as in the evaluation of Joan Crawford
and Marlene Dietrich cited above (*La Habana* 466), still form an
important element in the life of the narrator, who, says Cruz
Hernández, "...has an enormous passion for films..." (40). The
generic preferences shown by Cabrera Infante in his critical work and
in his other works of fiction are present as well in this book.

The detective and gangster genres are well represented here. The
narrator mentions at some length (97-98) the women who populate
"el cine negro," or the *film noir*, "a type of film that is characterized by
its dark, somber tone and cynical, pessimistic mood" (Katz, *Film* 418).[9]
These were often detective, thriller, or gangster movies. The narrator
shows an interest in several of the actresses who appeared in this
kind of film, naming not only Gail Russell and Veronica Lake but also
several others: "...no otras actrices sino otras mujeres: Priscilla Lane,
Anne Sheridan, Joan Leslie, Brenda Marshall, Ida Lupino y la falsa y
fatal Mary Astor: un amor en cada parte" (98; my ellipsis).[10]

Besides his specific reference to *film noir*, the narrator mentions
other examples of detective and gangster movies. These include
Double Indemnity and *The Postman Always Rings Twice* (214); *Mientras la
ciudad duerme* (*The Asphalt Jungle* [248]), an important film for Cabrera

Infante (see *Siete voces* 410; *Oficio* 156, 158); *The Third Man* (e.g., 254); *Dead End* (27); and *The Suspect* (214).

Of particular importance is his reference to Edward G. Robinson and Paul Muni as examples for him of gangsters (29-30). He says, alluding to *The Whole Town's Talking*, that:

> Más que el inolvidable Paul Muni de *Caracortada*, Robinson vendría a personificar al gangster, tanto como a su revés; el hombre ingenuo: uno todo sabiduría del mal, el otro todo ignorancia en el bien—y aquí estaban los dos a un tiempo, el malvado y el doble que es su contrario. (30)[11]

The "double" motif, important elsewhere in the work of Cabrera Infante (see Nelson, "El doble"), appears here with marked significance because of the dual nature of the narrator himself. Outwardly, he is a more or less bourgeois young man who works as a movie critic.[12] But he pursues another career, that of a Don Juan, often deceiving his wife or his parents about his activities (see, e.g., 200-01).

Another genre figuring prominently in the book is the horror or thriller film. Thus, the narrator mentions movies such as *Dr. Jekyll and Mr. Hyde* (99, 556) and refers to Larry Talbot, the protagonist of *The Wolf Man* and its sequels (471, 478). The narrator in fact implies an identification between himself and the Wolf Man. In a scene reminiscent of the original film, the narrator is in a room with his companion at the time, Dulce, and sees the moonlight after she opens a window: "Dulce salió disparada de la cama y se fue hacia la ventana. La abrió y por ella entró la luna, todavía llena, *like the moon that cursed Larry Talbot*" (471; original emphasis). The Wolf Man was afraid to marry his fiancée because of his condition, in which he became a wolf and killed the people (especially the women) he loved. His fear of transformation relates to the destructive release of his libido;[13] perhaps the narrator has a similar fear or wants to portray himself, whimsically, as such a potentially destructive person. He also uses imagery (523-27) which connects him to vampirism and to films like *Dracula*: " . . . así el sábado por la tarde era una ocasión perfecta para una cita judía. ¿Era ella judía? No, ella era católica húngara: la cruz la defendería del vampiro" (523). The double motif appears again in connection with the horror movie references, in particular with regard to *Dr. Jekyll and Mr. Hyde*, *The Wolf Man*, and *Dracula. King Kong*, a horror film, is the central movie allusion in the book.

Westerns, comedies, and dramas also appear in the book. *The Razor's Edge* (182-83) and *Camille* (618) are examples of dramas mentioned here. The narrator refers to figures from comedy such as Buster Keaton (288); Laurel and Hardy (373); and Charles Chaplin, whose *The Gold Rush* is seen by the narrator and one of his girlfriends so that he can review it in *Carteles* (497). The Western is referred to explicitly in connection with an encounter with a girl "a la hora señalada":

> (no puedo evitar sonreír al escribir la frase que era el título habanero para *High Noon*: como si la confrontación de Gary Cooper y los cuatro villanos fuera una ocasión amorosa o como si mi cita cuasi amorosa fuera un duelo del oeste).... (550)

Musicals are also a significant part of the film references in the book. The narrator comments that:

> Había también las películas musicales. Entre las que recuerdo mejor están las de Carlos Gardel en que pululuban los tangos, muchos de ellos tan deprimentes que me producían una tristeza incoercible, sentimiento inolvidable. Por supuesto que veía muchos musicales americanos pero no guardo recuerdo de sus melodías, con excepción de la temprana tonada "La carioca", entre los pies parlantes de Fred Astaire y las piernas que cantan de Ginger Rogers. (106)

He also speaks in this context of his introduction to "la música americana":

> Vine a descubrir la música americana ya adolescente en Zulueta 408 (hubo un avance de lo que vendría en una película vista en el cine Actualidades, *Sun Valley Serenade*, que caminé desde la muy alejada cuartería de Monte 822 para verla—y, sobre todo, oírla), no sólo en las películas sino en las victrolas automáticas, como la radiante, multicolor, cromada Wurlitzer... Me hice un fanático de la orquesta de Glenn Miller (la culpa inicial la tuvo *Sun Valley Serenade*, pecadora originaria).... (106-07; my ellipsis)

His interest in dancing is connected to the musical through *An American in Paris* (643), recalling the great interest of Cabrera Infante in Vincente Minnelli; and, apparently, through *The Red Shoes*, which, though not referred to by name in this instance, is recalled by a reference to "las zapatillas rojas de la ballerina del cine" (492).

King Kong, itself a parodist as well as a generator of Hollywood myth, is the central film of the iconography of the book. The "love" story between King Kong and the Fay Wray character, a woman who is not so unsympathetic to the monster as she may appear, is of the same order as the love story presented in *Bride of Frankenstein*. Both parody Hollywood conventions of love stories, with their repetitive generic structures.[14] The central position of *King Kong* in the book places the narrator as a frustrated Beast who spends his life pursuing the elusive Beauty, seen in different disguises in the women of the book.

King Kong appears in the book in a concealed fashion during a discussion about Debussy (238-39). The fact that a hidden reference to a film which is itself parodic should appear in a less than serious discussion on Debussy lends comic depth to the book, for *La Mer* of Debussy is the music to which Julia and the narrator make love and which is subjected to considerable frivolous treatment at the hands of Branly, a friend of the narrator. Branly here, Cabrera Infante has said, becomes a kind of Erik Satie figure, making a sarcastic remark about Debussy which recalls the sarcasm of Satie about the music of the same composer.

The joking of Branly leads Catia to ask "—¿Es que es loco?", receiving the answer "—Es entusiasta." Here, *King Kong* is directly quoted by Cabrera Infante, a fact he revealed in a class lecture. The subject of the conversation in the movie is Carl Denham, the originator of the epigraph which introduces *La Habana para un Infante Difunto*. Denham is a movie entrepreneur who "discovers" Kong.

The concealment of a reference to a camp film such as *King Kong* within a passage which is quite ironic adds to the impression of satire given by the entire passage and gives an additional dimension to the section, which is a sort of résumé of the parodies used in the novel. The title of the book appears in the passage in disguised form, or rather in the form which it parodies, as *"'La pavana para un gracioso difunto'"* (*Pavane pour une infante défunte*) (238). The *Pavane* was itself, as Cabrera Infante pointed out in his class at Wellesley, a parody by Ravel of a Debussy piece. Ravel and Satie are significant to Cabrera Infante, he also said, because of their strong impulse towards parody. Satie in particular is a favorite of Cabrera because of his revolutionary and iconoclastic nature.

The *Bolero* of Ravel provides an interesting sidelight on the relationship between film and *La Habana*. In the movie *10*, as is well known, the *Bolero* was the background music and the catalyst for the seduction of the hero, played by Dudley Moore, by the ironically named Virginia (Bo Derek). Virginia, a married woman, has few scruples about extramarital affairs and seems rather indifferent about her husband. In *La Habana*, published before *10* was released, Julia insists on *La Mer* as lovemaking music during her affair with the narrator. Like Virginia, Julia is married and less than concerned about her husband. Both women play assertive roles in their relationships, Julia by manipulating the Don Juanism of the narrator and Virginia by overcoming the shy befuddlement of the songwriter played by Moore.

The similarities between the two plots are evident. Perhaps the filmmakers may even have been inspired by the novel. Cabrera Infante pointed out the similarities but did not assert that any plagiarism had occurred. In any case, the near identity of the situations is good evidence of the cinematic possibilities built into the work of Cabrera Infante. The scenes from the book seem as though they should have been written for the Blake Edwards film.[15]

The narrator, while ironic and "sacrilegious" about movies, is nevertheless imbued with their mystique and participates in it, at times seemingly without much consciousness of his involvement in the reference points of cinema. His comment that he was in one instance "siguiendo el consejo de Oliver Hardy a Stan Laurel y tratando de ser nonchalant" (373) is an example of his easy, nearly unconscious tendency to slip into film lore.

The narrator is often more deliberate in his usage of film terminology or allusion and in fact transfers to his Don Juanism the ambience of certain movies, placing himself in the position of a romantic martyred by unfeeling or indifferent women. While he is closer than he would perhaps care to admit to the great Don Juan figure of Kierkegaard, the aesthetically motivated Seducer of *Either/Or*, the narrator wishes to cast himself in the mold of the heroes of movies such as *The Third Man*, or even, in a rather different sense, of *King Kong*. The heroes or male protagonists of both movies suffer disillusionment or even death because of their passion, an unrequited one in both instances. The narrator identifies himself directly with the writer hero Holly Martins of *The Third Man*:

Así, como él, calamitoso Cotten, escritor engañado por su único amigo y despreciado por la mujer amada, me sentía yo caminando de regreso a mi casa, todavía tocado por la música de cítara...llevando conmigo su final infeliz. (254; my ellipsis)

The romantic Don Juanism of the narrator, which is seen in examples such as the link with *The Third Man*, is thoroughgoing. He is the blasphemer who loves the object of his blasphemy. Movies and women are the two objects of his sacrilege. He desecrates the "temple" of film by worshipping, or actually attempting to possess, another image, that of a woman, within its walls. Like the Don Giovanni of Mozart, he falls into an inferno at the end of the book; but the inferno is a grotesque one: the body of the woman whom he tries to seduce in a moviehouse. The dialectic between blasphemy and worship, as between condemnation and redemption, comes full circle here.

Surely it is not coincidental that King Kong, as one of the major film analogues of the narrator, falls to his death from the height of his masculine assertiveness, having taken the heroine to the top of the Empire State Building. Neither does the end of Harry Lime, the antihero and twisted double of *The Third Man* (who dies in the underworld of the Vienna sewers, thus allowing Holly Martins to play the role of a mock Orpheus by ascending to the light without a look back at his friend Lime only to lose his beloved because she does *not* look back at him), seem unrelated to the "fall" motif of the book.

Movies are a significant force in *La Habana para un Infante Difunto* in a manner more religious than *Tres tristes tigres*. The terms of the later book are very familiar to, say, a practicing Catholic; and movies are the backdrop against which the conflict between heaven and hell is played out. The conflict between the profane and sacred impulses of the narrator is expressed in terms which seem to recall the decadent attitudinizing of a Huysmans character, Des Esseintes, but which actually express on another level the contrast between, in the words of Cabrera Infante, "real life" and "Hollywood" (Interview with author):

...yo no quería ver París antes de morir, ni siquiera visitar París realmente: el París con que yo soñaba era aquel en que Gene Kelly enamoraba bailando a la deliciosa Leslie Caron—era el París de *Un americano en París*, un París hecho en Hollywood, el París del cine, no del Sena, éstos fueron mis únicos viajes de entonces.... (643)

Despite his separation of himself from "los fanáticos fundadores de la Cinemateca," the narrator does speak in the same passage of such matters as the religious fervor of the dancers in La Habana during a religious festival. The religious and the profane are mixed in the mind of the narrator, as the subtle mention of a dance film in the present connection attests.

The association of religious fervor with film, even in the rather oblique fashion which appears here, recalls the work of Manuel Puig, for whom "'Films are holy'" (Katz, *Symposium* 9). The attitude of the work of Puig is indeed, as Cabrera Infante has noted in conversation, very different from that of his own work. The key to the difference is aesthetic distance, or more precisely irony.

In *El beso de la mujer araña*, some close identification between one of the protagonists, Molina, and Puig is neither difficult to make nor even discouraged by Puig himself, who shares with his character much of his fascination with movies and a particular set of actresses (see Corbatta, *Mito* 59; Morando Maza 297; Stone 70). In *La Habana para un Infante Difunto*, on the other hand, the sense of artifice, of the use of genre to present a character who fits into a typology, in this case that of Don Juan, is everywhere present and discourages such identification, adding to the strong warnings given by Cabrera Infante about identifying the narrator with himself. The book becomes a treatise on, or a lampoon of, a fanatic possessed of a fascination for movies—a movie critic gone wild—and for women. Movies function much more complexly and subtly within the book than they do within the work of Puig; if they are in any sense a sacred text for the narrator, that text is desecrated in ways not to be tolerated by the fervent Molina.

La Habana develops and extends the role of film in the work of Cabrera Infante. The allusions to movies do not differ greatly from those in his earlier works, preserving the line of continuity from his critical work; but the game of satire and parody, of sustained comic play on a conceit, has become paramount in this book, placing movie myths at the service of debunking their own tradition as well as that of other myths surrounding sexual role. Movie myths are used to parody and to deflate the Don Juan myth as well as to form a subtext for the Menippean satire of which, as Nelson argues, the book is a fine example. An instance of the satiric nature of the enterprise can be seen when Cabrera Infante relates the page numbering directly to a film, with Edward G. Robinson, about the discovery of the cure for syphilis, called *Dr. Ehrlich's Magic Bullet*:

> It took me three years to finish this daft divertimento, which is now 606 pages long. As you remember, 606 is the number of the fantastic formula with which Dr. Ehrlich conquered syphilis, a concoction called the Magic Bullet by the good doctor Edward G. Robinson in the moving movie of the same name. It's my homage to their last failure, formula 605, Fracastoro's fracaso.... (Cabrera Infante, "From 5 to 7" 41-42)[16]

The syphilis reference is also amusing, given the promiscuity of the narrator.

The approach taken by Cabrera Infante in *La Habana para un Infante Difunto* is quite ironic with respect to film as well as to the characters in the book. The irony does not, however, prevent the treatment of film from being an integral part of the work or from extending the line of continuity from the criticism of Cabrera Infante to his fiction. This continuity is extended into his recent non-fiction work, *Holy Smoke*, a book which shares some of the mechanism of parody operating in *La Habana para un Infante Difunto*.

NOTES

[1] Cruz Hernández also notes this tendency (40).

[2] Note the similarity here to the image of Ana/El Ama, in *Pubis angelical*, by Manuel Puig, as Hedy Lamarr. The analogy between El Ama and Lamarr is suggested in Corbatta 73. The film referred to by the narrator is *White Cargo* (1942). I owe the connection of Tondelayo to Lamarr to Halliwell, who included mention of her role (*Film Guide* 962-63).

[3] Note also the similarity of 'Magaly' to 'Lamarr.'

[4] Note the demonic parody of the relationship between Fay Wray and King Kong, as well as the implicit irony in the fact that the Bergman character is a prostitute—certainly no Vestal Virgin.

[5] See, in this connection, González and Sanborn. These critics argue that

> El héroe innominado de *La Habana para un Infante Difunto* se basa menos en el modelo del burlador de Sevilla, que conquistaba almas a la vez que cuerpos, que en el concepto del mito del 'burlador' o 'trickster'...." (87)

This interpretation seems to downplay the more serious side of the book, its revelation of the basic amorality of the narrator, who does perpetrate blasphemies and acts in bad faith with his wife and family in a manner not at all dissimilar to the procedure followed by Don Juan.

6 As Cabrera Infante informed my editor, the quotation is not exact. Denham has not only "taken a good look" at the natives; he has entered their village and talked to them through an interpreter (the ship's captain). Denham, responding to the captain, actually says, "'Yeah—blondes *are* scarce around here'" (original emphasis).

7 Note that Lisa (Grace Kelly) uses the term "'ghouls'" to refer to herself and Jefferies; the narrator of *La Habana para un Infante Difunto* is likened to Dracula, also in some respects a voyeur. The connection may only be coincidental, but the demonic is sensed in both texts in a very similar way.

8 Note the sly connection to *Rear Window* in the hen-pecked quality of the conversation imagined by the narrator: in the film, Stewart sees such arguments between Thorwald and his wife and becomes more interested in investigating the "crime," indeed ascribes a motive to it, precisely because of witnessing such "neorealisms." The reversal is interesting in view of the aesthetic character of the narrator as opposed to the essentially Philistine attitudes of Stewart.

9 For a good treatment of the nature of *film noir*, see Paul Schrader, "Notes on *Film Noir*."

10 "Un amor en cada parte" appears to parody the title of the Howard Hawks film *A Girl in Every Port* (1928), a movie mentioned by Cabrera Infante in an interview with me.

11 In the film, Robinson plays a dual role of a timid office worker and a gangster, his double. The plot revolves around the confusion of their identities.

12 The disarming appearance of the narrator was suggested to me by González and Sanborn, who compare him physically to "Woody Allen en *Manhattan*" (88).

13 For this notion, see Freud, *Three Case Histories* 226-34.

14 The parody of Hollywood love stories in *Bride of Frankenstein* was suggested to me by Gifford (*Pictorial* 105).

15 The remarks in the preceding five paragraphs are based in part on remarks of Cabrera Infante in a class lecture at Wellesley (21 November 1985).

16 The book, as printed, now has 711 pages. The significant point here, however, is the link made by Cabrera Infante between the film and the novel.

8

Holy Smoke

N *Holy Smoke*, CABRERA INFANTE extends his fascination with movies into the realm of cigar lore. The book has received mixed reviews, probably because the reviewers have not perceived its underlying structure, its organizing principle of "anatomy" or "Menippean satire" (see, e.g., the review by Rubin).[1] The book is indeed analogous to the *Satyricon*, since it deals with prandial and postprandial imagery (in this case concerning cigars and tobacco), pseudophilosophical discussion, the unveiling of appearances, and the journey of a mock hero through a labyrinth of allusions to pop art and cigars. *Holy Smoke* bears important similarities to *La Habana para un Infante Difunto* and *Tres tristes tigres*, as well as to other books by Cabrera Infante, in its use of epigraphs which provide keys to its structure. Somewhat like *La Habana para un Infante Difunto*, for which *King Kong*, quoted in the epigraph, provides a structuring motif, *Holy Smoke*, operating on a parodic level of greater complexity than one might think on a first reading, uses a particular film reference as a point of departure for a large structure of allusiveness. The film, *Bride of Frankenstein*, is not mentioned as an epigraph, but rather at the beginning of the main text. At least one of the epigraphs does, however, closely relate to *Bride of Frankenstein*, sharing with it certain motifs important to the book. While the use of films in *Holy Smoke* is truly extensive, many recurring concepts and puns seen in the book can be traced to this specific movie.

Cigars are treated as a civilizing force by Cabrera Infante, as a basis for gentlemanly conversation and as an important component of man-woman relationships. *Bride of Frankenstein* centers on the creation of a woman to act as a partner for a likewise artificially created man. The artificial creation of the Monster and his bride relates to a central motif of the book: the conflict between nature and civilization, between innocence and vice, between purity and sophistication. The connection between the movie and the topic of the book is made explicit on p. 2:

> These two short sequences in a most felicitous film [*Bride of Frankenstein*] contain the entire history of the five-century-old relationship between the European gentleman and his smoke. It all started in the New World, where smoking was not for gentlemen but for sorcerers [like Dr. Pretorius]—and for the incumbent Indian chief: he who wore the feathers.

The reference to *Bride of Frankenstein* begins by connecting cigars to civilized dining, here in a parodic setting:

> In *Bride of Frankenstein* the infamous Dr Pretorius, a vicious but vivacious villain, is seen supping in a cavernous crypt deep in the churchyard of the Baron's domain. With a large, crisp and spotlessly white napkin tucked under his stand-up collar, the prim old scientist is using as a table an empty coffin—from which his minions have just evicted the beautiful corpse of the village virgin. (1)

The scene, from the latter half of the film, combines the elements of vice, sex, culture, innocence (the "virgin"), and death which are played upon in different cinematic and literary contexts throughout the book. These elements, as well as other related ones, will appear in different linguistic guises during the course of the book. For example, the notion of vice, as oversophistication or sin, is seen repeatedly in *Holy Smoke*, often in contrast either with commonly accepted morality or with the idea of saintliness (as in "holy" smoke). The treatment of this notion by Cabrera Infante is a good illustration of his technique of conceptual transformation.

The idea of vice first appears explicitly when the Monster calls Pretorius "a vicious but vivacious villain." The movie is soon referred to explicitly in this connection, with regard to the liking of Pretorius for cigars: offering the Monster a cigar, Pretorius says that "'It's my only vice'" (1). Cabrera Infante has altered the citation here, whether deliberately or not; if a deliberate alteration, the change from the

"'Its my only weakness'" of the film to "'It's my only vice,'" while perhaps explicable for linguistic reasons, allowing Cabrera Infante to pun alliteratively on "vice, violin, virgin, vivacious, villain" and later on "vitola, *Vivacious Lady*," and by implication on "Victor" Frankenstein,[2] may also indicate an intent to put cigar-smoking into a moral realm. Vice may contrast with innocence, while weakness would be opposed to strength. Significant as well is the fact that Pretorius uses the same line earlier in the movie to refer to his drinking.[3] At any rate, the line is seen in many forms throughout the book.

A partial treatment of the allusions to this line will demonstrate the fugal quality of the book, akin perhaps to the punning technique of Marx Brothers movies (as in the "Why a duck?" scene from *Cocoanuts*). The notion of vice recurs, for instance in connection with "Queen Victoria," whose name is linked to other imagery in the book, such as "The Queen of Spades,"[4] and is a feminine form of "Victor." A complex pun is made on her name and that of Pretorius:

> In Victorian times English gentlemen could get away with murder (Jack the Ripper did) but not with smoking in front of a lady — Pretoria never dared to show in public her private vice. Accordingly a gentleman never smoked if there were ladies present. (166)

The image of dinner is also present, recalling the dining scene from *Bride of Frankenstein*, as well as the joking about the Monster becoming a gentleman who, incidentally, murders his intended bride and Pretorius but only "gets away" with it in the sense of being liberated from his sad existence. Other examples include a reference to *Pierrot le Fou*, in which Samuel Fuller is quoted as saying "'This is my only vice'" (189-90). This allusion is interesting in terms of the very complex fugal or contrapuntal structure of the book: "Then he smiles his New York Jewish smile, like a wise Norman Mailer whose Nile is the Hudson River. Now he opens an old humidor[5] (to maintain your cigars fresh all you need is a sense of humidor) a crimson crypt..."[6] (189-90; my ellipsis). From even such few examples as these of the use of "vice",[7] the extremely complex system of allusions in the book should be apparent.

The notions of vice and innocence found in *Bride of Frankenstein* suggest the contrast between artifice and nature which is so important to the book. Cigar-making, like cinema and literature, is based on artifice, and Cabrera Infante devotes much space to the technique of cigar-making and rolling. Similarly, *Bride of Frankenstein* and its forerunner, *Frankenstein*, as well as its many sequels and spinoffs, explain in at least some detail the method of creating a man (or a woman), a procedure based on piecing together dead tissue, rolling it in bandages, and bringing it to life with an apparatus which focuses the electricity of the universe. The monsters in *Bride of Frankenstein*, like cigars or cigarettes, rolled in wrappings, are made of dead tissue, are often "machine-made" (a frequent image in *Holy Smoke*), and react strongly when in contact with fire. Significantly, the Monster fears fire because it created him and can destroy him; similarly, a cigar is "created" by fire, in the sense that the sun cures green tobacco as well as in the more literal sense that fire liberates the essence of tobacco, "animates" its "holy smoke" much as the vital essence of the Monster was animated by electricity;[8] nevertheless, in its creation lie the seeds of its destruction.[9] The process of creation of the Bride thus foreshadows the method of creation and use of cigars which is detailed, often parodically, in *Holy Smoke*, and is also connected to the frequently appearing quotation from Kipling, "And a woman is only a woman, but a good cigar is / a Smoke."[10]

Cabrera Infante discusses cigar wrapping and rolling in a relatively serious fashion (34-42). Many allusions to rolling are found in the book. The description of the art of the cigar roller, found on page 39, is one of the most interesting with regard to *Bride of Frankenstein*. The mention of "tools," "skilled hands," and the worktable have an eerie resemblance to the creation scenes in the *Frankenstein* movies. The artifice of the cigar-roller is emphasized; like Dr. Frankenstein, he lends a special skill and dexterity to his work. The individual creativity of Dr. Frankenstein, akin to that of God creating Adam (and Eve) is alluded to by Cabrera Infante in connection with the machining of cigars:

> There are, alas, machine-rolled Havanas too. On my desk I keep an empty box of Partagas that wears a notice specifying that the cigars are all machine-made, to maul Mitty's myth. Soon even the Monster will be made at the Frankenstein plant near Düsseldorf. (232-33)

The importance of the creativity of Dr. Frankenstein, the "god" of "a new race," as Pretorius, who would presumably be its Lucifer, calls the monsters who will putatively mate, is in line with the sensibilities of Cabrera Infante during his auteurist phase, when he spoke of the director as "un poeta" (*Oficio* 377; see above, 13). The romantic focus of the films on the new Fall of man is another element which recurs importantly in *Holy Smoke*, as do the related images of Adam and Eve and of a Garden of Eden corrupted by outside influence.

Paradisiacal imagery is to be found in *Holy Smoke* as in other books by Cabrera Infante such as *Tres tristes tigres* and *Vista del amanecer en el trópico*. The discovery by Columbus of the Indies and tobacco, as well as the mention of Las Casas, call to mind the Noble Savage, an Enlightenment version of the Adam and Eve myth complex, and tie in with other imagery from *Holy Smoke*, such as its repeated references to Adam and Eve and to Paradise and Hell. The Eve imagery in turn suggests the leaf motif which pervades the book, as in this excerpt which deals with the tobacco industry in Cuba:

> He [one of the owners of the firm of Hunters & Frankau] summed all his courage to add: 'Anyway the whole point is futile as all the cigar factories in Havana are now closed.' Why was that? 'Lack of leaf.' He meant not to describe Eve before the Fall but not having enough tobacco in Cuba to roll one cigar. (123-24)

Film titles such as *All about Eve* (91, 144), *Bright Leaf* (185), and *It Started with Eve* (196) further extend the Eve imagery. The use of Paradise motifs as well as the references to Adam are even more extensive and should be treated individually.

The Paradise (or Heaven) imagery which runs throughout *Holy Smoke* (of course suggested in the title and its variants or metonymies—"holy ghost," "gaseous ghosts," "*Saint-Jack*," and so forth) is familiar to readers of *Arcadia todas las noches*, with its equivalence between the cinema and the bliss of Arcadia. The contrast between the native paradise of the New World and its violation by a corrupt Europe is important to the book and is seen in microcosm in *Bride of Frankenstein*. The Monster is shown in this film as spending a brief time in a "green world,"[11] in which he finds a blind Hermit who teaches him to smoke and to talk; in a sense, he loses his innocence—criminal though that may be under the terms of the film—and begins to become "civilized," much as the Indians of the New World did. But the Monster lives in a sadly ironic "paradise," since he has no Eve, is persecuted by the vengeful "angels" of the town's justice, and has already fallen from innocence by killing. He tries to reconstruct his paradise, or to discover a true paradise, by demanding that his "father" make a woman for him. Here the Biblical terms are reversed, since God took pity on Adam and created Eve rather that being forced to do so. The theme of the creation of a woman and its satiric "antitype"[12] in the manufacture of cigars is central to *Holy Smoke*.

The attempt of the Monster to reach a state of Paradise is partially seen in his pathetic desires for civilized comforts, parodied, as Cabrera Infante notes, by Mel Brooks in *Young Frankenstein*. This desire to belong to civilization conflicts with social reality as well as with the darker impulses of the Monster, but it ties in nevertheless to the idea of cigar-smoking as a social lubricant and as an index of culture which is treated in rather tongue-in-cheek fashion in *Holy Smoke*. The longing of the Monster for his own civilized paradise, or at least for a paradise removed from the frequently savage civilization in which he finds himself, is mirrored in many film titles in *Holy Smoke* which recall the idea of paradise: for example, *Heaven Can Wait* (200, 207, 221), *Trouble in Paradise* (suggested, as is *Heaven Can Wait*, by the phrase "a ladder to paradise" [207]), and *Rage in Heaven* (215). *Trouble in Paradise* is an especially outstanding example of the notion of paradise in unison with the desire for civilized comforts. Like the Monster and his Bride, the Herbert Marshall and Miriam Hopkins characters in *Trouble in Paradise* are misfits in normal social terms because of their *métier* as thieves; but unlike the Monster and his mate, the two protagonists of the Lubitsch film are depicted as fitting quite well into the cynicism of the civilization which surrounds and supports them.

The fact that the Monster wants a woman to be created for him is significant in view of another important motif of *Holy Smoke* (and of other work by Cabrera Infante), the Pygmalion-Galatea relationship. This motif was central to *Vertigo*[13] and was important to Josef von Sternberg, one of the directors whom Cabrera Infante has mentioned as influencing him as well as Manuel Puig (Interview with author). The impulse to idealize and thereby to control the desired woman (or to create an ideally desired woman) fits well into the schema of a character such as Códac. The analogy to *Bride of Frankenstein* is clear, with the center shifting from the desire of the Monster for a perfect mate to the fascination of Frankenstein (and his demonic double Pretorius—"the man beyond" [*praeter*] the pale of morality) with creating a woman whom he could educate or perhaps even exploit.[14] Cabrera Infante suggests this motif when writing of the scene in which the Monster comes to ask Pretorius for help (*Holy Smoke* 1-2). In order to perceive the connection being made here, a knowledge of the film is necessary, since Cabrera Infante does not mention the insistence of the Monster towards Frankenstein at the urging of Pretorius, who has ambitions of his own. Nevertheless, the Pygmalion motif is present, both in terms of control and of artificial creation. The artificiality of the Monster and, by extension, of the bride, is linked explicitly with cigars: "Undaunted, Dr Pretorius offers the man-made wanderer a man-made wonder: 'Have a cigar.'" (1). In a good example of the subtle allusive technique employed in the book, which is a kind of cyclotron in which allusions acquire a centripetal force, flying off to surface later in comically but poetically suggestive ways,[15] Cabrera Infante mentions *The Band Wagon* (90-91), in which, "Like Paul Henreid in *Now Voyager*, Fred [Astaire] keeps inducing Cyd [Charisse] to smoke cigarettes." (Similarly, the Hermit had induced the Monster to smoke in *Bride of Frankenstein*.) "She is reluctant but he is relentless. She becomes firm:[16] Adamant Eve" (91). Here, the insistence of the Monster on having a bride is combined with the "firmness" of Cyd Charisse to form a punning, hermaphroditic image which seems to comment on the strange relationship between Pygmalion and Galatea figures like the Monster (or Dr. Frankenstein) and the Bride.

The two sequences from *Bride of Frankenstein* do contain, in germ, two preoccupations of the book with respect to smoking: its association with civilization and its connection with character, self-importance, and self-worth in a society which values it. The book, like much of the work of Cabrera Infante, betrays a certain nostalgia for a period—here, generally the late nineteenth century, in which smoking was, under the right circumstances, a respectable and respected activity, at least for men.[17] Thus, Cabrera Infante quotes Oscar Wilde frequently in defense of smoking, mentioning repeatedly his "success de steam" when smoking on stage, and using some dialogue from *The Importance of Being Earnest* as an epigraph:

LADY BRACKNELL: ...Do you smoke?
ERNEST: Well, yes, I must admit I smoke.
LADY BRACKNELL: I am glad to hear it. A man should always have an occupation of some kind. (Front.)

The impulse towards sociability and self-importance as well as the elegant behavior connected in many minds with cigar-smoking are present—though not exempt from parody—in *My Fair Lady*, another key film for the book. A Pygmalion story with some interesting similarities to *Bride of Frankenstein*[18] (and, curiously, in an even more overt fashion to *The Bride*, a recent remake of *Bride of Frankenstein*), *My Fair Lady* is a movie set in the period which seems dear to the narrator of *Holy Smoke*, the epoch of Kipling, Wilde, and Yeats. The attempt of Professor Henry Higgins to "civilize" the flower-girl Eliza Doolittle (interestingly named, since Henry Frankenstein's wife is named "Elizabeth" and he, like Higgins, is actually civilized by her) is noteworthy for readers of Cabrera Infante for several reasons. Like Silvestre and Cué with Beba and Magalena, Higgins and, to some extent, his friend Pickering, speak in terms often unintelligible to the uneducated Eliza and treat her coldly after her coming-out at the Embassy ball.[19] The central issue and joke of the movie revolves around the use of language, since "Enry Iggins" (*Holy Smoke* 212) equates culture with good use of language. The contrast between the urban and the rural, or between intellectualized or sophisticated and non-academic cultures is strikingly present here as in *Tres tristes tigres* and *La Habana para un Infante Difunto*, or in *Frankenstein* and *Bride of Frankenstein*.[20] The Pygmalion and Galatea motif is crucial to *My Fair Lady* and bears odd similarities to *Bride of Frankenstein*: Higgins protests to his mother about Eliza that he does not have to be courteous to "'this creature I made from cabbage leaves.'" The apparent lightness of *Holy Smoke* conceals a carefully worked out system of allusions which mirrors many of the concerns of Cabrera Infante found in his earlier works.

Many film genres are represented in *Holy Smoke*, extending and expanding upon the choices made by Cabrera Infante in his criticism and narrative. The book contains many examples of comedy, drama, and adventure, as well as Western and horror films. Welles, Minnelli, and Hitchcock are especially well represented among the directors who interest Cabrera Infante, as are actors such as the Marx Brothers, W. C. Fields, Bogart, and Edward G. Robinson, one of whose movies, *Little Caesar*, provides the basis for the running puns on his "last words" "'Mother of Mercy, is this the end of Rico [Bandello[21]]?'" and shows Cabrera Infante to be preserving his interest in that movie on which he commented so strongly in *Siete voces*.

The truly eclectic film tastes of Cabrera Infante, then, form much of the subtext of *Holy Smoke*. The book is more subtly constructed than may be readily apparent upon a first reading, as some of the examples cited should demonstrate. The richness of the humor in the book depends on its interweaving of cinematic, literary, and musical allusions with rather arcane tobacco lore, but it is significant that several literary references are added as a sort of afterthought (in the section entitled "Ta Vague Littérature" [239-325]. As Ardis Nelson has noted, the title of the book is echoed in a line of Charles Coburn, who, "When it comes to cigars," "can go very far even when he is unmoved." In *Heaven Can Wait*, "... every now and then he exclaims boisterously, 'Holy smoke!' and puffs at his perennial Partagas. The best plug [a double entendre on chewing tobacco, also recurrent in the book] ever for this book" (200).[22] The tongue-in-cheek nature of the parody in *Holy Smoke* in the book is quite fittingly contained in one of the epigraphs, which, when followed on the next page by the first reference to *Bride of Frankenstein*, comments on that masterful cinematic parody of Hollywood romance which is at the center of *Holy Smoke*:

Lastly (and this is, perhaps, the golden rule), no woman should marry a man who does not smoke.

ROBERT LOUIS STEVENSON
Virginibus Puerisque (1881). (Front.)

Although the Monster never marries his bride-to-be, he at least becomes "a connoisseur of some import" (*Holy Smoke* 2) and helps to provide a satiric and cinematic model for a compendium of popular myths and technical lore which has aptly been called an "anatomy of a vice."

NOTES

[1] The notion of *Holy Smoke* as an "anatomy" was suggested to me by Ardis Nelson and is discussed in her "*Holy Smoke*: Anatomy of a Vice."

[2] As Prawer explains (22), Dr. Frankenstein is called "Victor" in the Shelley novel but "Henry" in the Whale *Frankenstein* films.

[3] This is, Everson suggests, perhaps due to injudicious cutting (45). See also the remarks by Bilyeau in her "Frankie's Back."

[4] This name is reminiscent of *Vanishing Point* and is itself tied to the frequent references to card- and dice-playing in *Holy Smoke*, as well as recalling *Bride of Frankenstein*, with the creation by Pretorius of a king and queen.

[5] References to humidors abound in the book; as with other images in

Holy Smoke, the mention of "humidor" sets off a chain of associations in the reader, who may recall, for instance, *My Fair Lady*, or other connections in which humidors appear. ⟍

6 The link between "humidor" and "crypt" may remind a careful reader—and movie watcher—of the need for "a fresh heart" for the Bride and its theft from a "crypt," here called "crimson" as a metonymy for blood, roses—another recurring image in the book—and perhaps even implying *The Crimson Pirate*, with its motif of a thieving hero.

7 Some of the other examples appear on pp. 193 ["'my only grime'"], 237, and 238.

8 See the amusing apothegmic reference to the process in *Holy Smoke* 265.

9 Such ideas are parodied in *Holy Smoke* in the piece quoted from Robert Louis Stevenson (254-55).

10 For the complete poem, see 281-83; note in this poem the idea of "a rival bride," an element figuring importantly in *Bride of Frankenstein* in the implicit conflict between Elizabeth, the wife of Dr. Frankenstein, and the Bride. The idea of sexual pairings between the monsters and the Frankensteins has been ingeniously brought out, as John G. Cawelti notes ("*Chinatown*" 192), in *Young Frankenstein* by Mel Brooks, a movie important to *Holy Smoke* (see 225).

11 The phrase is Northrop Frye's. See, e.g., *Anatomy* 182-84.

12 Here I employ the term of Northrop Frye, used at length in his *The Great Code: The Bible as Literature*.

13 But note the differing opinion by Barthélemy Amengual: "Il y a plus de savoir-faire que d'art inspiré dans la «reconversion» [sic] que Scottie réalise, de Judy en Madeleine. Travail de détective, de médecin légiste, davantage que de Pygmalion" (40).

14 My use of the term "demonic" derives from Frye, *Great Code*.

15 I am borrowing here the imagery used by Cabrera Infante in referring to *Kiss Me Deadly* (*Oficio* 85-86).

16 Note that Pretorius had worried about the firmness of a female corpse's legs (1).

17 See, however, the comments by Cabrera Infante on the problems encountered by Oscar Wilde with smoking on a public stage (*Holy Smoke* 187-88).

18 The connection between *My Fair Lady* and the Pygmalion myth was suggested to me by Maltin (*TV* 665).

19 Notice also that *Tres tristes tigres* has a section entitled "Los debutantes" and that much emphasis is placed on a naïve character from the provinces, Vivian Smith-Corona, who, like Eliza, undergoes a "coming-out" ritual which is, however, destructive of her innocence and good nature. Eliza gains considerably from her experience.

20 See Prawer, e.g. 58-59, 70, for comments on the conflicts between social classes in horror movies.

21 Notice the implicit pun on cigar-bands.

22 Nelson, "*Holy Smoke*" 9, suggested this citation to me. She also notes the way in which "movie stars" are "dethroned" in a parodic context, much as I have argued with respect to *La Habana para un Infante Difunto*, and mentions several instances of the use of film elements in *Holy Smoke*.

Conclusion

ANUEL PUIG HAS SAID that "'el cine de Hollywood de los años treinta y cuarenta'" survives because of its evocation of the imagery of dreams and because of the power of its storytelling ("Encuentros" 606-07; "Narrativa" 22). He contrasts this endurance of the Hollywood movie with the fading of trends such as neorealism and even of socially oriented mainstream movies such as *The Best Years of Our Lives* ("Síntesis" 486-87).

Guillermo Cabrera Infante would surely agree with such an assessment. Like Puig, he has worked with dreams and their imagery, and finds in the movies a great range of evocation of fantasy, as his focus on genre demonstrates.[1]

In much of the work of Cabrera Infante, the critic is offered a cross-section of Hollywood genres. The urge towards storytelling which is basic to the novelist is evidenced in his interest in films such as *Rio Bravo*, *The Asphalt Jungle*, and *The Set Up*. These movies, and most of the others mentioned or used in his fiction, are distinguished by their narrative power. Mirroring such narrative films, the recounting by Códac of the history of La Estrella, though appearing in literary form, demonstrates a capacity to express remembered experiences in visual terms. Several of the directors important to Cabrera Infante, such as Alfred Hitchcock, Orson Welles, Vincente Minnelli, and Josef von Sternberg, are notable both for the visual strength of their films and for their storytelling capability.[2]

Movies, and other types of popular culture forms, are neither uncritically accepted nor sardonically rejected in the works of Cabrera Infante. The prejudices against Hollywood which are harbored by many are absent from his criticism and fiction. Nevertheless, he does not accept the Hollywood tradition in a completely open-eyed manner, saying that "'...I have always been a staunch defender of Hollywood against charges of commercialism and vulgarity. Hollywood is commercial and vulgar—and a purveyor of popular entertainment'" ("Art" 183; my ellipsis). Cabrera Infante may defend Hollywood, but he does not pretend to ignore its less attractive qualities.

The position taken by Cabrera Infante is a defense of the value of movies and an insistence that they not be considered worthless or "trashy." Cabrera Infante, as has been noted, sees no difference "'betwen [sic] high and low culture'" ("Art" 183).

The interest of Cabrera Infante in popular culture is not only visible in the interpretations of movies and music in his books, but also in his own contributions to the fund of pop culture. *Vanishing Point*, itself based on both cultural elements generally called "high," such as the myths of antiquity, and those forms usually termed "low," such as the Hollywood movie, has become "'a piece of Americana, a cult film'" (Cabrera Infante, "Art" 182) and thus part of the culture of myths shared by its viewers. *Holy Smoke* is itself a pop art work, being a mock-serious treatment of a cultural artifact.

The importance of popular culture, and, within the confines of this study, of film, to the work of Cabrera Infante has been noted by numerous critics. Further detailed study of works by Cabrera Infante, such as his books of criticism, would surely yield results of interest to the critic concerned with comparative study.

Such works by Cabrera Infante, while of minor diffusion in publicity terms, are hardly unimportant in tracing the development of his fictional and essayistic style. One can certainly conclude that the theme of myth, the importance given to mannerism and rhetoric, the interest in generic forms such as the Western, the detective and thriller film, and the comedy, as well as the generally ironic cast of these critical works has carried over into the fiction of Cabrera Infante and is intensified in *Holy Smoke*. His well-known mythic treatment of the city can now be better understood with reference to his film tastes, in particular to the genres of the gangster and detective film and the musical. Film is not just another mine for allusion in the work of Cabrera Infante, but instead an integrated part of the structure of his fiction, contributing to it not only technically but also thematically.

Thus, the literary output of Cabrera Infante should not be

thought of as lacking in continuity because of the disruption due to his leaving Cuba. As I have tried to show, film has been a constant in his writing. His claims as to its influence on him are clearly not inaccurate.

The emphasis on film culture in the work of Cabrera Infante, through its nature, extent, and concentration, sets his writing apart from that of most other Latin-American authors with much interest in film, such as Fuentes and García Márquez.[3] Cabrera Infante can be as readily identified with film, especially the Hollywood film, as he can with language or with the evocation of La Habana in the 1950s. He transcends literary boundaries through his immersion in film, producing work which gains in richness by its association with the artistic tradition of cinema.

NOTES

[1] See Merrim, "Through"; Cabrera Infante, *Arcadia*, e.g., 31-32.

[2] Puig affirms the narrative ability of Hitchcock (and Hollywood) in an interview with Nora Catelli: "'Hollywood había sabido narrar. Imagínate cómo sabe narrar Hitchcock y las cosas han hecho que los norteamericanos en este sentido'" ("Narrativa" 22). Weinberg, in *Josef von Sternberg*, suggested to me the idea of von Sternberg as storyteller (see, e.g., 97-98).

[3] Manuel Puig would be a significant exception to this statement.

Selected List of Works Consulted

(For references to films, see filmography below.)

Acosta Cruz, María. *The Discourse of Excess: The Latin American Neobaroque and James Joyce*. Diss. State U of New York at Binghamton, 1984. Ann Arbor: UMI, 1985. 8417472.

Agee, James. *Agee on Film: Reviews and Comments by James Agee*. Introd. W. H. Auden. Illus. Tomi Ungerer. New York: McDowell, Obolensky, 1958. Vol. 1 of *Agee on Film*. 2 vols. 1958-60.

Agramonte, Arturo. *Cronología del cine cubano*. La Habana: ICAIC, 1966.

Alegría, Fernando. *Nueva historia de la novela hispanoamericana*. 4th ed. Hanover, NH: Serie Rama-Ediciones del Norte, 1986.

Almendros, Néstor. "Cinema and Culture in Cuba: An Interview with Néstor Almendros." With William Luis. Trans. Virginia Lawreck. *Review* 37 (1987): 14-20.

———. "Photography as a Passion: An Interview with Néstor Almendros." With Jorge Posada. *Sight and Sound* 53 (1984): 124-29.

Alter, Robert. "Mimesis and the Motive for Fiction." *Tri-Quarterly* 42 (1978): 228-49.

Alvarez-Borland, Isabel. "El cine documental y las viñetas de G. Cabrera Infante." *Explicación de textos literarios* 11 (1982-83): 3-10.

———. *Discontinuidad y ruptura en Guillermo Cabrera Infante*. Gaithersburg, MD.: *Hispamérica*-Montclair State College, 1982.

———. "Los ensayos de G. Cabrera Infante: fragmentos y experimentos." *Revista canadiense de estudios hispánicos* 11 (1986): 160-69.

———. "*La Habana para un Infante difunto*: Cabrera Infante's Self-Conscious Narrative." *Hispania* 68 (1985): 44-48.

Amengual, Barthélemy. "A propos de *Vertigo* où Hitchcock contre Tristan." *Alfred Hitchcock*. Ed. Michel Estève. *Etudes cinématographiques* 84-87. Paris: Lettres Modernes-Minard, 1971. 37-55.

Andrew, J. Dudley. *The Major Film Theories: An Introduction*. New York: Oxford UP, 1976.

Anger, Kenneth. *Hollywood Babylon*. 1975. New York: Dell, 1981.

Aparecida da Silva, Maria. "*Tres tristes tigres* de Cabrera Infante e o Neobarroco hispano-americano." *Letras de hoje* 14.45 (1981): 112-22.

Armour, Robert A. *Film, a Reference Guide*. American Popular Culture. Westport, CT: Greenwood, 1980.

Arnheim, Rudolf. "The Complete Film." Mast and Cohen 27-31.

———. "Film and Reality." Mast and Cohen 195-99.

———. "The Making of a Film." Mast and Cohen 199-203.

Bakhtin, Mikhail. *Problems of Dostoevsky's Poetics*. Trans. R. W. Rotsel. Ann Arbor: Ardis, 1973.

————. *Rabelais and His World.* Trans. Helene Iswolsky. Cambridge: MIT, 1968.

Bann, Stephen, and John E. Bowlt, eds. *Russian Formalism: A Collection of Articles and Texts in Translation.* 20th Century Studies. Edinburgh: Scottish Academic P, 1973.

Barr, Charles. "Cinemascope: Before and After." Mast and Cohen 120-46.

Batty, Linda. *Retrospective Index to Film Periodicals 1930-1971.* New York: Bowker, 1975.

Bazin, André. "An Aesthetic of Reality: Neorealism. (*Cinematic Realism and the Italian School of the Liberation*)." Graham 16-40.

————. *The Cinema of Cruelty from Buñuel to Hitchcock.* Ed. and introd. François Truffaut. Trans. Sabine d'Estrée and Tiffany Fliss. New York: Seaver, 1982.

————. "The Evolution of Film Language." Graham 25-50.

————. "*Le Journal d'un curé de campagne* and the Stylistics of Robert Bresson." *What Is Cinema?* 1: 125-43.

————. *Orson Welles: A Critical View.* Foreword François Truffaut. Profile by Jean Cocteau. Trans. Jonathan Rosenbaum. New York: Harper Colophon-Harper, 1979.

————. "*La Politique des auteurs.*" Graham 137-55.

————. *What Is Cinema?* Ed. and trans. Hugh Gray. Introd. François Truffaut. 2 vols. Berkeley: U of California P, 1967-71.

Berrong, Richard M. *Rabelais and Bakhtin: Popular Culture in* Gargantua and Pantagruel. Lincoln: U of Nebraska P, 1986.

Bilyeau, Nancy. "Frankie's Back." *American Film* Apr. 1986: 10.

Bitsch, Charles. "Surmultipliée." Rev. of *Kiss Me Deadly,* dir. Robert Aldrich. *Cahiers du cinéma* Oct. 1955: 42-43.

Bluestone, George. *Novels into Film.* Berkeley: U of California P, 1957.

Bordwell, David, and Kristin Thompson. *Film Art: An Introduction.* Addison-Wesley Series in Speech, Drama, and Film. Reading, MA: Addison-Wesley, 1979.

Borges, Jorge Luis. "La casa de Asterión." *Laberintos.* By Borges. Illus. Zdravko Ducmelic. Prol. José Edmundo Clemente. Buenos Aires: Joraci, 1977. 9-13.

Bowles, Stephen E., comp. and ed. *Index to Critical Film Reviews in British and American Film Periodicals* and *Index to Critical Reviews of Books about Film.* 3 vols. New York: Burt Franklin, 1974-75.

Braudy, Leo. *The World within a Frame: What We See in Films.* 1976. Garden City, NY: Anchor-Doubleday, 1977.

Braun, Eric. Rev. of *Vanishing Point,* by Guillermo Cain [Guillermo Cabrera Infante]. *Films and Filming* Oct. 1971: 60.

Brosnan, John. *Future Tense: The Cinema of Science Fiction.* New York: St. Martin's, 1978.

Brown, Curtis F. *Ingrid Bergman.* Pyramid Illustrated History of the Movies. New York: Pyramid, 1973.

Buñuel, Luis. Interview. *The Cinema of Cruelty from Buñuel to Hitchcock.* André

Bazin. Ed. and introd. François Truffaut. Trans. Sabine d'Estrée and Tiffany Fliss. New York: Seaver, 1982.

Burn, A. R. *The Pelican History of Greece.* Harmondsworth, Eng.: Penguin, 1965.

Burton, Julianne. "Learning to Write at the Movies: Film and the Fiction Writer in Latin America." *Texas Quarterly* 18.1 (1975): 92-103.

Burton, Robert S. "Taking Control of the Stage: Art and Politics in Hitchcock's *The Thirty-Nine Steps* (1935)." Unpublished essay and lecture, 1987.

Cabrera, Vicente. "La destrucción de la creación de *Tres tristes tigres.*" *Revista iberoamericana* 42 (1976): 553-59.

Cabrera Infante, Guillermo. *Arcadia todas las noches.* Barcelona: Biblioteca Breve-Seix Barral, 1978.

———. "The Art of Fiction LXXV: Guillermo Cabrera Infante." With Alfred MacAdam. *Paris Review* 25 (1983): 154-95.

———. "*Bajo el volcán*: Scenario. O de la novela al cine sin pasar por la pantalla." *Vuelta* Apr. 1985: 28-31.

———. "Blonde on Blonde: A Love Letter to Melanie Griffith." *American Film* Mar. 1988: 48-52.

———. "Cabrera Infante habla de su obra." With Jorge Nieto. *Razón y fábula* Dec. 1973: 64-83.

———. "Caín by Himself. Guillermo Cabrera Infante: Man of Three Islands." Comp. William L. Siemens. *Review* 28 (1981): 8-11.

———. "(C)ave Attemptor! A Chronology of GCI (After Laurence Sterne's)." *Review* 9 (1971-72): 5-9.

———. "Chaplin resucitado." *Cambio 16* 7 Mar. 1983: 104-06.

———. Class Lecture. Wellesley College. Wellesley, MA, 21 Nov. 1985.

———. "La confundida lengua del poeta." *Primera plana* 14 Jan. 1969: 64-65.

———. "Cuba's Shadow." *Film Comment* May-June 1985: 43-45.

———. "Entrevista: Cabrera Infante cantando *las 40.*" With John Brookesmith. *Imagen: Quincenario de arte, literatura e información cultural* (Caracas) 1 Feb. 1969: 9+ .

———. "Una entrevista con Cabrera Infante." With Kjell A. Johansson. *Alacrán azul* 1.1 (1970): 12-17.

———. "Entrevistas: Guillermo Cabrera Infante." With Albert Bensoussan. *Insula* Sept. 1970: 4.

———. *Exorcismos de esti(l)o.* Barcelona: Biblioteca Breve-Seix Barral, 1976.

———. "From 5 to 7: An Interview with Guillermo Cabrera Infante." With Regina M. Janes. *Salmagundi* 52-53 (1981): 30-56.

———. "Las fuentes de la narración." With Emir Rodríguez Monegal. *Mundo nuevo* July 1968: 41-48.

———. "Guillermo Cabrera Infante: El más triste (y alegre) de los tigres." *Son así: Reportaje a nueve escritores latinoamericanos.* Comp. Eligio García Márquez. Bogotá: La Oveja Negra, 1982. 181-231.

———. "Guillermo Cabrera Infante: Memories of an Invented City." *Faces, Mirrors, Masks.* Prod. and dir. "The Kitchen Sisters" (David Nelson and Nicky Silva). Proj. dir. Frank Tavares. Series ed. Julio Marzán. Natl. Public Radio, 1984.

————. *La Habana para un Infante Difunto*. Barcelona: Biblioteca Breve-Seix Barral, 1979.

————. *Holy Smoke*. New York: Harper, 1985.

————. "Include Me Out." Minc and Frankenthaler 9-20.

————. Interview. *De la literatura considerada como una forma de urticaria*. Carlos Alberto Montaner. Madrid: Colección Nova Scholar-Playor, 1980. 165-70.

————. Interview. *Siete voces*. Comp. Rita Guibert. México: Novaro, 1974. 351-446.

————. Interview with author. 20 Nov. 1985.

————. "Meta-final." *Alacrán azul* 1.1 (1970): 18-22.

————. *O*. Barcelona: Biblioteca Breve-Seix Barral, 1975.

————. *Un oficio del Siglo 20: G. Caín 1954-60*. 1963. Barcelona: Biblioteca Breve-Seix Barral, 1973.

————. "Orígenes (Cronología a la manera de Laurence Sterne)." *Guillermo Cabrera Infante*. Ed. Rosa Mª Pereda. Escritores de todos los tiempos 3. Madrid: EDAF, 1979. 233-48.

————. "Piñera's Virgil." *Review* 35 (1985): 19.

————. "A Portrait of Ardis Reading My Books." *Cabrera Infante in the Menippean Tradition*. By Ardis L. Nelson. Juan de la Cuesta Hispanic Monographs. Newark, DE: Juan de la Cuesta, 1983. xiii-xx.

————. "El presentador presentado." *Vuelta* Jan. 1980: 10-11.

————. "Remington Visits with Edison." *American Film* Jan.-Feb. 1986: 14+ .

————. "Retrato del artista ya maduro." *Cambio 16* 10 Sept. 1984: 74-75.

————. "Salsa para una ensalada." Minc, *Literatures* 21-36.

————. "Sobre tigres e Infantes." With Adelfa Fernández. *Américas* (Span. ed.) Mar.-Apr. 1982: 11-14.

————. "Talent of 2wo Cities." *Review* 35 (1985): 17-18.

————. *Tres tristes tigres*. Barcelona: Biblioteca Breve de Bolsillo-Seix Barral, 1965.

————. "21 en el 21: Una entrevista de larga distancia con Cabrera Infante." With Sharon Magnarelli. *Prismal/Cabral* Fall 1979: 23-42.

————. "Viaje Verbal a la Habana, ¡Ah Vana! *Entrevista de Isabel Alvarez-Borland con G. Cabrera Infante, Arquitecto de una Ciudad de Palabras Erigida en el Tiempo*." With Isabel Alvarez-Borland. *Hispamérica* Apr. 1982: 51-68.

————. *Vista del amanecer en el trópico*. Barcelona: Biblioteca Breve-Seix Barral, 1974.

Cachán, Manuel. "*La Habana para un Infante Difunto*: Choteo, erotismo y la nada." *Explicación de textos literarios* 15.1 (1986-87): 33-45.

Caín, G. [Guillermo Cabrera Infante]. *Vanishing Point: Screenplay by G. CAIN*. First draft, June 1969. Unpublished ts. London: Cupid Productions, Ltd. Theatre Arts Library, U of California, Los Angeles.

Calder, Jenni. *There Must Be a Lone Ranger*. London: Hamish Hamilton, 1974.

Campbell, Joseph. *The Hero with a Thousand Faces*. 2nd ed. Bollingen Series 17. Princeton: Princeton UP, 1968.

————. *The Masks of God.* 4 vols. 1959-68. Rev. ed. vol. 1, 1969. New York: Penguin, 1976.

Campos, René Alberto. *Espejos: La textura cinemática en* La traición de Rita Hayworth. Madrid: Colección Pliegos de Ensayo-Pliegos, 1985.

Carilla, Emilio. *Estudios de literatura hispanoamericana.* Publicaciones del Instituto Caro y Cuervo 42. Bogotá: Instituto Caro y Cuervo, 1977. 345-58.

Carrabino, Victor, et al., eds. *The Power of Myth in Literature and Film.* Selected Papers from the 2nd Annual Florida State University Conference on Literature and Film. Tallahassee: Florida State U-University Presses of FL, 1980.

Carroll, Jon. Rev. of *Vanishing Point,* by Guillermo Cain [Guillermo Cabrera Infante]. *Take One.* Sept.-Oct. 1970: 25-26.

Carroll, Lewis [Charles Lutwidge Dodson]. *Alice's Adventures in Wonderland. The Complete Works of Lewis Carroll.* Introd. Alexander Woollcott. Illus. John Tenniel. New York: Vintage-Random, 1976. 11-132.

Cavell, Stanley. *The World Viewed: Reflections on the Ontology of Film.* Enl. ed. Cambridge: Harvard UP, 1979.

Cawelti, John G. "*Chinatown* and Generic Transformation in Recent American Films." Grant, *Film Genre Reader* 183-201.

————. *The Six-Gun Mystique.* 2nd. ed. Bowling Green: Bowling Green UP, 1984.

Champlin, Charles. Rev. of *Vanishing Point,* by Guillermo Cain [Guillermo Cabrera Infante]. *Filmfacts* 4 (1971): 130-31.

Chanan, Michael, ed. *Chilean Cinema.* Introd. Michael Chanan. London: British Film Institute, 1976.

Chandler, Raymond. *The Long Goodbye.* 1953. New York: Ballantine, 1971.

Clarens, Carlos. *Crime Movies: From Griffith to* The Godfather *and Beyond.* New York: W. W. Norton, 1980.

————. *George Cukor.* Cinema One 28. London: Secker and Warburg; British Film Institute, 1976.

————. *An Illustrated History of the Horror Films.* New York: Putnam's, 1967.

Connolly, Cyril. *Enemies of Promise.* Rev. ed. New York: Stanley Moss-Persea, 1983.

————. *The Unquiet Grave: A Word Cycle by Palinurus.* Introd. Cyril Connolly. Rev. ed. New York: Persea, 1981.

Corbatta, Jorgelina Fidia. *Mito personal y mitos colectivos en las novelas de Manuel Puig.* Diss. U of Pittsburgh, 1983. Ann Arbor: UMI, 1983. 8411626.

Corliss, Richard. *Talking Pictures: Screenwriters in the American Cinema.* Introd. Andrew Sarris. 1974. New York: Penguin, 1975.

Cozarinsky, Edgardo. "Páginas del libro de la noche." Rev. of *Arcadia todas las noches,* by Guillermo Cabrera Infante. *Escandalar* 3.1 (1980): 91-92. [Cozarinsky notes several elements of the book which I had already developed when I recently read his review.]

D'Amico, Alicia, and Sara Facio, comps. and photogs. *Retratos y autorretratos: Escritores de América Latina.* With texts. Buenos Aires: Crisis, 1973. 29-37.

Davison, Peter, Rolf Meyersohn, and Edward Shils, eds. *Culture and Mass Culture*. Cambridge, Eng.: Chadwyck-Healey; Teaneck, NJ: Somerset House, 1978. Vol. 1 of *Literary Taste, Culture, and Mass Communication*. 14 vols. 1978-80.

Del Monte, Esteban. "Trotes tras *Tres tristes tigres*." *Mundo nuevo* Mar. 1968: 69-71.

Deutelbaum, Marshall, and Leland Poague, eds. *A Hitchcock Reader*. Ames: Iowa State UP, 1986.

Dorfles, Gillo, et al. *Kitsch: The World of Bad Taste*. New York: Universe, 1969.

Durgnat, Raymond. *The Crazy Mirror: Hollywood Comedy and the American Image*. 1969. New York: Delta-Dell, 1970.

Eagle, Herbert. *Russian Formalist Film Theory*. Michigan Slavic Materials 19. Ann Arbor: Michigan Slavic Publications-U of Michigan, 1981.

Eisenstein, Sergei M. *The Film Sense*. Trans. and ed. Jay Leyda. New York: Harvest-Harcourt, 1947.

Eliade, Mircea. *The Myth of the Eternal Return*. Trans. Willard R. Trask. New York: Pantheon, 1954.

Eloy Martínez, Tomás. "América: Los novelistas exilados." *Primera plana* 30 July 1968: 40-50 [includes questionnaire answers by Cabrera Infante].

Elsaesser, Thomas. "Tales of Sound and Fury: Observations on the Family Melodrama." Grant, *Film Genre Reader* 278-308.

Everson, William K. *Classics of the Horror Film*. Secaucus, NJ: Citadel, 1974.

Eyzaguirre, Luis B. *El héroe en la novela hispanoamericana del siglo XX*. Santiago de Chile: Universitaria, 1973. 313-23.

Farber, Manny. *Movies*. New York: Hillstone-Stonehill, 1971.

Feal, Rosemary Geisdorfer. *Novel Lives: The Fictional Autobiographies of Guillermo Cabrera Infante and Mario Vargas Llosa*. North Carolina Studies in the Romance Languages and Literatures 226. Valencia, Sp.: Artes Gráficas Soler, 1986.

————. "Autobiography and the Identity Game in Cabrera Infante's *La Habana para un infante difunto*." *Folio* Dec. 1984: 36-49.

Fell, John L. *Film and the Narrative Tradition*. Norman: U of Oklahoma P, 1974.

Ferguson, Christina Pokrivnak. *Sustained Game Metaphors in Contemporary Novel: The Game Is Life*. Diss. U of Arkansas, 1985. Ann Arbor: UMI, 1985. 86-18073.

Fernández, Enrique. "Miami's 'Autores.' " *Film Comment* May-June 1985: 46-48.

Fernández, Pablo Armando. "Autopsia de *Lunes de Revolución*." With William Luis. Annot. William Luis. *Plural* Mar. 1982: 52-62.

Finch, Christopher. *Pop Art: Object and Image*. London: Studio Vista; New York: Dutton Pictureback, 1968.

Foster, David William. *Cuban Literature: A Research Guide*. Garland Reference Library of the Humanities 511. New York: Garland, 1985. 125-33.

————. "Manuel Puig and the Uses of Nostalgia." *Latin American Literary Review* 1.1 (1972): 79-81.

Frederick, Bonnie K. "*Tres tristes tigres*: The Lost City." *Mester* May 1978: 21-30.

French, William. *The Movie Moguls: An Informal History of the Hollywood Tycoons.* 1969. Harmondsworth, Eng.: Pelican/Penguin, 1971.

Freud, Sigmund. *Moses and Monotheism.* Trans. Katherine Jones. New York: Vintage-Random House, 1939.

———. *Sexuality and the Psychology of Love.* Introd. and ed. Philip Rieff. 1963. New York: Collier-Macmillan, 1972.

———. *Three Case Histories.* Introd. and ed. Philip Rieff. New York: Collier-Macmillan, 1963. 226-34.

Frye, Northrop. *Anatomy of Criticism: Four Essays.* 1973, 1971. Princeton UP: 1957.

———. *The Great Code: The Bible and Literature.* 1981. New York: Harcourt, 1982.

Gallagher, David P. "Guillermo Cabrera Infante (Cuba 1929)." *Guillermo Cabrera Infante.* Ed. and comp. Julián Ríos. Caracas: Espiral/Fundamentos, 1974. 47-49.

———. *Modern Latin American Literature.* New York: Oxford UP, 1973. 164-88.

García, Franklin. "Distintas formas de montaje en la novelística hispano-americana contemporánea." *Revista canadiense de estudios hispánicos* 3 (1978): 1-25.

Gifford, Denis. *The British Film Catalogue 1895-1970: A Reference Guide.* New York: McGraw-Hill, 1973.

———. *A Pictorial History of Horror Movies.* London: Hamlyn, 1973.

Gilbert, Stuart. *James Joyce's* Ulysses: *A Study.* Rev. ed. New York: Vintage-Random, 1955.

Gilliatt, Penelope. *Jacques Tati.* London: Woburn, 1976.

Gimferrer, Pere. "Aproximaciones a Manuel Puig." *Plural* June 1976: 21-25.

Giordano, Jaime. "Función estructural del bilingüismo en algunos textos contemporáneos (Cabrera Infante, Luis R. Sánchez)." *Minc, Literatures* 161-75.

González, Eloy R., and Barbara G. Sanborn. "Un nuevo burlador: La fantasía erótica de *La Habana para un Infante Difunto* de Guillermo Cabrera Infante." *Explicación de textos literarios* 14 (1985-86): 85-90.

González Echeverría, Roberto. *The Voice of the Masters: Writing and Authority in Modern Latin American Literature.* Latin American Monographs 64. Austin: Institute of Latin American Studies-U of Texas P, 1985. 137-68, 186-87.

Goodman, Ezra. *The Fifty Year Decline and Fall of Hollywood.* New York: Mac-Fadden, 1961.

Graham, Peter, ed. and comp. *The New Wave: Critical Landmarks Selected by Peter Graham.* Cinema World 5. Garden City, NY: Doubleday, 1968.

Grant, Barry K., ed. *Film Genre: Theory and Criticism.* Metuchen, NJ: Scarecrow, 1977.

———. , ed. *Film Genre Reader.* Austin: U of Texas P, 1986.

Graves, Robert. *The Greek Myths.* Rev. ed. 2 vols. Harmondsworth, Eng.: Penguin, 1960.

Gray, Hugh. Introduction. *What Is Cinema?* 2: 1-15.

Guérin, Miguel Alberto. Rev. of *Tres tristes tigres,* by Guillermo Cabrera

Infante. *Sur* Mar.-Apr. 1968: 85-87.

Guillermo, Edenia, and Juana Amelia Hernández. "*Tres tristes tigres.*" *Papeles de Son Armadans* 65 (1972): 25-48.

Hall, Kenneth E. "Cabrera Infante and the Work of Alfred Hitchcock," *World Literature Today* 61 (1987): 598-600.

————. *The Function of Cinema in the Works of Guillermo Cabrera Infante and Manuel Puig.* Diss. U of Arizona, 1986. Ann Arbor: UMI, 1986. 8613818.

Halliwell, Leslie. *The Filmgoer's Companion.* 6th ed. New York: Avon, 1977.

————. *Halliwell's Film Guide.* 2nd ed. 1979. New York: Scribner's, 1980.

Haskell, Molly. *From Reverence to Rape: The Treatment of Women in the Movies.* New York: Holt, 1973.

Hazera, Lydia D. "Cinematic Influences in the Works of Cabrera Infante, Puig, and Vargas Llosa." *New Orleans Review* 12.3 (1985): 43-52.

————. "Strategies for Reader Participation in the Works of Cortázar, Cabrera Infante and Vargas Llosa." *Latin American Literary Review* 13.26 (1985): 19-34.

Hemingway, Ernest. *The Old Man and the Sea.* New York: Scribner's, 1952.

Hernández, Cruz. "Oh, You Sexy Kid You." Rev. of *La Habana para un infante difunto,* by Guillermo Cabrera Infante. *Caribbean Review* 9.4 (1980): 40-41.

Hernández-Lima, Dinorah. "Guillermo Cabrera Infante: Los clásicos en *Vista del amanecer en el trópico.*" Lecture, 36th Mountain Interstate Foreign Language Conference, Wake Forest University, 11 Oct. 1986.

————. *Versiones y re-versiones históricas en la obra de Guillermo Cabrera Infante.* Diss. U of Maryland, 1983. Ann Arbor: UMI, 1983. 12146713.

Higham, Charles, and Joel Greenberg, comps. and eds. *The Celluloid Muse: Hollywood Directors Speak.* Chicago: Regnery, 1969.

Hillier, Jim, ed. Cahiers du Cinéma: *The 1950s: Neo-Realism, Hollywood, New Wave.* Cambridge: Harvard UP, 1985. Vol. 1 of *Cahiers du Cinéma* [an anthology in English]. 2 vols. to date. 1985- .

Hitchcock, Alfred. *Hitchcock.* With François Truffaut. With the Collaboration of Helen G. Scott. Trans. Helen G. Scott. New York: Simon, 1967.

Hodges, Devon L. *Renaissance Fictions of Anatomy.* Amherst: U of Massachusetts P, 1985.

Huizinga, Johan. *Homo Ludens: A Study of the Play-Element in Culture.* 1950. Boston: Beacon, 1955.

Huss, Roy, and T. J. Ross, eds. *Focus on the Horror Film.* Englewood Cliffs: Spectrum-Prentice, 1972.

Huysmans, J[oris]-K[arl]. *Against Nature: A New Translation of A Rebours.* Trans. Robert Baldick. Harmondsworth, Eng.: Penguin, 1959.

Ingarden, Roman. *The Literary Work of Art: An Investigation on the Borderlines of Ontology, Logic, and Theory of Literature. With an Appendix on the Functions of Language in the Theater.* Trans. and introd. George G. Grabowicz. Northwestern University Studies in Phenomenology and Existential Philosophy. Evanston, IL: Northwestern UP, 1973.

Jiménez, Reynaldo L. *Guillermo Cabrera Infante y* Tres tristes tigres. Miami: Colección Polymita-Universal, 1976.

Johnson, William, ed. *Focus on the Science Fiction Film*. Englewood Cliffs: Spectrum-Prentice, 1972.

Jordan, René. *Gary Cooper*. Pyramid Illustrated History of the Movies. New York: Pyramid, 1974.

Kadir, Djelal. "Nostalgia or Nihilism: Pop Art and New Spanish American Novel." *Journal of Spanish Studies: Twentieth Century* 2 (1974): 127-35.

————. "Stalking the Oxen of the Sun and Felling the Sacred Cows: Joyce's *Ulysses* and Cabrera Infante's *Three Trapped Tigers*." *Latin American Literary Review* 4.8 (1976): 15-22.

Kael, Pauline. *The Citizen Kane Book*. 1971. Toronto: Bantam, 1974.

————. "Orson Welles: There Ain't No Way." *Kiss Kiss Bang Bang*. New York: Bantam, 1954.

————. "Trash, Art, and the Movies." *Going Steady*. 1970. New York: Bantam, 1971. 103-58.

Kahn, Gordon. *Hollywood on Trial: The Story of the 10 Who Were Indicted*. Foreword Thomas Mann. The Literature of Cinema. 1948. New York: Arno/The New York Times: 1972.

Kaminsky, Stuart. *American Film Genres: Approaches to a Critical Theory of Popular Film*. 1974. New York: Laurel-Dell, 1977.

Katz, Ephraim. *The Film Encyclopedia*. New York: Perigee-Putnam's, 1979.

Katz, Lisa E., ed. *A Symposium of Latin American Writers, May 10, 1978: The Artist in an Alien Culture*. The City College Papers 17. The Jacob C. Saposnekow Memorial Lectures. New York: City College of the City U of New York, 1979.

Kennedy, William. "Island of Luminous Artifact." Rev. of *View of Dawn in the Tropics*, by Guillermo Cabrera Infante. *Review* 25-26 (1980): 136-37.

Kierkegaard, S. *Either/Or*. Trans. David F. Swenson and Lillian Marvin Swenson. Rev. and introd. Howard A. Johnson. 1959. 2 vols. Princeton: Princeton UP, 1971-72. Vol. 1.

Kirk, G. S. *The Nature of Greek Myths*. Harmondsworth, Eng.: Pelican-Penguin, 1974.

Kitses, Jim. *Horizons West. Anthony Mann, Budd Boetticher, Sam Peckinpah: Studies of Authorship within the Western*. Cinema One 12. 1969. Bloomington: Indiana UP, 1970.

Knight, Arthur. *The Liveliest Art: A Panoramic History of the Movies*. New York: Mentor-NAL, 1959.

Kracauer, Siegfried. *From Caligari to Hitler: A Psychological History of the German Film*. New York: Dennis Dobson, 1947.

————. *Theory of Film: The Redemption of Physical Reality*. London: Oxford UP, 1960.

Lachenay, Robert [François Truffaut]. "Portrait d'Humphrey Bogart." With filmography by Charles Bitsch. *Cahiers du cinéma* Nov. 1955: 30-37.

Laura, Ernesto G. Rev. of *Invasion of the Body Snatchers*. *Focus on the Science Fiction Film*. Ed. William Johnson. Englewood Cliffs: Spectrum-Prentice, 1972. 71-73.

La Valley, Albert J., ed. *Focus on Hitchcock*. Englewood Cliffs: Spectrum-Prentice, 1972.

Levine, Suzanne Jill. "La escritura como traducción: *Tres tristes tigres* y una *Cobra*." *Revista iberoamericana* 41 (1975): 557-67.

Lewis, L. M. Rev. of *Holy Smoke*, by G. Cabrera Infante. *Library Journal* 15 Mar. 1986: 69.

Limbacher, James L., comp. and ed. *Feature Films on 8mm, 16mm and Videotape*. 7th ed. New York: Bowker, 1982.

Lindgren, Ernest. *The Art of the Film*. 2nd ed. New York: Collier, 1963.

Lindstrom, Naomi. "The Problem of Pop Culture in the Novels of Manuel Puig." *The American Hispanist* Nov.-Dec. 1978: 28-31.

Little, William. "Notas acerca de *Tres tristes tigres* de Cabrera Infante." *Revista iberoamericana* 36 (1970): 635-42.

Ludmer, Josefina. "*Tres tristes tigres*: Ordenes literarios y jerarquías sociales." *Revista iberoamericana* 45 (1979): 493-503.

Luhr, William. "The Function of Narrative in Literature and Film: Some Issues." *Ideas of Order in Literature and Film*. Selected Papers from the Fourth Annual Florida State University Conference on Literature and Film. Ed. Peter Ruppert et al. Tallahassee: FL State U-University Presses of FL, 1980. 32-38.

McArthur, Colin. *Underworld U.S.A.* Cinema One Series 20. London: Secker & Warburg-British Film Institute, 1972.

McConnell, Frank D. *The Spoken Seen: Film and the Romantic Imagination*. Baltimore: Johns Hopkins UP, 1975.

————. *Storytelling and Mythmaking: Images from Film and Literature*. New York: Oxford UP, 1979.

McMurray, George R. *Spanish American Writing since 1941: A Critical Survey*. New York: Ungar, 1987. 75-80, 327-32.

Magill, Frank N., ed. *Magill's Survey of Cinema: Silent Fiilms*. Assoc. eds. Patri King Hanson and Stephen L. Hanson. Vol. 2. Englewood Cliffs, NJ: Salem, 1982. 3 vols.

Magny, Claude-Edmonde. *The Age of the American Novel: The Film Aesthetic of Fiction between the Two Wars*. Trans. Eleanor Hochman. New York: Ungar, 1972.

Malcuzynski, M.-Pierrette. "*Tres tristes tigres*, or the Treacherous Play on Carnival." *Ideologies and Literature* 15 (1981): 33-56.

Maltin, Leonard, ed. *Leonard Maltin's TV Movies*. New York: Signet-NAL, 1987, 1984.

————, ed. *The Whole Film Sourcebook*. New York: NAL, 1983.

Marín Morales, José Alberto. "Siete novelistas hispano-americanos." *Arbor: Revista general de investigación y cultura* 76 (1970): 27-43.

Mast, Gerald, and Marshall Cohen, comps. and eds. *Film Theory and Criticism: Introductory Readings*. New York: Oxford UP, 1974.

Matas, Julio. "Orden y visión de *Tres tristes tigres*." *Revista iberoamericana* 40 (1974): 87-104.

————. Rev. of *Tres tristes tigres*, by Guillermo Cabrera Infante. *Revista ibero-americana* 35 (1969): 418-20.

Menton, Seymour. *Prose Fiction of the Cuban Revolution*. Latin American Monographs 37. Austin: U of Texas P, 1975.

Merrim, Stephanie. "*La Habana para un infante difunto* y su teoría topográfica de las formas." *Revista iberoamericana* 48 (1982): 403-13.

————. *Logos and the Word: The Novel of Language and Linguistic Motivation in Grande Sertao: Veredas and Tres tristes tigres*. Utah Studies in Literature and Linguistics 23. Berne: Lang, 1983.

————. "Through the Film Darkly: Grade 'B' Movies and Dreamwork in *Tres tristes tigres* and *El beso de la mujer araña*." *Modern Language Studies* 15.4 (1985): 300-12.

Mickelsen, Vicki Gillespie. *Games Novelists Play*. Diss. Indiana U, 1974. Ann Arbor: UMI Research P, 1974. 75-1724.

Minc, Rose S., ed. *Latin American Fiction Today: A Symposium*. Takoma Park, MD: Hispamérica-Montclair State College, 1979.

————, ed. *Literature and Popular Culture in the Hispanic World: A Symposium*. Gaithersburg, MD: Hispamérica-Montclair State College, 1981.

————, ed. *Literatures in Transition: The Many Voices of the Caribbean Area. A Symposium*. Gaithersburg, MD: Hispamérica-Montclair State College, 1982.

Minc, Rose S., and Marilyn R. Frankenthaler, eds. *Requiem for the "Boom"—Premature? A Symposium*. Gaithersburg, MD: Montclair State College, 1980.

Mitchell, Phyllis. "The Reel against the Real: Cinema in the Novels of Guillermo Cabrera Infante and Manuel Puig." *Latin American Literary Review* 6.11 (1977): 22-29.

Monaco, James. *How to Read a Film: The Art, Technology, Language, History, and Theory of Film and Media*. With diagrams by David Lindroth. Rev. ed. New York: Oxford UP, 1981.

Monaco, Paul. "Film as Myth and National Folklore." Carrabino 35-49.

Monsiváis, Carlos. "Pop Culture and Literature in Latin America." Trans. Lydia Hunt. *Review* 34 (1985): 9-13.

Montaner, Carlos Alberto. *De la literatura considerada como una forma de urticaria*. Madrid: Colección Nova Scholar-Playor, 1980.

Montes-Huidobro, Matías. Rev. of *La Habana para un infante difunto*, by Guillermo Cabrera Infante. *Chasqui* May 1979: 90-91.

Morando Maza, Saúl L. "Manuel Puig." *Gente que conocí*. By Morando Maza. Buenos Aires: Corregidor, 1980. 297-302.

Morello-Frosch, Marta. "The New Art of Narrating Films." *Review* 4-5 (1971-72): 52-55.

Morin, Edgar. *The Stars*. Trans. Richard Howard. Evergreen Profile Book 7. New York: Grove, 1960.

Nachbar, Jack. *Focus on the Western*. Englewood Cliffs: Spectrum-Prentice, 1974.

Navasky, Victor S. *Naming Names*. 1980. Harmondsworth, Eng.: Penguin, 1981.

Nelson, Ardis L. "Betrayal in *Tres tristes tigres* and Petronius' *Satyricon*." Minc, *Latin* 153-62.

————. *Cabrera Infante in the Menippean Tradition*. Prologue by Guillermo Cabrera Infante. Juan de la Cuesta Hispanic Monographs. Newark, DE: Juan de la Cuesta, 1983.

————. "El doble, el recuerdo y la muerte: Elementos de fugacidad en la narrativa de G. Cabrera Infante." *Revista iberoamericana* 49 (1983): 509-21.

————. "*La Habana para un infante difunto*: Cabrera Infante's 'Continuous Showing.'" *Revista canadiense de estudios hispánicos* 5 (1981): 216-18.

————. "*Holy Smoke*: Anatomy of a Vice." *World Literature Today* 61 (1987): 598-600.

————. "*Tres tristes tigres* y el cine." Indiana University-Department of Spanish and Portuguese. J. M. Hill Monograph Series 3. N.p.: Indiana U, 1976. 1-25.

Older, Dora Vázquez. *El juego contradictorio en Cabrera Infante*. Diss. Brown U, 1977. Ann Arbor: UMI, 1977. 7732616.

Ortega, José. *La estética neobarroca en la narrativa hispanoamericana*. Madrid: José Porrúa Turanzas, 1984. 49-55.

Ortega, Julio. *Relato de la utopía: Notas sobre narrativa cubana de la Revolución*. Barcelona: La Gaya Ciencia, 1973. 141-60.

Panofsky, Erwin. "Style and Medium in the Motion Pictures." Mast and Cohen 151-69.

Peavler, Terry J. "Guillermo Cabrera Infante's Debt to Ernest Hemingway." *Hispania* 62 (1979): 289-96.

Pereda, Rosa Mª *Guillermo Cabrera Infante*. Escritores de todos los tiempos 3. Madrid: EDAF, 1978.

Powdermaker, Hortense. *Hollywood: The Dream Factory*. New York: Universal Library—Grosset; Little, 1950.

Prawer, S. S. *Caligari's Children: The Film as a Tale of Terror*. Oxford: Oxford UP, 1980.

Pudovkin, Vsevolod. "On Editing." Mast and Cohen 67-74.

Puig, Manuel. *El beso de la mujer araña*. Nueva narrativa hispánica. Barcelona: Seix-Barral, 1983.

————. "Conversación con Manuel Puig: la redención de la cursilería." With Danubio Torres Fierro. *Eco* 173 (1975): 507-15.

————. "Encuentros con Manuel Puig." With Jorgelina Corbatta. *Revista iberoamericana* 49 (1983): 591-620.

————. Entrevista. With Saúl Sosnowski. *Hispamérica* May 1973: 70-80.

————. "Entrevista con Manuel Puig: Una narrativa de lo melifluo." With Nora Catelli. *Quimera* April. 1982: 22-25.

————. "An Interview with Manuel Puig." With Ronald Christ. *Partisan Review* 44 (1973): 49-54.

————. "Síntesis y análisis: Cine y literatura." *Eco: Revista de occidente* 42 (1977): 483-88.

————. *La traición de Rita Hayworth*. Colección "El espejo." 6th. ed. rev. Buenos Aires: Sudamericana, 1972.

Radice, Betty. Introduction. *Terence: The Comedies*. By Terence. Trans. and introd. Betty Radice. Rev. ed. Harmondsworth, Eng.: Penguin, 1976. 11-29.

Reisz, Karel, and Gavin Millar, writs. and comps. *The Technique of Film Editing*. Introd. Thorold Dickinson. 2nd ed., enl. New York: Communications Arts-Hastings House, 1968.

Rela, Walter. *Spanish American Literature: A Selected Bibliography: Literatura hispanoamericana: Bibliografía selecta. 1970-1980*. East Lansing; Montevideo: Michigan State U: Dept. of Romance and Classical Languages, 1982.

Richardson, Robert. *Literature and Film*. Bloomington: Indiana UP, 1969.

Rivero, Eliana. "Hacia un análisis feminista de *Tres tristes tigres*." *Theory and Practice of Feminist Literary Criticism*. Ed. Gabriela Mora and Karen S. Van Hooft. Studies in Literary Analysis. Ypsilanti, MI: Bilingual, 1982. 279-91.

Robinson, Sharon Denise. "Women on the Edge: A Study of the Female Characters in Cabrera Infante's *Así en la paz como en la guerra*." Thesis U of NC-Chapel Hill, 1985.

Rodríguez-Luis, Julio. "Dos versiones del subdesarrollo: 'Tres tristes tigres', de Cabrera Infante, y 'Temporada de duendes', de Pedro Juan Soto." *Sin nombre* 12.1 (1981): 39-45.

—————. *La literatura hispanoamericana: Entre compromiso y experimento*. Madrid: Espiral/Fundamentos, 1984.

Rodríguez Monegal, Emir. "Cabrera Infante: La novela como autobiografía total." *Revista iberoamericana* 47 (1981): 265-71.

—————. "Estructura y significaciones de *Tres tristes tigres*." *Narradores de esta América*. Ed. Rodríguez Monegal. 2 vols. Buenos Aires: Alfa Argentina, 1974. 2: 331-64.

—————. "The New Latin American Novelists." *Partisan Review* 44 (1977): 40-51.

Rohmer, Eric, and Claude Chabrol. *Hitchcock: The First Forty-four Films*. Trans. Stanley Hochman. Ungar Film Library. New York: Ungar, 1979.

Rosen, Marjorie. *Popcorn Venus: Women, Movies and the American Dream*. New York: Coward, 1973.

Rubins, Josh. "Puffs." Rev. of *Holy Smoke*, by G. Cabrera Infante. *New York Review of Books* 8 May 1986: 35.

Sainz, Gustavo. "La novela de los nuevos." With Emir Rodríguez Monegal. *Mundo nuevo* Apr. 1968: 4-11.

Sánchez-Boudy, José. *La nueva novela hispanoamericana y Tres tristes tigres*. Miami: Universal, 1971.

Sarris, Andrew, ed. *Hollywood Voices: Interviews with Film Directors*. Indianapolis: Bobbs-Merrill, 1971.

—————. Introduction. *Morocco and Shanghai Express: Two Films by Josef von Sternberg*. Josef von Sternberg. Classic Film Scripts. New York: Simon, 1973.

—————. "Rerunning Puig and Cabrera Infante." *Review* 9 (1973): 46-48.

Scheybeler, C. A. H. J. "A Critical Study of *Tres tristes tigres* by Guillermo Cabrera Infante." Bachelor's Thesis, St. Antony's College, Latin American Centre, Oxford U, 1972.

Schrader, Paul. "Notes on Film Noir." Grant, *Film Genre* 169-82.

Schwartz, Ronald. "*Cobra* Meets the *Spiderwoman*: Two Examples of Cuban and Argentinian 'Camp.' " Minc and Frankenthaler 137-49.

————. *Nomads, Exiles, and Emigrés: The Rebirth of the Latin American Narrative, 1960-80.* Metuchen, NJ: Scarecrow, 1980.

Siegel, Joel E. *Val Lewton: The Reality of Terror.* Cinema One 22. New York: Viking, 1973.

Siemens, William L. "The Antichrist-Figure in Three Latin American Novels." Carrabino 113-21.

————. "The Devouring Female in Four Latin American Novels." *Essays in Literature* 1 (1974): 118-29.

————. *Guillermo Cabrera Infante: Language and Creativity.* Diss. U of Kansas, 1971. Ann Arbor: UMI, 1972. 72-11804.

————. "Mirrors and Metamorphosis: Lewis Carroll's Presence in *Tres tristes tigres.*" *Hispania* 62 (1979): 297-303.

————. "Serving up the Campbells: The 'Los visitantes' Segment of Guillermo Cabrera Infante's *Tres tristes tigres.*" *West Virginia University Philological Papers* 30 (1984): 102-08.

————. *Worlds Reborn: The Hero in the Modern Spanish American Novel.* Morgantown: West Virginia UP, 1984. 138-71.

Sobchack, Vivian. *Screening Space: The American Science Fiction Film.* 2nd enl. ed. New York: Ungar, 1987.

Solomon, Stanley J. *Beyond Formula: American Film Genres.* New York: Harcourt, 1976.

Sontag, Susan. "Notes on 'Camp.'" *Partisan Review* 31 (1964): 515-30.

Souza, Raymond D. *Major Cuban Novelists: Innovation and Tradition.* Columbia: U of Missouri P, 1976. 80-100 and throughout.

————. Rev. of *La Habana para un Infante Difunto,* by Guillermo Cabrera Infante. *Cuban Studies/Estudios cubanos* 11.1 (1981): 95-97.

Spiegel, Alan. *Fiction and the Camera Eye: Visual Consciousness in Film and the Modern Novel.* Charlottesville, UP of Virginia, 1976.

Steinbrunner, Chris, and Burt Goldblatt. *Cinema of the Fantastic.* New York: Saturday Review P, 1972.

Stephenson, Ralph, and Jean R. Debrix. *The Cinema as Art.* 2nd ed. Harmondsworth, Eng.: Penguin, 1976.

Stone, Judy. "On Edge." *American Film* Oct. 1984: 68+ .

Sypher, Wylie. *Four Stages of Renaissance Style: Transformations in Art and Literature 1400-1700.* Garden City, NY: Anchor-Doubleday, 1965.

Tarratt, Margaret. "Monsters from the Id." Grant, *Film Genre* 161-81.

Thomson, David. *America in the Dark: The Impact of Hollywood Films on American Culture.* New York: Morrow, 1977.

Tittler, Jonathan. "Intratextual Distance in *Tres tristes tigres.*" *Modern Language Notes* 93 (1978): 285-96.

————. *Narrative Irony in the Contemporary Spanish-American Novel.* Ithaca: Cornell UP, 1984. 78-125.

Todorov, Tzvetan, comp. and ed. *Teoría de la literatura de los formalistas rusos.* Trans. Ana María Nethol. Crítica literaria. México: Siglo Veintiuno, 1970.

Torres Fierro, Danubio. Rev. of *La Habana para un infante difunto*, by Guillermo Cabrera Infante. *Vuelta* May 1980: 37-39.

Tyler, Parker. *The Hollywood Hallucination*. New York: Creative Age, 1944.

———. *Magic and Myth of the Movies*. Introd. Richard Schickel. 2nd ed. New York: Simon, 1970.

———. *The Three Faces of the Film: The Art, the Dream, the Cult*. New York: Yoseloff, 1960.

Tynan, Kenneth. "Garbo." Mast and Cohen 569-74.

Updike, John. "Infante Terrible." *New Yorker* 29 Jan. 1972. 91-94.

Volek, Emil. *Cuatro claves para la modernidad: Análisis semiótico de textos hispánicos. Aleixandre, Borges, Carpentier, Cabrera Infante*. Biblioteca Románica Hispánica 2. Estudios y Ensayos 35. Madrid: Gredos, 1984. 154-78.

Von Sternberg, Josef. *Fun in a Chinese Laundry*. New York: Macmillan, 1965.

———. *Morocco and Shanghai Express: Two Films by Josef von Sternberg*. Introd. Andrew Sarris. Classic Film Scripts. New York: Simon, 1973.

Wagner, Geoffrey. *The Novel and the Cinema*. Cranbury, NJ: Associated University Presses; London: Tantivy, 1975.

Walker, John. "Havana in Slow Motion." Rev. of *La Habana para un Infante Difunto*, by Guillermo Cabrera Infante. *Américas* (Eng. ed.) Nov-Dec. 1980: 47-48.

Warshow, Robert. *The Immediate Experience: Movies, Comics, Theatre & Other Aspects of Popular Culture*. Introd. Lionel Trilling. New York: Atheneum, 1970.

Weinberg, Herman G. *Josef von Sternberg: A Critical Study*. New York: Dutton, 1967.

———. *The Lubitsch Touch: A Critical Study*. 3rd rev. and enl. ed. New York: Dover, 1977.

Welsch, Janice R. *Film Archetypes: Sisters, Mistresses, Mothers and Daughters*. Diss. Northwestern, 1975. The Arno Press Cinema Program. New York: Arno-New York Times, 1978.

Willis, Donald C. *The Films of Howard Hawks*. Metuchen, NJ: Scarecrow, 1975.

Wolfenstein, Martha, and Nathan Leites. *Movies: A Psychological Study*. 2nd ed. New York: Atheneum, 1970.

Wollen, Peter. *Signs and Meanings in the Cinema*. Bloomington: Indiana UP, 1969.

Wood, Michael. *America in the Movies: Or, "Santa Maria, It Had Slipped My Mind."* New York: Basic Books, 1975.

Wood, Robin. *Hitchcock's Films*. New York: A. S. Barnes, 1965.

———. *Howard Hawks*. The Cinema World Series 7. Garden City, NY: Doubleday, 1968.

World Literature Today 61 (1987). Focus on Guillermo Cabrera Infante.

Yúdice, George. "Synchronic Narrative Structures in Contemporary Spanish American Fiction." *Minc, Latin* 185-96.

Zierold, Norman. *The Moguls*. New York: Avon, 1969.

Zimmerman, J.E. *Dictionary of Classical Mythology*. New York: Bantam, 1964.

Filmography

(I have drawn extensively on
Halliwell's Film Guide in preparing this list.)

Abbott, Bud, and Lou Costello. "Who's on First?" *Abbott and Costello Live*. Writ.
Eddie Forman. Mus. dir. Al Goodman. Prod. and dir. Charles Friedman.
The Colgate Comedy Hour, NBC. N.d.

Aldrich, Robert, dir. *The Big Knife*. With Jack Palance, Ida Lupino, and Rod
Steiger. UA/Aldrich and Associates, 1955.

———, dir. *Kiss Me Deadly*. With Ralph Meeker, Cloris Leachman, and
Maxine Cooper. UA/Parklane, 1955.

———, dir. *Vera Cruz*. With Gary Cooper and Burt Lancaster. UA/Hecht-
Hill-Lancaster, 1953.

All about Eve. Dir. Joseph L. Manckiewicz. With Bette Davis, George Sanders,
and Anne Baxter. Twentieth Century-Fox, 1950.

Berkeley, Busby, dir. *Footlight Parade*. Chor. Busby Berkeley. With James
Cagney and Joan Blondell. Warner Bros., 1933.

Blood and Sand. With Rita Hayworth, Tyrone Power, and Linda Darnell. Dir.
Rouben Mamoulian. Twentieth Century-Fox, 1941.

Bresson, Robert, dir. *Journal d'un curé de campagne*. With Claude Laydu and Jean
Riveyre. Union Générale Cinématographique, 1950

Bride of Frankenstein. Dir. James Whale. With Boris Karloff, Colin Clive, Elsa
Lanchester, and Ernest Thesiger. Universal, 1935.

Brooks, Mel, dir. *Young Frankenstein*. With Gene Wilder, Marty Feldman,
Madeleine Kahn, and Peter Boyle. Writ. Gene Wilder and Mel Brooks.
TCF/Gruskoff/Venture/Jouer/Crossbow, 1974.

Buñuel, Luis, dir. *Ensayo de un crimen*. [*The Criminal Life of Archibaldo de la Cruz*].
With Ernesto Alonso and Ariadna Welter. Alianza Cinematográfica, 1955.

The Caine Mutiny. With Humphrey Bogart, José Ferrer, Van Johnson, and Fred
MacMurray. Dir. Edward Dmytryk. Columbia/Stanley Kramer, 1954.

Capra, Frank, dir. *Lost Horizon*. With Ronald Colman, H. B. Warner, and
Thomas Mitchell. Columbia, 1937.

———, dir. *Mr. Smith Goes to Washington*. With James Stewart, Claude Rains,
and Jean Arthur. Columbia, 1939.

Chaplin, Charles, dir. *City Lights*. With Charles Chaplin and Virginia Cherrill.
Charles Chaplin, 1931.

————, dir. *The Gold Rush*. With Chaplin, Georgia Hale, and Mack Swain. UA/Charles Chaplin, 1925.

————, dir. *The Great Dictator*. With Chaplin, Paulette Goddard, and Jack Oakie. Charles Chaplin, 1940.

————, dir. *The Immigrant*. With Chaplin and Edna Purviance. Mutual, 1917.

————, dir. *Limelight*. With Chaplin, Claire Bloom, and Buster Keaton. Charles Chaplin, 1952.

————, dir. *Monsieur Verdoux*. With Chaplin and Martha Raye. Charles Chaplin, 1947.

————, dir. *A Woman of Paris*. With Edna Purviance, Adolphe Menjou, and Carl Miller. Charles Chaplin, 1923.

Clair, René, dir. *Entr'acte*. Ballets Suédois, 1924.

Cocteau, Jean, dir. *Orphée*. With Jean Marais, François Perier, and María Casares. André Paulve 1/Films du Palais Royal, 1949.

Corman, Roger, dir. *Not of This Earth*. With Paul Birch and Beverly Garland. Allied Artists, 1957.

————. dir. *The St. Valentine's Day Massacre*. With Jason Robards, Jr., George Segal, and Ralph Meeker. TCF/Los Altos, 1967.

The Creature from the Black Lagoon. Dir. Jack Arnold. With Richard Carlson, Julie Adams, and Richard Denning. Universal-International, 1954.

Cukor, George, dir. *Dinner at Eight*. With Marie Dressler, John Barrymore, Wallace Beery, and Jean Harlow. MGM, 1933.

————, dir. *A Double Life*. With Ronald Colman and Signe Hasso. Kanin Productions, 1947.

————, dir. *My Fair Lady*. With Rex Harrison, Audrey Hepburn, Stanley Holloway, and Wilfrid Hyde White. CBS/Warner Bros., 1964.

————, dir. *A Star Is Born*. With Judy Garland and James Mason. Warner Bros., 1954.

————, dir. *The Women*. With Norma Shearer, Joan Crawford, and Rosalind Russell. MGM, 1939.

Curtiz, Michael, dir. *Mildred Pierce*. With Joan Crawford, Zachary Scott, and Ann Blyth. Warner Bros., 1945.

————, dir. *Young Man with a Horn*. With Kirk Douglas, Lauren Bacall, Doris Day, and Hoagy Carmichael. Warner Bros., 1950.

De Sica, Vittorio, dir. *Ladri di biciclette [Bicycle Thieves]*. Writ. Cesare Zavattini. With Lamberto Maggiorani and Enzo Stabiola. PDS-ENIC, 1948.

Dr. Ehrlich's Magic Bullet. With Edward G. Robinson, Ruth Gordon, and Otto Kruger. Dir. William Dieterle. Warner Bros., 1940.

Dr. Jekyll and Mr. Hyde. Dir. Victor Fleming. With Spencer Tracy, Ingrid Bergman, and Lana Turner. MGM, 1941.

Donen, Stanley, dir. *Funny Face*. With Fred Astaire and Audrey Hepburn. Paramount, 1956.

————, dir. *Seven Brides for Seven Brothers*. With Howard Keel and Jane Powell. MGM, 1954.

Dracula. Dir. Tod Browning. With Bela Lugosi, David Manners, and Edward Van Sloan. Universal, 1930.

Duck Soup. With Groucho, Chico, Harpo, and Zeppo Marx. Dir. Leo McCarey. Paramount, 1933.

Edwards, Blake, dir. *Breakfast at Tiffany's.* With Audrey Hepburn, George Peppard, and Buddy Ebsen. Paramount, 1961.

——, dir. *S.O.B.* With Julie Andrews, William Holden, and Robert Preston. Lorimar, 1981.

——, dir. *10.* With Dudley Moore and Bo Derek. Orion, 1979.

Eisenstein, Sergei M., dir. *Bronenosets Potemkin* [*The Battleship Potemkin*]. Goskino, 1925.

Fellini, Federico, dir. *La dolce vita.* With Marcello Mastroianni and Anita Ekberg. Riama/Pathé Consortium, 1960.

——, dir. *La strada.* With Giulietta Masina, Anthony Quinn, and Richard Basehart. Ponti/De Laurentiis, 1954.

Five Million Years to Earth [*Quatermass and the Pit*]. With Andrew Keir, James Donald, Barbara Shelley, and Julian Glover. Dir. Roy Ward Baker. Writ. Nigel Kneale. Hammer/Anthony Nelson Keys, 1967.

Flying Down to Rio. Dir. Thornton Freeland. With Dolores del Rio, Ginger Rogers, and Fred Astaire. RKO, 1933.

Ford, John, dir. *The Searchers.* With John Wayne, Jeffrey Hunter, and Natalie Wood. Warner Bros./C. V. Whitney, 1956.

——, dir. *Stagecoach.* With Claire Trevor, John Wayne, and Thomas Mitchell. Walter Wanger, 1939.

——, dir. *Wagonmaster.* With Ben Johnson, Joanne Cru, and Ward Bond. RKO/Argosy, 1950.

——, dir. *The Whole Town's Talking.* With Edward G. Robinson and Jean Arthur. Columbia, 1935.

Gilda. With Rita Hayworth, Glenn Ford, and George Macready. Dir. Charles Vidor. Columbia, 1946.

Grand Hotel. Dir. Edmund Goulding. With Greta Garbo, John Barrymore, and Lionel Barrymore. MGM, 1932.

Hawks, Howard, dir. *The Big Sleep.* With Humphrey Bogart and Lauren Bacall. Warner Bros., 1946.

——, dir. *Hatari!.* With John Wayne, Elsa Martinelli, and Red Buttons. Paramount/Malabar, 1962.

——, dir. *His Girl Friday.* With Rosalind Russell and Cary Grant. Columbia, 1940.

——, dir. *Red River.* With John Wayne, Montgomery Clift, and Walter Brennan. UA/Monterey, 1948.

——, dir. *Rio Bravo.* With John Wayne, Dean Martin, Ricky Nelson, Walter Brennan, and Angie Dickinson. Warner Bros., 1959.

——, dir. *Scarface.* With Paul Muni, Ann Dvorak, George Raft, and Boris Karloff. Howard Hughes, 1932.

——, prod. *The Thing from Another World.* Dir. Christian Nyby [actually dir. Howard Hawks (see Brosnan 86-87)]. With Robert Cornthwaite, Kenneth Tobey, and Margaret Sheridan. RKO/Winchester, 1951.

Hitchcock, Alfred, dir. *The Lady Vanishes*. With Margaret Lockwood, Michael Redgrave, and Dame May Whitty. Gaumont British, 1938.

————, dir. *The Man Who Knew Too Much*. With James Stewart and Doris Day. Alfred Hitchcock, 1956.

————, dir. *Marnie*. With Tippi Hedren and Sean Connery. Universal/ Geoffrey Stanley, 1964.

————, dir. *Notorious*. With Ingrid Bergman, Cary Grant, and Claude Rains. David O. Selznick, 1946.

————, dir. *Psycho*. With Anthony Perkins, Vera Miles, and Janet Leigh. Shamley/Alfred Hitchcock, 1960.

————, dir. *Rear Window*. With James Stewart, Grace Kelly, Thelma Ritter, and Raymond Burr. Alfred Hitchcock, 1954.

————, dir. *Rebecca*. With Laurence Olivier, Joan Fontaine, and Judith Anderson. David O. Selznick, 1940.

————, dir. *Rope*. With James Stewart, John Dall, and Farley Granger. Transatlantic, 1948.

————, dir. *Sabotage*. With Oscar Homolka and Sylvia Sidney. Gaumont British, 1936.

————, dir. *The Secret Agent*. With John Gielgud, Robert Young, Peter Lorre, and Madeleine Carroll. Gaumont British, 1936.

————, dir. *Shadow of a Doubt*. With Joseph Cotten, Teresa Wright, and Henry Travers. Universal, 1943.

————, dir. *Spellbound*. With Ingrid Bergman, Gregory Peck, and Leo G. Carroll. David O. Selznick, 1945.

————, dir. *Suspicion*. With Joan Fontaine and Cary Grant. RKO, 1941.

————, dir. *The Thirty-Nine Steps*. With Robert Donat and Madeleine Carroll. Gaumont British, 1935.

————, dir. *To Catch a Thief*. With Cary Grant and Grace Kelly. Paramount/ Alfred Hitchcock, 1955.

————, dir. *The Trouble with Harry*. With Edmund Gwenn, Mildred Natwick, John Forsythe, and Shirley MacLaine. Alfred Hitchcock, 1955.

————, dir. *Vertigo*. With ʻJames Stewart, Kim Novak, and Barbara Bel Geddes. Photog. Robert Burks. Alfred Hitchcock, 1958.

Horse Feathers. With Groucho, Chico, Harpo, and Zeppo Marx. Dir. Norman Z. McLeod. Paramount, 1932.

The Horse's Mouth. With Alec Guinness. Dir. Ronald Neame. UA/Knightsbridge, 1958.

Huston, John, dir. *The Asphalt Jungle*. With Sterling Hayden, Sam Jaffe, Louis Calhern, and Marilyn Monroe. MGM, 1950.

————, dir. *Beat the Devil*. With Humphrey Bogart, Gina Lollobrigida, and Robert Morley. Romulus/Santana, 1953.

————, dir. *Key Largo*. With Humphrey Bogart, Lauren Bacall, Claire Trevor, and Edward G. Robinson. Warner Bros., 1948.

————, dir. *The Maltese Falcon*. With Humphrey Bogart, Mary Astor, Sydney Greenstreet, and Peter Lorre. Warner Bros., 1941.

————, dir. *The Misfits*. With Marilyn Monroe, Clark Gable, and Montgomery Clift. UA/Frank E. Taylor, 1961.

————, dir. *Moby Dick*. With Gregory Peck, Richard Basehart, and Orson Welles. John Huston, 1956.

————, dir. *Moulin Rouge*. With José Ferrer and Zsa Zsa Gabor. Writ. John Huston. Romulus, 1952.

————, dir. *The Night of the Iguana*. With Richard Burton, Deborah Kerr, and, Ava Gardner. MGM/Seven Arts, 1964.

————, dir. *The Treasure of the Sierra Madre*. With Humphrey Bogart, Walter Huston, and Tim Holt. Warner Bros., 1948.

I the Jury. With Biff Elliott and Peggie Castle. Parklane, 1953.

Johnny Belinda. Dir. Jean Negulesco. With Jane Wyman, Lew Ayres, and Charles Bickford. Warner Bros., 1948.

Kazan, Elia, dir. *Baby Doll*. With Karl Malden, Eli Wallach, and Carroll Baker. Warner Bros./Elia Kazan, 1956.

————, dir. *East of Eden*. With James Dean, Raymond Massey, and Julie Harris. Warner Bros., 1954.

————, dir. *A Face in the Crowd*. With Andy Griffith, Lee Remick, Walter Matthau, and Patricia Neal. Newton, 1957.

————, dir. *The Goddess*. With Kim Stanley and Lloyd Bridges. Writ. Paddy Chayevsky. Columbia, 1958.

————, dir. *The Set Up*. With Robert Ryan. RKO, 1949.

Kelly, Gene, and Stanley Donen, dirs. and chors. *On the Town*. With Kelly, Frank Sinatra, Jules Munshin, and Vera-Ellen. MGM, 1949.

————, dirs. and chors. *Singin' in the Rain*. With Kelly, Donald O'Connor, and Debbie Reynolds. MGM, 1952.

The Killers. With Lee Marvin, John Cassavetes, Angie Dickinson, Ronald Reagan, and Clu Gulager. Dir. Don Siegel. Universal-International, 1964.

King Kong. Dir. Merian C. Cooper and Ernest Schoedsack. With Fay Wray, Robert Armstrong, and Bruce Cabot. RKO, 1933.

Kubrick, Stanley, dir. *The Killing*. With Sterling Hayden, Marie Windsor, and Jay C. Flippen. UA/Harris-Kubrick, 1956.

————, dir. *Paths of Glory*. With Kirk Douglas, Adolphe Menjou, and George Macready. UA/Bryna, 1957.

Lang, Fritz, dir. *You Only Live Once*. With Sylvia Sidney and Henry Fonda. Walter Wanger, 1937.

Letter from an Unknown Woman. With Joan Fontaine and Louis Jourdan. Dir. Max Ophuls. Universal, 1948.

Lewton, Val, prod. *Bedlam*. Dir. Mark Robson. With Boris Karloff and Anna Lee. RKO, 1946.

————, prod. *The Body Snatcher*. Dir. Robert Wise. With Henry Daniell and Boris Karloff. RKO, 1945.

————, prod. *Cat People*. Dir. Jacques Tourneur. With Simone Simon, Kent Smith, and Jane Randall. RKO, 1942.

————, prod. *I Walked with a Zombie*. Dir. Jacques Tourneur. With Frances Dee and Tom Conway. RKO, 1943.

————, prod. *Isle of the Dead*. Dir. Mark Robson. With Boris Karloff and Ellen Drew. RKO, 1945.

————, prod. *The Leopard Man*. Dir. Jacques Tourneur. With Dennis O'Keefe, Jean Brooks, and Margo. RKO, 1943.

Little Caesar. With Edward G. Robinson and Douglas Fairbanks, Jr. Dir. Mervyn LeRoy. Warner Bros., 1930.

The Long Wait. With Anthony Quinn, Charles Coburn, and Peggie Castle. UA/Parklane, 1954.

Lubitsch, Ernst, dir. *Heaven Can Wait*. With Don Ameche, Gene Tierney, and Charles Coburn. Twentieth Century-Fox, 1943.

————, dir. *Ninotchka*. With Greta Garbo and Melvyn Douglas. MGM, 1939.

————, dir. *The Shop around the Corner*. With James Stewart, Margaret Sullavan, Frank Morgan, and Felix Bressart. MGM, 1940.

————, dir. *To Be or Not to Be*. With Jack Benny, Carole Lombard, and Robert Stack. Ernst Lubitsch, 1942.

————, dir. *Trouble in Paradise*. With Herbert Marshall, Miriam Hopkins, Kay Francis, and Edward Everett Horton. Paramount, 1932.

Manhattan Melodrama. With Clark Gable, William Powell, and Myrna Loy. Dir. W. S. Van Dyke. MGM, 1932.

Mann, Anthony, dir. *Bend of the River*. With James Stewart and Arthur Kennedy. Universal-International, 1952.

————, dir. *The Far Country*. With James Stewart and Walter Brennan. Universal-International, 1955.

————, dir. *The Man from Laramie*. With James Stewart, Arthur Kennedy, and Donald Crisp. Columbia, 1955.

————, dir. *Man of the West*. With Gary Cooper, Lee J. Cobb, Julie London, and Arthur O'Connell. UA/Ashton, 1958.

————, dir. *The Naked Spur*. With James Stewart, Robert Ryan, and Janet Leigh. MGM, 1952.

————, dir. *Winchester '73*. With James Stewart, Stephen McNally, Shelley Winters, and Dan Duryea. Universal-International, 1950.

Milius, John, dir. *Dillinger*. With Warren Oates and Ben Johnson. Writ. John Milius. American International Pictures, 1973.

Minnelli, Vincente, dir. *An American in Paris*. With Gene Kelly, Nina Foch, Leslie Caron, and Oscar Levant. MGM, 1951.

————, dir. *The Band Wagon*. With Fred Astaire, Jack Buchanan, Oscar Levant, and Cyd Charisse. MGM, 1953.

————, dir. *Bells Are Ringing*. With Judy Holliday and Dean Martin. MGM, 1960.

————, dir. *Brigadoon*. With Gene Kelly, Cyd Charisse, and Van Johnson. MGM, 1954.

————, dir. *The Four Horsemen of the Apocalypse*. With Glenn Ford, Ingrid Thulin, and Charles Boyer. MGM, 1961.

————, dir. *Gigi*. With Leslie Caron, Louis Jourdan, and Maurice Chevalier. MGM, 1958.

————, dir. *Home from the Hill*. With Robert Mitchum, George Peppard, and George Hamilton. MGM/Sol C. Siegel, 1959.

————, dir. *Kismet*. With Howard Keel and Ann Blyth. MGM, 1955.

————, dir. *Lust for Life*. With Kirk Douglas and Anthony Quinn. MGM, 1956.

————, dir. *Madame Bovary*. With Jennifer Jones, Van Heflin, James Mason, and Louis Jourdan. MGM, 1949.

————, dir. *Meet Me in St. Louis*. With Judy Garland, Margaret O'Brien, and Tom Drake. MGM, 1944.

————, dir. *The Pirate*. With Gene Kelly, Judy Garland, and Walter Slezak. MGM, 1948.

————, dir. *The Reluctant Debutante*. With Rex Harrison, Kay Kendall, Sandra Dee, and John Saxon. MGM/Avon, 1958.

————, dir. *Some Came Running*. With Frank Sinatra, Shirley MacLaine, and Dean Martin. MGM/Sol C. Siegel, 1959.

————, dir. *Undercurrent*. With Katharine Hepburn, Robert Taylor, and Robert Mitchum. MGM, 1946.

Monroe, Marilyn, actress. *Bus Stop*. Dir. Joshua Logan. With Don Murray and Betty Field. Twentieth Century-Fox, 1956.

————, actress. *Gentlemen Prefer Blondes*. Dir. Howard Hawks. With Jane Russell and Charles Coburn. Twentieth Century-Fox, 1953.

My Little Chickadee. With Mae West, W. C. Fields, and Joseph Calleia. Dir. Edward Cline. Universal, 1939.

The Old Man and the Sea. With Spencer Tracy. Dir. John Sturges. Photog. James Wong Howe. Warner/Leland Hayward, 1958.

Preminger, Otto, dir. *Anatomy of a Murder*. With James Stewart, Lee Remick, and Ben Gazzara. Columbia/Otto Preminger, 1959.

————, dir. *Angel Face*. With Robert Mitchum and Jean Simmons. RKO, 1952.

Pudovkin, Vsevolod, dir. *Mat'* [*Mother*]. Mezhrabpom-Russ, 1926.

Rebel without a Cause. With James Dean, Natalie Wood, Jim Backus, and Sal Mineo. Dir. Nicholas Ray. Warner Bros., 1955.

Red Dust. With Clark Gable and Jean Harlow. Dir. Victor Fleming. MGM, 1932.

The Red Shoes. Writ. and dir. Michael Powell and Emeric Pressburger. With Anton Walbrook, Moira Shearer, and Marius Goring. GFD/The Archers, 1948.

Renoir, Jean, dir. *La Grande illusion*. [*Grand Illusion*]. With Pierre Fresnay, Erich von Stroheim, and Jean Gabin. RAC, 1937.

Sarafian, Richard, dir. *Vanishing Point*. Writ. Guillermo Cain [Guillermo Cabrera Infante]. Photog. John A. Alonzo. With Barry Newman, Cleavon Little, and Dean Jagger. TCF/Cupid, 1971.

Siodmak, Robert, dir. *The Killers*. With Burt Lancaster, Edmond O'Brien, and Ava Gardner. Universal-International, 1946.

Sun Valley Serenade. With Sonja Henie, Glenn Miller and his Orchestra, John Payne, and Milton Berle. Dir. H. Bruce Humberstone. Twentieth Century-Fox, 1941.

Tati, Jacques, dir. *Jour de fête*. [*Playtime*]. With Tati. Writ. Tati. Specta Films, 1960.

————, dir. *Les Vacances de M. Hulot* [*Monsieur Hulot's Holiday*]. With Tati. Writ. Tati. Cady/Discina, 1953.

Them!. Dir. Gordon Douglas. With James Whitmore, Edmund Gwenn, and James Arness. Warner Bros., 1954.

They Live by Night. With Farley Granger and Cathy O'Donnell. Dir. Nicholas Ray. RKO, 1948.

The Third Man. Dir. Carol Reed. With Joseph Cotten, Trevor Howard, Valli, and Orson Welles. British Lion/London Films/David O. Selznick/Alexander Korda, 1949.

Tourneur, Jacques, dir. *Out of the Past*. With Robert Mitchum, Jane Greer, and Kirk Douglas. RKO, 1947.

Vivacious Lady. With Ginger Rogers, James Stewart, and Charles Coburn. RKO, 1938.

Von Sternberg, Josef, dir. *Der Blaue Engel* [*The Blue Angel*]. With Emil Jannings and Marlene Dietrich. UFA, 1930.

————, dir. *Blonde Venus*. With Marlene Dietrich, Cary Grant, and Herbert Marshall. Paramount, 1932.

————, dir. *The Devil Is a Woman*. With Marlene Dietrich and Lionel Atwill. Paramount, 1935.

————, dir. *Dishonored*. With Marlene Dietrich, Victor McLaglen, and Warner Oland. Paramount, 1931.

————, dir. *Docks of New York*. With George Bancroft and Betty Compson. Paramount, 1928.

————, dir. *The Last Command*. With Emil Jannings and William Powell. Paramount, 1928.

————, dir. *Morocco*. With Marlene Dietrich, Gary Cooper, and Adolphe Menjou. Paramount, 1930.

————, dir. *The Scarlet Empress*. With Marlene Dietrich, John Lodge, and Sam Jaffe. Paramount, 1934.

————, dir. *Shanghai Express*. With Marlene Dietrich, Clive Brook, Warner Oland, and Anna May Wong. Paramount, 1932.

Weekend in Havana. With Alice Faye, John Payne, and Carmen Miranda. Dir. Walter Lang. Twentieth Century-Fox, 1941.

Welles, Orson, dir. *Citizen Kane*. With Welles, Joseph Cotten, Everett Sloane, and Dorothy Comingore. Photog. Gregg Toland. RKO, 1941.

————, dir. *Confidential Report* [*Mr. Arkadin*]. With Welles, Michael Redgrave, and Akim Tamiroff. Sevilla Studios, 1955.

————, dir. *The Lady from Shanghai*. With Welles, Rita Hayworth, Everett Sloane, and Glenn Anders. Columbia, 1948.

————, dir. *The Magnificent Ambersons*. With Tim Holt, Joseph Cotten, Agnes Moorehead, and Anne Baxter. RKO, 1942.

————, dir. *Touch of Evil*. With Charlton Heston, Orson Welles, Janet Leigh, and Akim Tamiroff. Universal-International, 1958.

Wilder, Billy, dir. *Love in the Afternoon*. With Gary Cooper, Audrey Hepburn, and Maurice Chevalier. Allied Artists, 1957.

————, dir. *Some Like It Hot*. With Jack Lemmon, Tony Curtis, and Marilyn Monroe. UA/Mirisch, 1959.

————, dir. *Sunset Boulevard*. With Gloria Swanson, William Holden, and Erich von Stroheim. Paramount, 1950.

The Wolf Man. With Lon Chaney Jr., Claude Rains, and Maria Ouspenskaya. Dir. George Waggner. Universal, 1940.

Wyler, William, dir. *The Best Years of Our Lives*. With Fredric March and Myrna Loy. Photog. Gregg Toland. Samuel Goldwyn, 1946.

————, dir. *The Little Foxes*. With Bette Davis, Herbert Marshall, and Teresa Wright. Photog. Gregg Toland. Samuel Goldwyn, 1941.

————, dir. *Wuthering Heights*. With Laurence Olivier, Merle Oberon, and David Niven. Photog. Gregg Toland. Samuel Goldwyn, 1939.

Subject Index

Name-Title-Place Index

Film Index